GENDER SEGREGATION

Gender Segregation
Divisions of Work in Post-Industrial Welfare States

Edited by

LENA GONÄS and JAN CH KARLSSON
Karlstad University, Sweden

ASHGATE

Published by
Ashgate Publishing Limited
Gower House
Croft Road
Aldershot
Hampshire GU11 3HR
England

Ashgate Publishing Company
Suite 420
101 Cherry Street
Burlington, VT 05401-4405
USA

Ashgate website: http://www.ashgate.com

British Library Cataloguing in Publication Data
Gender segregation : divisions of work in post-industrial
  welfare states
  1.Sexual division of labor 2.Women employees 3.Employee
  rights 4.Sexual division of labor - Sweden 5.Women
  employees - Sweden 6.Employee rights - Sweden
  I.Gonäs, Lena, 1945- II.Karlsson, Jan, 1948-
  306.3'615

Library of Congress Cataloging-in-Publication Data
Gender segregation : divisions of work in post-industrial welfare states / edited by
Lena Gonäs and Jan Ch Karlsson.
        p. cm.
  Includes index.
  ISBN 0-7546-4453-7
  1. Sexual division of labor--Europe--Case studies. 2. Sexual division of labor--
United States. I. Gonäs, Lena, 1945- II. Karlsson, Jan, 1948-

  HD6060.65.E85G455 2005
  306.3'615094--dc22

                                                                        2005030367

ISBN-10: 0 7546 4453 7

Printed and bound in Great Britain by Antony Rowe Ltd, Chippenham, Wiltshire.

Contents

List of Figures

List of Tables

List of Contributors

Lisbeth Bekkengen is a Researcher and has a PhD in Working Life Science from the University of Karlstad, Sweden.

Ann Bergman is a Senior Lecturer and has a PhD in Working Life Science at the University of Karlstad, Sweden.

Rosemary Crompton is Professor of Sociology at the City University London, UK.

Ruth Emerek is Associate Professor at the Institute for History, International and Social Studies at Aalborg University Centre.

Lena Gonäs is Professor in Working Life Science at the University of Karlstad, Sweden.

Liselotte Jakobsen is Associate Professor in Sociology at the University of Karlstad, Sweden.

Jan Ch. Karlsson is Professor of Sociology at the University of Karlstad.

Diane Perrons is Reader in Economic Geography and Gender Studies and Director of the Gender Group at London School of Economics, UK.

Chris Tilly is Professor at the Department of Regional Economic and Social Development, University of Massachusetts Lowell, USA.

Foreword

Gender segregation in the labour market has been studied by researchers from different disciplines for decades. Studies have been performed on the labour market level and in work organizations. Also individual outcomes in relation to wages, working contracts and working conditions have been in focus as well as health effects.

The objective with this book is to give a picture of the contemporary social science research in the field and with an international comparative perspective. A background to work is to be found in the research and development project 'Gender and Work' that was launched at the National Institute for Working Life in Stockholm, Sweden in 1999. It was a project uniting research and more practical development work on work place level based on a multidisciplinary approach. A specific task was to study relations between segregation and health.

The project group 'Gender and Work' arranged the third international congress on Women, Work and Health held in Stockholm in June 2002. At the congress two symposia were arranged in cooperation with researchers from the department of Working Life Science at the University of Karlstad. One seminar was arranged by professor Lena Gonäs and the other by professor Jan Ch Karlsson at the University of Karlstad. This book contains papers from these symposia.

Lena Gonäs
Jan Ch Karlsson

Acknowledgements

Chapter 6, 'The New Economy and the Work Life Balance: Conceptual Explorations and a Case Study of New Media', by Diane Perrons. Published in *Gender, Work and Organisations*, 2003, vol. 10, no. 1, pp. 65–93.

Chapter 8, 'Employment, Flexible Working and the Family', by Rosemary Crompton. Published in *British Journal of Sociology*, 2002, vol. 53, no. 4, pp. 537–558.

We gratefully acknowledge the permission from the publishers to include these articles in our book.

Chapter 1

Divisions of Gender and Work

Lena Gonäs and Jan Ch Karlsson

Introduction

The objective of this book is to discuss if and to what extent gender divisions in working life are changing. In doing so, we will explore implications of gender segregation and possible openings for integration at different levels in society. Gender segregation is discussed from two perspectives; a labour market perspective and a family-work level perspective. The authors unite these perspectives and discuss if and where we can find patterns of gender integration and where there still is stability and continuity in gender relations. By applying a multidisciplinary approach and illustrating our problem area with development on different analytical levels we hope to further the discussion on how and in what ways integration can be pursued.

Stability and change

In a long perspective the segregation patterns have changed towards a more even distribution of women and men over occupations and sectors in the labour market in most countries (Rubery et al., 1999). At the same time, countries with high female employment rates have high segregation levels. Studies on the development in the European Union show that there is a positive correlation between employment rates and segregation levels (Rubery et al., 1999; Emerek et al., 2001). As more women enter the labour market they are recruited into sectors and work tasks that already are defined as 'female' jobs, and they are doing service jobs earlier performed in the household but now transformed into market work. Growing welfare state labour markets produce health, education and services and have become major employers of women. The dual dependency between the post industrial welfare state and the growing female labour force has formed new relations in the labour market and in the political arena. Women are dependent on the welfare state for the supply of child and elderly care to be able to take a job at the same time as these services are their major labour market, at least in the Nordic welfare states. In other welfare state regimes the relations are different, and as can be seen from many studies, the support from the state to develop a social infrastructure that support women's paid employment varies (Lewis, 1993; Orloff, 1993; Plantenga and Hansen, 1999a and b; Sainsbury, 1999). The retrenchment of the welfare state during the crises of the

1990s had gendered consequences. Plantenga and Hansen cited the Spanish expert in a benchmarking report from the EU network Gender and Employment:

> Women are not only late comers in the labour market, but they arrive massively in the middle of an employment crisis without precedence... In addition, the underdevelopment of the welfare state in Spain and the aging of the population increase the work load of women. (Plantenga and Hansen, 1999a, p. 41)

Swedish experiences during the 1990s showed that certain groups were more vulnerable than others. In February 1999 the Swedish Government set up a commission of researchers to review welfare development in Sweden during the 1990s. The commission took the name 'A Balance Sheet for the Welfare in the 1990s'. One conclusion from this work is that single mothers during the 1990s lived under worse conditions than other comparable groups in society (single fathers, single without children, cohabiting with and without children). Four patterns were prevailing:

1. Already in the beginning of the 1990s, single mothers had worse economic conditions than other comparable groups.
2. This relatively bad economic situation was consolidated during the decade.
3. The big changes occurred during the first half of the decade, the income level was reduced and the economic buffers were decreasing.
4. Other groups that had experienced negative changes had an increase in the income level during the second part of the decade, but this was not happening for the single mothers (Gähler, 2001).

The study is based on the Level of Living Study performed by Statistics Sweden. For lone mothers the results showed that by the end of the decade, the adjusted disposable median income was 5 percent lower in the beginning, half of them had no economic margins and more than 60 percent had difficulties in coping with the current expenditures.

What explanations are to be found? Is it related to the income composition or to the employment pattern? The answers were found in the labour market. The main explanation is that the development of the number of working hours among employed single mothers had developed negatively. While full time wage labour had generally been on a constant level during the 1990s for single mothers, it had increased substantially for mothers in two-parent families. The weekly working hours had increased for both full time and part time working mothers in two-parent families, but been constant for full time working single mothers and decreased for part time working single mothers. The analysis in the report concludes that when asked single mothers say that an increase in working hours would be the best solution to their economic difficulties. Problems with day care or that it is uneconomical to work are not referred to as reasons for not increasing working hours or entering the labour force, if they for example are in education and training. The obstacles were found in the labour market, for example discrimination on the basis of being a single parent.

Diane Sainsbury has in her report to the 'Balance Sheet Commission' discussed the welfare changes for women and men in Sweden during the 1990s (Sainsbury, 2000). The gender differences in entitlement to both health insurance and unemployment benefits have decreased during the period. Even through the crisis in the 1990s one can say that the gender differences in these two systems have at least not increased. For the pension system the gender differences are still substantial when it comes to income related pensions over the minimum level. Here still just two thirds of women belonged to this category in 1997, while over 90 percent of all men belonged to it.

The divisions of paid and unpaid work on societal level have to be considered when analysing gender relations in the labour market. The role of the state, its policies, laws and regulations are shaped by ideas and traditions that are gendered. The need for women as a labour force has varied during decades. War time needs for women in factories was transformed to its opposite in the post war period of the 1950s. And nowadays, the reserve army concept seems to be outdated when it comes to describing women's position in the labour market. But the increase in all age groups of female employment levels has not been followed by stable positions in the labour market for all. Part-time jobs, temporary jobs and short term contracts by temporary agents are to a large extent characterizing the female labour force, universally. Again policies, laws and regulations differ between countries, but a common feature seems to be a gender segregation where the outcome of higher education, distribution of the well paid jobs, and career possibilities are unevenly distributed to the negative for women.

A consequence of gender segregation is uneven economic conditions. Empirical studies estimate that gender segregation explain a large proportion of the gender wage gap. How much the gender segregation shall be accounted for varies, but according to Blau et al. (1998) it might in the United States be between 12 and 37 percent of the gender wage gap. A Swedish study concerning the development of the gender pay gap during the period 1981 to 2000 found that the traditional explanations of gender difference in education and skill do not any longer explain the gender wage differences. A standardized calculation showed an increase in the wage gap that had to be explained by other factors (SOU, 2001:53). Given the trend in women's educational level and working experience the gender pay gap should have decreased much more than it has. Labour market segregation looks more as a possible explanation. The hierarchical segregation and the under representation of women as managers and executives probably affects the overall gender gap.

Let us also look at data on the division of labour between men and women in housework in Sweden. Up to the 1970s – for as long as there have been statistics on the matter – women performed most of the housework, both if we count actual time and percentages. During the 1970s there was, however, a change: men spent more of their time doing housework and their share of it increased. Most people have since believed that this development towards gender equality has continued. But if we scrutinize the data we find that this is a truth with modifications. Men's share in percentages of housework has indeed increased considerably – but it is not due to the men themselves. In a time study comparing the years 1990/91 and 2000/01 it is laconically stated (Statistics Sweden, 2003, p. 22): 'For men there is no change to report when it comes to housework.'

What has happened is that women do *less* housework now than before. (The decrease during the 1990s is on average 40 minutes per day.) Today there are probably more dust angels under beds and behind chests of drawers, few iron underwear, there are more semi manufactures of food, more dishwashers and microwave ovens, and so on. The consequence of women's reduced time in housework and the status quo of that of men, is that the total amount of time spent on housework is less now than before. And that is why men's share has increased as long as we only consider percentages. But in that regard one might say that Swedish men have taken a great step towards gender equality – without having changed their behaviour at all.

Changing gender relations: Two strategies

There exist at least two standpoints in the debate on gender segregation and how to act in relation to this phenomenon. One line of argument says that gender segregation is not the problem; it is only the wage discrimination. If women and men were to get equal wage for work of equal value, the gender divisions would not matter. Supporters for the other standpoint argue that segregation is the major cause for wage differences. They say that equal wage for equal work will be an illusion as long as women and men are in separate segments of the labour market, divided by more or less clear barriers and demarcation lines. One process that results in segregation is the bare sorting of people according to gender, ethnicity, education and experience to fit the demands of different segments of the labour market. Recruitment strategies, contractual relations as well as remuneration differ between segments and their 'ideal' labour force.

To be able to explain labour market segregation one has to go from a societal or macro perspective to analyze mechanisms and decision-making processes on organizational and individual level.

In her article 'The Future of "Gender and Organizations": Connections and Boundaries', Joan Acker (1998) discusses how contemporary research on gender and organizations has broken down the boundaries between economics and organization – boundaries formed on disciplinary reasoning and not by the character of the problem to be solved. Studies on power and social relations cut across disciplines, not only in relation to gender but also to ethnicity and class.

But it is on the individual level and in the family that changing gender relations find its most profound expressions. It is here we can see if work arrangements and labour market conditions make it possible for men and women to change their roles and responsibilities. That is why we also present papers showing the relations between employment, work organization and family on one hand and on the other hand effects of new institutions and their practices from an individual and family perspective.

Are there openings towards integration? Of course we can register changes, occupations have changed their gender composition along the history as technology and organization of work has taken new forms. We find historical examples of office clerks once being a very male dominated task becoming one of the most 'female', continuing to be almost disappearing in the new technology developments and organizational changes of office work. Today higher education creates a skilled female labour force, but the opportunities for women to use these skills in the labour market have not increased correspondingly. One can say that education is more profitable for men than for women. Swedish data shows that changes in the wage structure from 1981 and forward have been unfavourable for women as a group. During this period there has been an increasing equality between women and men in experience and length of education (SOU, 2001:53, p. 155). If only these factors had influenced the wages, the gender wage gap would have decreased by 6.5 percent between 1981 and 2000. But the average wage difference between women and men decreased much less (around 1.5 percent). This is explained by the fact that wage differences have increased, given educational length and experience. Data gives the picture of women getting less out of their education in terms of economic reward than men.

Women's income from work in relation to men's can be seen as an illustration of the costs of having a family and children for a woman. In the year 2000 Swedish cohabiting women had 66 percent of men's incomes. If they had small children the relation between women's and men's incomes fell to 57 percent. Cohabiting women with children aged 7–17 had 64 percent of men's incomes, lower than single women with children of the same age. The latter had 68 percent of men's incomes. The economic penalty for women of having a family and children was substantial (Prop., 2002/03:1).

Content of the book

The choice of participating countries is based on the idea that we need to have a representation of studies from countries belonging to different welfare state regimes. Our decision has been to present studies performed in countries belonging to the liberal and the Scandinavian or so-called social democratic welfare state regime. As a basis for this book is a conference held in Stockholm – Women, Work and Health 2002, and two special seminars organized by the Department of Working Life Science at Karlstad University in Sweden and the publication of this book can also be seen as a presentation of young scholars from this department.

After this introduction, Chris Tilly (Chapter 2) takes his point of departure in the standard, efficiency-driven economic narrative of labour market inequality, which holds that such inequality results straightforwardly from the interplay of supply and demand in a market for individual skills. But much social science research points to a very different, socially driven account of labour market inequality. Norms and stereotypes channel action in labour markets. Power disparities and the imperatives of organizational maintenance decisively shape labour market outcomes. Labour markets are constructed not simply of striving individuals, but of pervasive networks.

The chapter reviews two bodies of evidence about labour markets in the United States that offer a test of the relative validity of these two views of the labour market. First, it examines how racial inequality in the labour market has changed over time. Second, it looks at differences across cities in class, gender, and racial gaps in earnings. In both cases, the socially driven model offers more satisfactory explanations.

After briefly addressing the generalizability of these US-based conclusions to other parts of the world, the chapter turns to predictions for future trends in labour market inequality. The efficiency-driven approach contends that the labour market has largely shed, and will continue to shed, distinctions of race, ethnicity, gender, and caste, and that the future will be determined above all by the evolution of technology and of skill development systems. The socially driven view, on the contrary, holds that categorical distinctions reappear in new forms, and that technological choices are a result as much as a cause of social arrangements. A distinction is suggested between the ranking of jobs and the sorting of people among jobs and employment statuses to explore the further implications of a socially driven perspective.

Lena Gonäs considers (in Chapter 3) a multilevel approach to gender and work on the Swedish scene. During the last decade, the Swedish labour market has undergone a severe transformation. The economic crisis that hit the country in the beginning of the decade caused an increase in the unemployment levels for both women and men, at first in the manufacturing, building, and construction industries. Change followed in the public sector, both in the number of employees and in the way production was organized. By the end of the decade, the situation had changed and there was a labour shortage in certain occupations and regions (that is, in the major metropolitan areas, both in new occupations, such as the IT-industry, and in more traditional occupations like nursing and teaching). Swedish women have almost the same employment rate as men, but the labour market is very segregated. Women are predominantly employed in the service sector and/or the public sector in health, education, and child and elder care. These employment patterns (that is, a situation with both labour shortage and unemployment) point to the importance of regionally specific analyses of gender patterns. In addition, since gender segregation at work is associated with both differential exposures to health and safety hazards and higher rates of absenteeism for both men and women, the mental and physical health status in the female workforce may be expected to vary tremendously among these subgroups of the economy.

Towards this background Gonäs describes an action-oriented, regional research project that involves collaboration between researchers and practitioners. The local actors have contributed with knowledge based on local conditions; researchers with gender theoretical perspectives, concepts, and general knowledge about working life, health, and organization. The overall aim is to study the origin of segregation, inequity, and gender-related ill health within the region and what mechanisms maintain deficiencies in equal opportunity. The central questions are: 1) What changes have taken place in the 1990s labour market and in work organizations, and how have these changes affected gender-based segregation patterns, working and living conditions, and health? 2) In what way does gender segregation affect different types of employment, working conditions, means of influence, and health/ ill-health for women and men? 3) What are the regional factors that influence these patterns? and 4) How can local actors within the framework of existing institutions and regulations affect the health and work outcomes for women through change in the gender segregation of the labour market and within organizations? The six-year project involves gathering both quantitative and qualitative data. The project brings together multidisciplinary competence from the fields of social science, behavioural, and medical science.

Ann Bergman discusses (in Chapter 4) the very concept of gender segregation in relation to one of the official political equal opportunity guiding principles in Sweden. Equal opportunities policies in Sweden imply striving for an equitable distribution of women and men in all areas of society in general and in working life in particular. There are in other words political ideas that an equal number of women and men in organizations, in jobs, in departments and so on will lead to integration. An empirical study of gender segregation in organizations shows that this is not necessarily the case. The study rather illustrates how complex the relations between segregation and integration are.

She therefore argues for the need to study different types of gender segregation in organizations – both separate and in relation to each other – and also for the need to focus on structures and mechanisms as a complement to observable gender patterns. The theoretical discussion concentrates on three sets of relations: gender, power and the division of labour. The theoretical argument also embraces a number of mechanisms that are of importance for our understanding of how gender segregation is reproduced in working life.

Bergman's theoretical standpoints are linked to the observable segregation patterns by a discussion of different types of gender segregation, namely job segregation, hierarchical segregation and departmental segregation, but also how they are related to each other. When the relations – that is, the patterns – are examined there are possibilities to compare the male dominated, female dominated and integrated departments, jobs and hierarchical positions. There are also possibilities to identify some of the mechanisms that are important for the reproduction and transformation of gender segregation. While doing that she shows that gender equality is not necessarily the outcome of an equivalent number of women and men. Segregation sometimes takes place within numerical integration and vice versa.

How can gender segregation be measured? – that is the topic of Ruth Emerek's contribution (Chapter 5). Gender segregation is a prevailing characteristic of European labour markets and desegregation has become one of the main objectives of the European action programme for equal opportunities and is considered an important task of the European Employment Strategy. The discussion of segregation and the levels of segregation are however based on measurement, which are open to discussion and criticism. A recent study for the European Commission reveals that none of the measures generally used are perfect, and that the special measure used by the Commission even involves a paradox, as less dissimilarity over occupations combined with a higher proportion of women in employment may result in a higher measure of segregation. The methodology should thus be improved or developed and at least discussed.

It is also important, Emerek argues, to question and discuss the concept of gender segregation. Segregation is a result of multidimensional processes, and the question is whether segregation is a problem, and if so why? One standpoint is that gender segregation reveals real gender differences, indicates discrimination towards women in the male-dominated labour market, and is a most important cause of wage differences. Another standpoint is that gender segregation would be no problem, if women and men held the same wage for equal work or work of equal value and the same working conditions. Segregation is mainly seen as a result of different choices of trade and profession between women and men, and it is (from this standpoint) questioned if gender segregation is a disadvantage.

Differences in gender segregation in various labour markets cannot be discussed without including a discussion of differences in the scale of women's employment and the division of work in households – that is the gender segregation in caring, maintenance and bread-winning. Other important dimensions are the difference in segregation for different generations and educational levels. The process of occupational integration and how new gender divisions in work places subsequently develop should be a main objective for more intensive future research of segregation – including longitudinal studies of occupations.

There is (according to generally used measurements) evidence of a desegregation process in labour markets over time. The long-term development is however a very slow process of desegregation. The continuation of gender segregation can of course be linked to differences in women's and men's choices of education and career paths. Some countries, such as Denmark, have tried, but with little success to pilot women's choice of education into male-dominated areas. The Danish labour market remains, however, still highly gender segregated. Emerek discusses the problem of segregation, the concept of segregation and the methodology of measuring segregation using a study of the Danish labour market. It compares horizontal as well as vertical segregation over generations and education using a highly differentiated occupational classification system.

Given the diverse nature, varied understandings and different claims made about the new economy Diane Perrons seeks (in Chapter 6) to empirically explore gendered employment practices at opposite ends of the hierarchy: new media and care-work and refuse collection, in one local labour market. New media employees/freelancers are generally highly qualified professionals who experience highly pressurized working patterns, individualized systems of pay determination and continuing gender segregation, all issues traditionally of trade union concern; yet this population rarely, if ever, turns to trade unions for support. The author explores what role trade unions might play in this context, whether alternative forms of representation have developed to deal with their concerns.

Care-workers and refuse collectors by contrast are more likely to be unionized, but generally have few formal skills and qualifications and their working conditions have recently been adversely affected by the private finance initiative (a contemporary form of privatization). Perrons explores the effects of this initiative on working conditions and systems of representation. She also explores the differential treatment of and response by these different groups of workers characterized by high levels of gender segregation (women care-workers and male refuse collectors). On a more conceptual level she explores the continuing foundations and implications of gender segregation at different levels in the new economy.

Liselotte Jakobsen is one of the developers of life mode theory, aiming at integrating class and gender analysis. Here she puts theory to use in a study of assistant nurses (Chapter 7). During the 1990s the Swedish public sector, as in many other countries, went through big reorganizations. The aim was to improve effectiveness and quality. Money should be saved through cut-downs in staff, at the same time as the level of qualification among remaining staff should be raised. This meant that many assistant nurses were given notice, and that assistant nurses' jobs were transformed into nurses' jobs. As a result, approximately two thirds of assistant nurses lost their jobs, entirely or partially. In order to study the possible consequences of such extensive cut-downs in the biggest women's occupation in the country, a case study was conducted. Twenty assistant nurses, 18 women and two men, were followed up during a period ranging from about five to eight years from the notice to quit.

The nurses were interviewed on two occasions. The first set of interviews showed that at this point in time, most of them were still working in their occupation in the public health sector, sometimes even at the same workplace. However, part time employment and temporary employment had increased within the group; there was a considerable deterioration in terms of employment and the nurses were experiencing economic problems. The interviewees also felt that they had been badly treated by the employer, they were worried about the future and they expressed anxiety about the way the reorganization had affected the situation of the patients. Yet the majority wanted to carry on within their occupation. A new job would call for education, and they did not think that they could afford or manage education, some of them because they had small children. Some could not think of anything else to do. But above all, and despite the recent negative experiences, they were almost all very happy with their work as assistant nurses. They believed that things would have to change. Only one of them, a man, had left for another job. Three younger women had started various kinds of education; the other man and one more woman were considering doing so.

When new interviews were carried out three and a half years later, conditions within the public health sector had changed rather dramatically. Now the organization was slimmed, but at the same time it was beginning to be difficult to get enough personnel; it was troublesome to fill the new nurses' posts and even assistant nurses were sometimes hard to find. The interviews showed that all assistant nurses who wanted to stay in their occupation, also had managed to do so. Furthermore they had improved their working conditions, most of them were permanently employed and most of them had achieved the working hours they wanted. So far they felt satisfied, but they complained about heavy work pressure and the situation of the patients. Some of those who went through education were on their way back to the health sector, but now aiming at higher positions within the organization.

In order to shed some light on what actually took place, and why it did so, in these processes, Jakobsen uses life mode analysis. She suggests that the mechanisms behind the events in large parts could be understood as interplay between the practices and ideologies of socio-structural life modes in modern western society, in this particular case the worker life mode, the housewife life mode and the career life mode.

Rosemary Crompton (in Chapter 8) weaves together two themes. The first theme relates to sociological arguments relating to growing individualism in 'late modernity'. These debates are seen as being associated with the turn to economic liberalism and its consequences. In employment, economic liberalism has been associated with the development of New Managerial Techniques, which include flexible working as well as the development of the 'entrepreneurial self' in the employment context. In the family, individualism has been associated with both family instability and falling birth rates. The second theme relates to the consequence (in Europe, US and Australasia at any rate) of changes in gender relations and the gender division of labour following the impact of 'second wave' feminism. In particular, Crompton focuses on arguments (from rather different quarters) that there has been 'no real change' in the gender division of labour – that is, that as women still retain the major responsibility for caring work, and men are still dominant in the market sphere, there has been a modification rather than fundamental shift in the gender division of labour.

Both flexible employment, and family instability, are critically examined. It is suggested that perceived current 'instabilities' in both families and employment are not, in fact, novel phenomena in market capitalism. However, what is new as far as the current situation is concerned is the substantial normative shift that has taken place in respect of gender relations and attitudes towards gender. A counter-argument is developed in respect of the second theme. It is suggested that parallel developments within, and the growing tensions between, employment and the family might be the source of 'counter-movements' against the effects of economic liberalism.

Lisbeth Bekkengen studies (Chapter 9) gender differences in parental leave. In Sweden fathers and mothers have had the equal and statutory right to take paid parental leave since 1974. But men do not use their rights to the same extent as women do, and both parental leave and parenthood are still the responsibilities of women. If the purpose is to understand why women – but not men – use the rights it is important to compare men's and women's conditions both in working life and in family life. The main difference between men and women is not the conditions at the workplace or the financial possibilities, but the fact that men have the freedom of choice whereas women have to adjust to the circumstances. Women as well as men can have problems at the workplace, but the problems become obstacles only when several alternatives exist. Men can decide if, when and for how long they want to be on parental leave. Women take parental leave when the baby is born, and they cannot negotiate and discuss whether they want to be on parental leave. If women should do so they would – by contrast to men – be regarded as bad parents. The main mechanism is therefore how fatherhood and motherhood is socially constructed.

The question of parental leave highlights three social structures: the relation between production (work) and reproduction (family), the relation of men and women to work and family, and finally the gender relation. In the interaction between these structures women become 'parents' whereas men are 'daddies'. This means that women have responsibilities in both working life and family life, both as parents and as employed. As employed men as well have responsibilities in working life, but in family life – and parenthood – men have rights, rights to take an active part in the parenthood or they can show a lack of commitment. The differences between men could be described as whether they have a 'children oriented masculinity'. This masculinity could exist on the discourse level only, but men who turn the children oriented masculinity into practice seem to take parental leave independent of the circumstances, if parental leave corresponds with their own wishes and needs. Men with this type of masculinity are not necessary equal men, because this masculinity highlights primarily men's relationship to children, not the gender relation.

In a final chapter the editors discuss methodological as well as theoretical questions raised by the contributors to the book.

References

Acker, J. (1998), 'The Future of "Gender and Organizations": Connections and Boundaries', in *Gender, Work and Organization*, vol. 5, pp. 195–206.

Blau, F. D., P. Simpson, and D. Anderson (1998), 'Continuing Progress?: Trends in the Occupational Segregation in the Unites States Over the 1970s and 1980s', *Feminist Economics*, vol. 4, pp. 29–71.

Emerek, R., H. Figureiredo, M. P. González, L. Gonäs, and J. Rubery (2001), 'Indicators on Gender Segregation', in J. Rubery, C. Fagan, D. Grimshaw, H. Figureiredo and M. Smith (eds), *Indicators on Gender Equality in the European Employment Strategy*, Report to the Equal Opportunities Unit, DG Employment, http://www.umist.ac.uk/management/ewerec/egge/egge.htm.

Gähler, M. (2001), 'Bara en mor – ensamstående mödrars ekonomiska levnadsvillkor i 1990-talets Sverige' ('Only a mother – The Economic Living Conditions for Lone Mothers in the 1990s in Sweden), *SOU*, 2001:54, Fritzes, Stockholm.

Lewis, J. (1993), 'Women, Work and Family Policies in Europe', in J. Lewis (ed.), *Women and Social Policies in Europe*, Edward Elgar, London.

Orloff, A. S. (1993), 'Gender and the Social Rights of Citizenship: The Comparative Analysis of Gender Relations and Welfare States', *American Sociological Review*, vol. 58, pp. 303–332.

Plantenga, J. and J. Hansen (1999a), *Benchmarking Equal Opportunities in the European Union*, Synthesis report based on eight European countries, Institute of Economics, Utrecht University, Utrecht.

Plantenga, J. and J. Hansen (1999b), 'Assessing Equal Opportunities in the European Union', *International Labour Review*, no. 138, pp. 351–379.

Prop., 2002/03:1, *Finansplanen, Utgiftsområde 14, Bilaga 1, Fördelningen av ekonomiska resurser mellan kvinnor och män* (The Division of Economic Resources between Women and Men), Finansdepartementet (Ministry of Finance), Stockholm.

Rubery, J., M. Smith, and C. Fagan (eds) (1999), *Women's Employment in Europe: Trends and Prospects*, Routledge, London.

Sainsbury, D. (ed.) (1999), *Gender and Welfare State Regimes*, Oxford University Press, Oxford.

Sainsbury, D. (2000), 'Välfärdsutvecklingen för kvinnor och män på 1990-talet', (Development of the level of living for women and men in the 1990s), *SOU*, 2000:40, Fritzes, Stockholm.

SOU, 2001:53, *Välfärd och arbete i arbetslöshetens årtionde*, Kommittén för Välfärdsbokslut, Norstedts, Stockholm.

Statistics Sweden (2003), *Tid för vardagsliv, Kvinnors och mäns tidsanvänding 1990/91 och 2000/2001*, Rapport 99, Statistics Sweden, Stockholm.

Chapter 2

Labour Market Inequality, Past and Future: A Perspective from the United States

Chris Tilly

Introduction

Social scientific analysis of labour market inequality has generated two main narratives: an efficiency-driven narrative and a socially driven narrative. The standard, *efficiency-driven* economic narrative of labour market inequality holds that such inequality results straightforwardly from the interplay of supply and demand in a market for individual skills. But much social science research points to a very different, *socially driven* account of labour market inequality. Norms and stereotypes channel action in labour markets. Power disparities and the imperatives of organizational maintenance decisively shape labour market outcomes. Labour markets are constructed not simply of striving individuals, but of pervasive networks.

I review four bodies of evidence about labour markets that offer a test of the relative validity of these two views of the labour market. First, I examine how racial inequality in the labour market in the United States has changed over time. Second, I look at differences across US cities in class, gender, and racial gaps in earnings. Third, I consider the growth of part-time and temporary work in the United States. Finally, I broaden my scope to international evidence, addressing the link between gender segregation and the gender pay gap. Despite appealing features of the efficiency-driven theory – chiefly simplicity and explanatory parsimony – in both cases, the socially driven model offers more satisfactory explanations of the evidence about labour market inequality.

In closing, I turn to predictions for future trends in labour market inequality. The efficiency-driven approach contends that the labour market has largely shed, and will continue to shed, distinctions of race, ethnicity, gender, and caste, and that the future will be determined above all by the evolution of technology and of skill development systems. The socially driven view, on the contrary, holds that categorical distinctions reappear in new forms, and that technological choices are a result as much as a cause of social arrangements. I distinguish between the *ranking* of jobs and the *sorting* of people among jobs and employment statuses to explore the further implications of a socially driven perspective.

Specifying the two narratives

The efficiency-driven narrative regarding labour markets is grounded in neoclassical economics. According to economist Gary Becker, 'The combined assumptions of maximizing behaviour, market equilibrium, and stable preferences, used relentlessly and unflinchingly, form the heart of the economic approach as I see it' (1976, p. 5). This outlook sees the labour market as the meeting place of two optimization processes. Prices (wages) are determined by the supply of and demand for skills possessed by individuals. The supply of skills is determined by the optimization processes of individuals and families. This optimization, in turn, is shaped by innate abilities, individuals' preferences (for example, the extent to which they are willing to forego consumption in order to invest in their own or their children's skills), as well as the available education and training system. Firms seek to maximize profits by deciding (among other things) the quantity and mix of labour with different types of skills that they can most efficiently use to produce their desired output. They base these choices on the demand for products, and on available production technology. In making these optimizing choices, they set the demand for skills. While advocates of an efficiency-driven narrative will readily acknowledge that the world deviates from this ideal type, they generally argue that the differences are sufficiently small and unsystematic that the model is adequate for making predictions and guiding policy.

The efficiency-driven narrative's key implication is that earnings inequality (as well as other types of labour market inequality, such as inequality in unemployment rates) is efficient, in the sense that it conveys information needed for households and firms to optimize. Market wages signal which skills are most scarce and therefore most productive, and which are less needed. If an industry expands or contracts, wage movements will tell workers to flock to the industry or flee it. The relative wages of labourers and engineers allow firms to figure out the most efficient combination of these two types of workers. Attempts to 'artificially' reduce earnings inequality corrupt this information, pushing the economy farther from efficiency. To the extent that society values equality, we should direct our efforts to helping increase the skills of the less-skilled.

To be sure, this simple efficiency-based account is not the only perspective emerging from standard economic theory. As George Akerlof (2002), Michael Spence (2002), and Joseph Stiglitz (2002) have pointed out, they and others have been constructing for more than 30 years an alternative economic paradigm built on departures from rationality and the unavailability or costliness of the information needed to optimize. However, as Stiglitz also noted, public policy in most of the world is still largely – indeed, increasingly – guided by the efficiency-based narrative.

Moreover, as I have argued elsewhere (Tilly and Tilly, 1998), the 'new information economics' itself includes contrary efficiency-based and socially based ideas.

The socially driven narrative has a more eclectic pedigree than its efficiency-driven counterpart, drawing on sociology and on Marxist and institutionalist approaches to economics. While these schools of thought disagree on much, they generally agree that skill has a large social component rather than consisting of cognitive ability and dexterity (Darrah, 1994; Vallas, 1990). That is, job performance depends greatly on social context. The nature of relationships with co-workers, supervisors, or customers, for example, can spell the difference between success and failure. More generally, the socially driven approach holds that the supply of and demand for labour are socially determined. As Tilly and Tilly put it, 'Work does not issue from the efforts of isolated individuals who respond to market cues but from social relations among workers, employers, and consumers' (1998, p. 4). Worker and employer preferences are shaped by norms, pre-existing social networks, and discrimination – with segregation as one result. In particular, employers' optimization deviates greatly from an objective calculation of how to maximize profits. It incorporates prejudices and beliefs, as well as managers' individual goals.

Labour supply and demand also depend on pre-existing social networks – indeed, a large fraction of recruitment and hiring takes place through network processes (Granovetter, 1995). Institutions such as child care systems and seniority rules also mould supply and demand. Wage-setting itself results from a wide range of norms (such as notions of fairness) and institutions (such as unions or business associations), not just from economic supply and demand. Overcoming inequality, therefore, does not simply call for additional investment in technical skills. It requires social change.

Evidence about labour market inequality

I review four bodies of evidence about labour market inequality. The first examines how earnings gaps between blacks and whites in the United States have changed over time. Over the 20th century, the black-white pay gap narrowed markedly. James Smith and Finis Welch (1989) offered an efficiency-driven account of this change. They explained the narrowing trend via two related forms of optimizing behaviour by African Americans: migration out of the South and acquisition of more education. But Martin Carnoy (1994) challenged this interpretation. He focused on blacks' rate of progress decade by decade, and noted that it was highly uneven (Table 2.1).

There is little question that migration and educational upgrading boosted African Americans' economic fortunes. But why the stop-start pattern? Two obvious factors to examine would be the availability of jobs (which drives many migrations) and the disposition of politics and public policy (which plays a key part in the quality of schools available to African Americans, among other issues). More broadly, we can look at macroeconomic and political conditions. Macroeconomic expansion, as manifested in lower unemployment rates, clearly aids African Americans (Cherry and Rodgers, 2000). But this generalization still does not offer a fully satisfactory explanation. How do we account for blacks' stagnant wage position relative to whites during the generally buoyant 1950s and late 1980s? Carnoy pointed to the federal level political stance toward African Americans, fluctuations in which followed this time pattern almost precisely. The broad political stance translated into a variety of specific policies over the decades in question: school desegregation and equalization of educational resources, passage and enforcement (or non-enforcement) of antidiscrimination laws, government employment of African Americans, and government purchasing from black-owned businesses. Moreover, he observed, federal governments favourable toward civil rights and affirmative action have also tended to place more emphasis on combating unemployment and less on reducing inflation, so that macroeconomic conditions were themselves mightily influenced by the political climate. Socially driven explanations appear to offer a superior explanation for these time patterns in racial inequality.

Table 2.1   Black wage levels relative to whites, United States

1940s: Rapid advance
1950s: Stagnation
1960-75: Rapid advance
1975-95: Stagnation and by some measures regression
1995-2000: Advance

Source: Adapted and updated from Carnoy 1994.

A second body of evidence assays US regional variation in inequality. Leslie McCall (2001) studied the variation of several forms of wage inequality across 500 geographic regions in the United States. She looked at gender, race, and the average gap between people with different levels of education, such as high school graduates and four year college graduates (a distinction McCall labels 'class', but which does not capture a broader conception of class). An efficiency-driven narrative would lead us to expect that skill differences are the key to all earnings differences (with some exceptions, such as compensating wage differentials for dangerous or unpleasant work) (Rosen, 1986; Willis, 1986). Therefore, racial and gender wage gaps should be wider where earnings disparities by education level yawn wider as well. In other words, all three dimensions of inequality should be positively correlated.

Table 2.2 shows how the gender wage gap is correlated with various other dimensions of inequality. Contrary to predictions based on the efficiency-driven account, the correlations are virtually all negative (and the one exception shows a negligible correlation). Can a socially driven narrative explain this result? McCall suggested that the explanations lie in regional 'configurations of inequality' – sets of relative wage positions grounded in institutional features of the labour market (see also Peck, 1996). Although she classified US regions into a set of four main configurations, a comparison of the two polar extremes illustrates the logic of her analysis.

Table 2.2   **Correlation of gender wage gap with other wage gaps, across 500 regions of the United States**

Wage gap	*Correlation*
Women: High school vs. college	(-)
Women: Less than high school vs. college	--
Men: High school vs. college	(-)
Men: Less than high school vs. college	(-)
Women: Black vs. white	(-)
Women: Latina vs. white	(-)
Men: Black vs. white	(-)
Men: Latino vs. white	(-)

Source: McCall, 2001.

The Detroit metropolitan area, capital of the US auto industry and of the still powerful United Auto Workers union, exemplifies the 'industrial' configuration. Gender inequality looms large, reflecting the importance of well paid, largely male manual jobs in heavy industry. Although unions moderate wage differences by educational level among men, the educational wage gap among women is large, reflecting the relative bifurcation of women's jobs between service and professional occupations. Unions and union-influenced politics (African-American Detroit mayor Coleman Young, who governed between 1973 and 1993, started out as a United Auto Workers activist) also mitigate racial wage differences.

At the other extreme lies the 'post-industrial' configuration, with the sunbelt metropolis of Dallas as its archetype. Dallas's economy is centred on high technology and services, and its labour markets are 'de-institutionalized', with low union density and high levels of contingent work. Although regional data on company policies are not available, we know from case study evidence that businesses in Dallas's key industries tend to adopt compensation policies with a relatively loose connection between job classification and seniority (Cappelli et al., 1997). The result is greater inequality by educational level among men, greater racial inequality, but diminished gender inequality. A nation of Dallases and Detroits would generate the negative correlation coefficients seen in Table 2.2. The general point is that historically formed labour market structures and institutions – not the simple supply and demand of the efficiency-based account – differentially shape the various axes of inequality.

A third phenomenon that allows us to weigh the relative merits of the efficiency-driven and socially driven viewpoints is the growth of part-time and temporary employment in the United States. Part-time employment trended upward as a share of total employment from the mid-1950s, when the level of part-time employment was first measured, to the mid-1990s, before levelling off (Tilly, 1996). Temporary agencies, invented in the late 1950s, saw their share of the workforce trend upward up to the present (Rogers, 2000).

Efficiency theory leads us to look to two likely sources of this growth. One is a shift in preferences of the workforce. If more workers prefer shorter hours or the flexibility that comes with short-term assignments, employers will find ways to accommodate these desires. The second is a shift in the technology of work itself that makes it more discontinuous, so that staffing with long-term, full-time employees becomes less efficient. This shift in the technology of work could result from a change in the composition of employment: for example, fewer people producing durable goods on assembly lines that companies seek to keep running as many hours are possible, and more people serving lunches at peak times during the day and week. The change in the composition of employment, in turn, could be due to changes in the mix of demand (more people eating meals outside the home as women enter the workforce in larger numbers) or in production technology (productivity advances in durable goods production that reduce its employment share relative to food service). Alternatively, work technology could shift simply because, within each industry, businesses have only now discovered efficient ways to match staff to workload that could have improved efficiency all along. One possible socially driven account would give the same pattern a different interpretation: the diffusion of part-time and temporary employment does not represent the spread of an innovation, but the breakdown of norms and institutions that historically barred the use of more exploitative forms of employment.

Analysis of the patterns of growth of part-time and temporary work in the United States suggests that a combination of efficiency-based and socially based factors are at work. In my own research (Tilly, 1996), I found that growing numbers of women and teenagers in the US labour market propelled the growth of part-time employment from the 1950s to the early 1970s. But the contribution of this demographic shift to part-time growth diminished. By the 1980s, the number of women and teens seeking part-time work was no longer increasing as a proportion of the workforce: women increasingly sought part-time work, and the exit of the 'baby boom' generation from their teenage years decreased the flow of teens. Indeed, the continuing trend toward a higher share of part-time employment was driven exclusively by growing 'involuntary' part-time employment – part-time workers who would prefer full-time work.

What about changes in the technology of work? Part of the rise in part-time employment resulted from growing employment shares claimed by retail trade and services, sectors which historically had high levels of part-time employment. But another portion arose from a growing proportion of part-time jobs *within* almost every industry. In-depth interviews with managers supported both interpretations of this within-industry trend suggested above. Managers most often cited two advantages of a part-time workforce: the ability to match staffing levels with peaks of work volume (an efficiency-based explanation), and savings due to the ability to offer lower wages and fringe benefits to part-time workers (suggesting new opportunities for exploitation resulting from weakened norms and institutions).

Particularly interesting was the evidence that I found that the retail industry had expanded part-time employment to a point that it led to diminished efficiency. Retail managers complained about the low commitment level and high turnover of part-time workers. In a fascinating pairing of comments, the human resource director of a supermarket chain described trying to convert as many jobs to part-time as possible because part-time compensation was half as much per hour, while a store manager estimated that a full-time produce clerk was three times as productive per hour as a part-timer! The scope of management miscalculation is suggested by the fact that as part-time employment grew, US grocery store productivity fell 23 percent in real terms between 1973 and 1992 (Tilly, 1996, p. 26). It is difficult to square these facts with a pure efficiency story.

Nonetheless, US businesses did not persist endlessly down the path of increasing part-time employment. During the long expansion of the 1990s, part-time employment declined significantly, snapping a thirty-plus year growth trend. As labour shortages heightened quit rates and lack of job commitment among low-paid workers including many part-timers, employers finally shifted to a more full-time workforce. As predicted by efficiency-based theories, employers responded to shifts in labour supply. But it is difficult to explain why they took so long to respond without drawing on socially driven theories.

In the case of temporary work, a socially based explanation is even more compelling. Whereas two-thirds to three-quarters of part-time workers in the United States are willingly working short hours (Tilly, 1996), 60 percent of temporary help employees would prefer a non-temporary job (Hudson, 1999). George Gonos (1997) demonstrated that at the dawn of the temporary help industry, agencies such as Manpower fought a concerted political and legal battle to avoid regulatory requirements, so that they could offer businesses a way to hire workers unencumbered by labour regulations. Thus, it appears to be the opening of a loophole in protective institutions that explains the rapid expansion of temporary jobs.

A final source of evidence is international comparisons of occupational segregation and pay inequality by gender. Occupational segregation by gender is virtually universal, as is gender-based pay inequality: women work in different jobs than men, and earn less than men, on average, all over the world. As Barbara Reskin and Heidi Hartmann (1986) described it:

> There is some division of labour by sex in most societies. Across all societies, moreover, there is a pattern to this division of labour. Women generally do those tasks that are compatible with child care – tasks that are not dangerous, do not take them far from the home, do not require close attention, and are readily interrupted…. Within the limits of female-assigned child care and sexual dimorphism in strength and energy, there is a great deal of variability across societies as to which gender is expected to do what job, even in the West. (p. 7, citations omitted)

Efficiency-based analysts attribute gender pay differences to productivity differences. According to these analysts, women may choose to work in different jobs from men for a variety of reasons, including individual preferences or a need for flexibility due to child care responsibilities – but if they are getting paid less on average, it is because they are less productive. After all, if women were being paid less than their productivity, alert employers would start hiring women into 'men's' jobs in order to save on wage payments, starting a bidding-up process that would only end when women's pay reflected their productive abilities. Women's lower average productivity could result from less work experience due to child-bearing and rearing, or to attention divided between duties in the workplace and home (England, 1992; Hersch and Stratton, 1997, 2002; Stratton, 1995).

The socially driven analysis, on the other hand, reasons that gender pay gaps are largely created by segregation between differently valued occupations. Such segregation, in turn, is reinforced by a set of institutions (England, 1992; Kilbourne, England and Beron, 1994). In some countries the institutions still include explicit legal barriers to women (or to subgroups of women, such as those who are married). But in richer countries, the main forces channelling women are strongly held norms about who is appropriate for a job and how a job must be performed (for example, how many hours a week a worker must put in to do the job adequately). Norms also reward work typically done by men more than work typically done by women; for instance, in the United States there is a wage penalty for jobs that include 'nurturing' activities (Kilbourne, England, and Beron, 1994).

The socially driven narrative about gender in the labour market would predict that where occupational segregation is greater, the wage gap between men and women will be wider as well. However, this turns out not to be true. David Anker (2001) summarized the research on the relationship between occupational differences and pay differences by gender, in international comparison. Estimates generally find a relationship that is not statistically significant and in some instances is unexpectedly negative. McCall, similarly, finds only a small correlation between these two measures of gender difference across US regions.

Does the missing correlation disprove the socially driven narrative, at least as it relates to gender differences in the labour market? Before giving up on the socially driven account, it makes sense to take a closer look at patterns of occupational segregation and gender pay disparities. As Table 2.3 shows, the potential for a negative correlation arises because of the position of the Scandinavian countries – with high segregation but a small pay gap – and Asian countries, with low segregation but a large wage differential.

To understand why these countries fall at the extremes of the grid, it is necessary to examine individual national cases. Consider Sweden and Japan (Anker, 2001; Hashimoto, 1990; Western, 1997). Sweden's labour market features centralized wage-setting by union federations and employer associations. The unions have pursued solidarity-oriented bargaining that has compressed wage differences. At the same time, Sweden has subsidized child care, and has created large numbers of part-time jobs concentrated in the public sector. The result is working women who are funnelled into particular jobs, but who receive wages not far below those of men. Japan's system of enterprise unionism, on the other hand, decentralizes wage-setting. Women work in the secondary fringe – in small firms, in part-time for short-term jobs – in almost every sector. In short, the unexpected cross-national pattern does not refute the importance of social institutions in the labour market, but rather reflects institutional patterns that are more complex than anticipated.

Table 2.3   The cross-national pattern of levels of occupational segregation and wage gap by gender

		Occupational segregation		
		Low	*Medium*	*High*
Wage gap	*Small*			Nordic countries
	Medium		Rest of Europe	
	Large	Asia		

Source: Based on Anker, 2001.

In summary, a variety of evidence about labour market inequality points to the importance of social factors. This does not deny the value of the efficiency-based notion that employers and workers respond to forces of supply and demand, at least if those forces loom large enough. As I noted in the discussion of part-time employment in the United States, businesses facing a labour shortage eventually backed off from excessive (by efficiency criteria) use of part-time workers. Similarly, David Card and Alan Krueger (1995) argued that although moderate increases in the US federally mandated minimum wage have not and will not lead to diminished employment, very large increases would likely lead to disemployment. The point is that much of the actual historical and cross-sectional variation we observe has little to do with efficiency-driven mechanisms, and instead reflects social forces and institutions.

The future of labour market inequality

The efficiency-driven narrative and the socially driven narrative forecast rather different futures for labour market inequality. In the efficiency-driven account, two main factors drive change. The first is the continuing decline of non-efficiency factors in shaping the labour market. Economies have and will continue to shed discriminatory distinctions and social democratic protections alike, as societies realize that these market distortions reduce economic well-being. As these other influences are stripped away, employment rates and wages will more and more reflect true differences in skill and productivity. Richard Herrnstein and Charles Murray (1994) put forward a particularly extreme version of this hypothesis, holding that labour market success increasingly reflects genetically grounded ability – though many other researchers have refuted this particular analysis of recent changes (see, for example, Devlin et al., 1997; Levine, 1999).

In any case, the supposed growing importance of skill points to the second factor driving the evolution of inequality: changes in the supply and demand for skill. Growing wage inequality within countries, on this account, results from 'skill-biased technological change' – technological shifts, notably computerization, that favour more highly skilled workers. As of 1999, two leading economists in the field declared that 'The [economics] profession seems to be near consensus' that skill-biased technological change is driving increased demand for skilled labour (Berman and Machin, 1999, p. 3). On the other hand, most efficiency-focused analysts attribute changes in earnings inequality *between* countries – such as the falling relative earnings of much of sub-Saharan Africa, or the surge in wages in some newly industrializing economies such as Korea – to the degree to which each nation has shed efficiency-hampering institutions. But to the extent that most countries *are* indeed dispensing with such fetters (Friedman, 2000), the efficiency framework would predict that cross-national differences should increasingly reflect differential success in imparting skills. In short, in the future, patterns of earnings inequality among individuals and nations alike will flow ever more directly from skill differences.

There are a variety of reasons for questioning the description of the recent past that underlies these predictions for the future. While institutional change has been unmistakable, it is debatable whether the changes have taken – and will continue to take – the form of widespread liberalization. As Stiglitz (2002) observed, post-communist marketization has generally lead to either highly regulated markets (as in China) or privatized plunder (as in Russia) – neither one a model of efficient, laissez-faire capitalism (see also Hohnen, 2003). The countries of Latin America, many of which liberalized their economies over the past two decades, are now turning the other way (Forero, 2002; Moffett, 2002; Semple, 2002). Bruce Western and Joshua Guetzkow (2002) posited that the emerging economic regime in the United States itself can be better characterized as 'punitive' than as 'neoliberal', given the huge prison population and the escalating controls imposed on recipients of social welfare payments.

Doubts also arise about the technologically driven story of growing earnings inequality (Moss, 2002; Moss and Tilly, 2001). Robert Gordon (2000) noted that contrary to 'new economy' claims about computers' impact on every sector of the economy, surging productivity in the United States has been confined almost entirely to the durable goods sector, with much of the measured gain coming from productivity improvements in the manufacturing of computers themselves. The timing of growing US earnings inequality does not match up with the timing of the technological shifts alleged to have fuelled that growth (Howell, Duncan and Harrison, 1998). And the much more rapid widening of disparities in the United States compared to other rich countries, despite similar technological changes sweeping all countries, suggests that technology can be at most one part of the cause.

What alternative explanation does a social driven perspective offer? The socially based view is by its nature less deterministic. In fact, this viewpoint starts from the premise that technological choices, far from being exogenous, are themselves socially determined. Persistent managerial attempts to take control of the labour process away from workers testify as much (Braverman, 1974; Noble, 1984). Skill development systems are *a fortiori* social outcomes, as evidenced by the very different skill systems found in different countries (Dertouzos, Lester and Solow, 1989). But beyond this social context for technological and skill change itself, a socially driven narrative would focus on factors other than skill in explaining the persistence and evolution of inequality.

One critical change, in this view, is the weakening of 'pure' categorical distinctions such as gender, race, and ethnicity – primarily as a result of social movements for equality and expanded democracy. In the United States, gender and ethnicity have come to matter less. Conversely, as overall inequality widens, class matters more. Inequality is growing *within* groups, such as women and African Americans, who were once largely confined to a narrow band of low earnings. To be sure, the impact of ethnicity and gender are not declining everywhere. The eruption of ethnically based conflicts and even civil wars in many parts of the world, and the resurgence of religious fundamentalism incorporating male supremacy, demonstrate that these ascriptive categories exert a growing grip in some settings. But their economic import in most wealthy countries have diminished.

Even so, research informed by a socially driven paradigm tells us that categorical distinctions are tenacious, and often reappear in new forms. Moss and Tilly (2001) found that US employers no longer feel comfortable saying that they do not like African Americans; instead, many employers state that African Americans lack necessary skills. Whereas blacks do indeed, on average, have lower levels of education than whites, these employer attitudes are widespread in low-level jobs that require little, if any, education – and for which the alternative workforce consists largely of immigrants with limited education themselves (Waldinger and Lichter, 2003). Instead of education, managers focus primarily on the 'soft skills' involved in social interaction – 'skills' that are assessed subjectively and that depend greatly on the friendliness of a work environment toward workers from a particular group. Racial (and gender) stereotypes have also become more likely to stigmatize particular subgroups: for instance, managers have particularly negative perceptions of less educated black men from the inner city (Kirschenman and Neckerman, 1991).

Lawrence Bobo, James Kluegel and Ryan Smith (1997) characterized new white prejudices toward blacks in the United States as 'laissez-faire racism'. The tenor of these beliefs is that civil rights laws have removed the obstacles to black advancement, so if African-Americans have failed to gain economically it is because they lack ability or are not exerting sufficient effort. A similar spirit motivated the 1996 welfare law placing strict work requirements, time limits, and other restrictions on single mothers receiving government assistance. Although the conservatives who drafted the bill justified it in terms of supporting marriage, the message that resonated most with the general public could be described as 'laissez-faire sexism': female welfare recipients should be subject to the same market discipline as the rest of the population. Much like laissez-faire racism, this ideology overlooks the multiple burdens and problems that hamper single mothers in the labour market (Albelda and Tilly, 1997). Thus, there seems little prospect that gender and race distinctions in the labour market will fade away.

So far, this discussion of socially driven narrative's insights about the future has examined *sorting* processes: how are people sorted among jobs, and who gets the good jobs? But labour market inequality also depends on *ranking* (Granovetter and Tilly, 1988): which jobs are the good jobs, and how different are pay and working conditions for good and bad jobs? As the late reggae musician Peter Tosh (1977) queried, 'Everybody's trying to reach the top / Tell me, how far is it from the bottom?'

Clearly, the top of the labour market has moved farther from the bottom. An efficiency-driven response would hold that the same mechanism determines both ranking and sorting: jobs are ranked based on productivity, and people are sorted among jobs based on their skill and consequent productivity. But a socially driven analysis of ranking changes directs attention to changes in institutions, norms, and rules (Tilly, 1997, 2000). In the United States, the most obvious changes are the declines of union density and of the real value of the mandated minimum wage. Processes that shift employment outside large organizations – such as subcontracting and temporary employment – have also contributed. Most fundamentally, basic norms that limited wage disparities have been weakened by the same resurgent laissez-faire ideology that rationalizes continued race and gender inequalities. Similar processes have stretched apart wages in other nations, though not to the same extent as in the United States.

The policy implications of the efficiency-driven framework and the socially driven one are quite different. If earnings inequalities result from efficiency-maximizing economic activity, then at best we can trade off efficiency for equity, sacrificing some economic output in order to distribute goods and services more equally (Okun, 1975). At worst, attempts to redistribute resources warp incentives to the point where they harm those they are intended to help (Murray, 1984). Active policy instruments for reducing inequality are limited to skill development systems, and in the United States the dominant reform proposals for such systems propose marketization through school vouchers and the like.

The socially driven narrative, on the other hand, describes a far more contingent relationship between efficiency and equity – one that I can only summarize very briefly here. Under many circumstances, redistribution boosts growth rather than dragging it down (Tilly, 2004; Tilly and Albelda, 1995). Varied institutional arrangements are all compatible with economic competitiveness (Christopherson, 2002; Ortmann and Salzman, 1998; Tilly and Tilly, 1998). The implication is that within limits, *we choose the amount of inequality* by the institutions, policies, and norms we adopt. This does not mean that it is easy to reduce inequality. But it does mean that current patterns of inequality are neither efficient nor inevitable, and that a variety of policy instruments can productively be used to attack inequality. The evidence presented in this chapter suggests that a socially driven narrative does a better job than an efficiency-driven one in explaining many current patterns and recent changes in labour market inequality. If so, the future of inequality will depend crucially on how we use this knowledge to guide the choices we make as societies.

References

Akerlof, George A. (2002), 'Behavioral Macroeconomics and Macroeconomic Behaviour', *American Economic Review*, vol. 92, pp. 411–433.

Albelda, Randy and Chris Tilly (1997), *Glass Ceilings and Bottomless Pits: Women's Work, Women's Poverty*, South End Press, Boston.

Anker, David (2001), 'Theories of Occupational Segregation by Sex: An Overview', in Martha Fetherolf Loutfi (ed.), *Women, Gender, and Work: What Is Equality and How Do We Get There?*, International Labour Office, Geneva, pp.129–156.

Becker, Gary S. (1976), *The Economic Approach To Human Behaviour*, University of Chicago Press, Chicago.

Berman, Eli and Stephen Machin (1999), 'SBTC Happens: Evidence on the Factor Bias of Technological Change in Developing and Developed Countries', paper presented at the *National Bureau of Economic Research Summer Conference, Labour Studies*, July 1999.

Bobo, Lawrence, James R. Kluegel and Ryan A. Smith (1997), 'Laissez-Faire Racism: The Crystallization of a "Kinder, Gentler" Anti-Black Ideology', in Steven A. Tuch and Jack K. Martin (eds), *Racial Attitudes in the 1990s: Continuity and Change*, Prager, Greenwood, CT.

Braverman, Harry (1974), *Labour and Monopoly Capital: The Degradation of Work in the Twentieth Century*, Monthly Review Press, New York.

Cappelli, Peter, Laurie Bassi, Harry Katz, David Knoke, Paul Osterman and Michael Useem (1997), *Change at Work*, Oxford University Press, New York.

Card, David and Alan Krueger (1995), *Myth and Measurement: The New Economics of the Minimum Wage*, Princeton University Press, Princeton, NJ.

Carnoy, Martin (1994), *Faded Dreams: The Politics and Economics of Race in America*, Cambridge University Press, Cambridge.

Cherry, Robert and William Rodgers (eds) (2000), *Prosperity For All? The Economic Boom and African Americans*, Russell Sage Foundation, New York.

Christopherson, Susan, (2002), 'Why Do National Labour Market Practices Continue to Diverge in the Global Economy? The "Missing Link" of Investment Rules', *Economic Geography*, vol. 78, pp. 1–20.

Darrah, Charles (1994), 'Skill Requirements at Work: Rhetoric Vs. Reality', *Work and Occupations*, vol. 21, pp. 64–84.

Dertouzos, Michael, Richard Lester, Robert Solow and the M.I.T. Commission on Industrial Productivity (1989), *Made in America: Regaining the Competitive Edge*, M.I.T. Press, Cambridge, MA.

Devlin, Bernie, Stephen E. Fienberg, Daniel P. Resnick and Kathryn Roeder (1997), *Intelligence, Genes, and Success: Scientists Respond to the Bell Curve*, Copernicus, New York.

England, Paula (1992), *Comparable Worth: Theories and Evidence*, Aldine, New York.

Forero, Juan (2002), 'Still Poor, Latin Americans Protest Push for Open Markets', *New York Times*, July 19, p. A1.

Friedman, Thomas L. (2000), *The Lexus and the Olive Tree: Understanding Globalization*, Updated and Expanded Edition, Anchor Books, New York.

Gonos, George (1997), 'The Contest over "Employer" Status in the Postwar US: The Case of Temporary Help Firms', *Law & Society Review*, vol. 31, pp. 81–110.

Gordon, Robert (2000), 'Does the "New Economy" Measure up to the Great Inventions of the Past?', *Journal of Economic Perspectives*, vol. 14, pp. 49–74.

Granovetter, Mark (1995), *Getting a Job: A Study of Contacts and Careers*, 2nd Edition, University of Chicago Press, Chicago (first published in 1974).

Granovetter, Mark and Charles Tilly (1988), 'Inequality and Labour Processes', in Neil J. Smelser (ed.), *Handbook of Sociology*, Sage Publications, Newbury Park, CA.

Hashimoto, Masanori (1990), *The Japanese Labour Market in a Comparative Perspective with the United States: A Transaction-Cost Interpretation*, W.E. Upjohn Institute for Employment Research, Kalamazoo, MI.

Herrnstein, Richard and Charles Murray (1994), *The Bell Curve: Intelligence and Class Structure in American Life*, Free Press, Kalamazoo, MI.

Hersch, Joni and Leslie Stratton (1997), 'Housework, Fixed Effects, and Wages of Married Workers', *Journal of Human Resources*, vol. 32, pp. 285–307.

Hersch, Joni and Leslie Stratton (2002), 'Housework and Wages,' *Journal of Human Resources*, vol. 37, pp. 217–229.

Hohnen, Pernille (2003), *A Market Out of Place? Remaking Economic, Social, and Symbolic Boundaries in Post-Communist Lithuania*, Oxford University Press, Oxford.

Howell, David R., Margaret Duncan and Bennett Harrison (1998), *Low Wages in the US and High Unemployment in Europe: A Critical Assessment of the Conventional Wisdom*, Working Paper No. 5, Center for Economic Policy Analysis, New School For Social Research, New York, NY.

Hudson, Ken (1999), *No Shortage of 'Nonstandard' Jobs*, Briefing Paper, Economic Policy Institute, Washington, DC, http://www.epinet.org/briefingpapers/hudson/hudson.pdf.

Kilbourne, Barbara S., Paula England and Katherine Beron (1994), 'Effects of Changing Individual, Occupational, and Industrial Characteristics on Changes in Earnings: Intersections of Race and Gender', *Social Forces*, vol. 72, pp. 1149–1176.

Kirschenman, Joleen and Kathryn M. Neckerman (1991), '"We'd Love to Hire Them, But...": The Meaning of Race For Employers', in Christopher Jencks and Paul E. Peterson (eds), *The Urban Underclass*, Brookings Institution, Washington, DC, pp. 203–232.

Levine, David I. (ed.) (1999), 'Symposium: (Attempts At) Replication of *The Bell Curve*', *Industrial Relations*, Vol.38, pp. 245–406.

McCall, Leslie (2001), *Complex Inequality: Gender, Class, and Race in the New Economy*, Routledge, New York.

Moss, Philip (2002), 'Earnings Inequality and the Quality of Jobs: What We Know, What We Don't Know, and How We Should Look', in William Lazonick and Mary O'Sullivan (eds), *Corporate Governance and Sustainable Prosperity*, Palgrave, New York.

Moss, Philip and Chris Tilly (2001), *Stories Employers Tell: Race, Skill, and Hiring in America*, Russell Sage Foundation, New York.

Moffett, Matt (2002), 'Going South: Old Demons Sap Signs of Progress in Latin America', *Wall Street Journal*, July 25, p. A1.

Murray, Charles (1984), *Losing Ground: American Social Policy, 1950–1980*, Basic Books, New York.

Noble, David (1984), *Forces of Production: A Social History of Industrial Automation*, Knopf, New York.

Okun, Arthur (1975), *Equality and Efficiency: The Big Trade-Off*, The Brookings Institution, Washington, DC.

Ortmann, Günther and Harold Salzman (1998), *Changing Corporate Structures in the Global Economy: Maximizing, Satisficing, and Viability*, Working Paper, University of Hamburg, Hamburg.

Peck, Jamie (1996), *Work/Place: The Social Regulation of Labour Markets*, Guilford Press, New York.

Reskin, Barbara and Heidi Hartmann (eds) (1986), *Women's Work, Men's Work: Sex Segregation on the Job*, National Academy Press, Washington, DC.

Rogers, Jackie Krasas (2000), *Temps: The Many Faces of the Changing Workforce*, Cornell University Press, Ithaca, NY.

Rosen, Sherwin (1986), 'The Theory of Equalizing Differences', in Orley Ashenfelter and Richard Layard (eds), *Handbook of Labour Economics I*, North-Holland, Amsterdam, pp. 641–692.

Semple, Kirk (2002), 'Turmoil in Latin America Threatens Decades of Reform', *Boston Globe*, August 18, p. A12.

Smith, James P. and Finis R. Welch (1989), 'Black Economic Progress after Myrdal', *Journal of Economic Literature*, vol. 27, pp. 519–564.

Spence, Michael (2002), 'Signaling in Retrospect and the Informational Structure of Markets', *American Economic Review*, vol. 92, pp. 434–459.

Stiglitz, Joseph (2002), 'Information and Change in the Paradigm in Economics', *American Economic Review*, vol. 92, pp. 4460–4501.

Stratton, Leslie (1995), 'The Effect Interruptions in Work Experience Have on Wages', *Southern Economic Journal*, vol. 61, pp. 955–970.

Tilly, Chris (1996), *Half a Job: Bad and Good Part-Time Jobs in a Changing Labour Market*, Temple University Press, Philadelphia.

Tilly, Chris (1997), 'Arresting the Decline of Good Jobs in the USA?', *Industrial Relations Journal*, December.

Tilly, Chris (2000), 'Falling Wages, Widening Gaps: US Income Distribution at the Millennium', in Ron Baiman, Heather Boushey, and Dawn Saunders (eds.), *Political Economy and Contemporary Capitalism: Radical Perspectives on Economy Theory and Policy*, M.E. Sharpe, Armonk, NY.

Tilly, Chris (2004), 'Geese, Golden Eggs, and Traps: Why Inequality Is Bad for the Economy', in Dollars and Sense and United For a Fair Economy (ed.), *The Wealth Inequality Reader*, Economic Affairs Bureau, Cambridge, MA, pp. 78–84.

Tilly, Chris and Randy Albelda (1995), 'Not Markets Alone: Enriching the Discussion of Income Distribution', in Robert Heilbroner and Charles Whalen (eds.), *Political Economy For the Next Century*, M. E. Sharpe, Armonk, NY.

Tilly, Chris and Tilly, Charles (1998), *Work Under Capitalism*, Westview Press, Boulder, CO.

Tosh, Peter (1977), 'Equal Rights', *Equal Rights*, Columbia Records, New York.

Vallas, Stephen (1990), 'The Concept of Skill: A Critical Review', *Work and Occupations*, vol. 17, pp. 379–398.

Waldinger, Roger and Michael I. Lichter (2003), *How the Other Half Works: Immigration and the Social Organization of Labour*, University of California Press, Berkeley, CA.

Western, Bruce (1997), *Between Class and Market: Postwar Unionization in the Capitalist Democracies*, Princeton University Press, Princeton, NJ.

Western, Bruce and Joshua Guetzkow (2002), 'Punitive Policy and Neoliberalism in the US Labour Market', paper presented at the *Annual Meetings of the American Sociological Association*, Chicago, August 16–18.

Willis, Robert J. (1986), 'Wage Determinants: A Survey and Reinterpretation of Human Capital Earnings Functions', in Orley Ashenfelter and Richard Layard (eds), *Handbook of Labour Economics I*, North-Holland, Amsterdam, pp. 525–602.

Chapter 3

Gendered Divisions of Work: A Multilevel Approach

Lena Gonäs

Introduction

In this chapter I will discuss gendered division of work in a regional context. I will use results from a research project 'Gender and Work' conducted at the National Institute for Working Life in Sweden during 2000–2004. It was a multidisciplinary project consisting of many different studies, performed in three municipalities in the region of Östergötland in Sweden (Gonäs, 2005). By multilevel approach I mean more than the common sense understanding of studying gender divisions on different analytical levels. I try to analyze gendered structures and processes on societal and organizational levels and the outcomes for single individuals. By doing so I will illustrate the differentiated pattern, where we on the one hand can see openings for a more integrated and egalitarian society and on the other hand the mechanisms of re-segregation and what that can mean for the single individual, female or male. The chapter starts with a discussion of labour market trends and continues with discussing the opening question if we are moving towards an egalitarian labour market. This is done with the help of a scenario presented in the mid-1970s. One of the conditions put down for that scenario is very relevant for our discussion, namely an equal division of paid and unpaid work between women and men. After that I take up some international studies to illustrate common and different developments in gender divisions between countries. To illustrate processes on labour market and organizational levels I use our studies from the Östergötland region and an analysis of individual labour market histories.

Towards an egalitarian labour market?

In many European countries, women comprise almost half of the labour force (*Employment in Europe*, 2003). But a variety of measures indicate that the labour markets of all European countries remain segregated by gender. Further, there appears to be a direct relationship between pronounced gender segregation and increasing rates of female employment (Emerek et al., 2001).

During the 1990s, there was both change and continuity in the gender segregation of the labour market. Changes in gender distribution occurred in occupations that require higher levels of education. According to a Swedish public inquiry which submitted its report in 2004 (SOU, 2004:43), there has been a generation shift towards a more equal gender distribution among members of younger age-groups entering such occupations. Conversely, there has been little change in occupations that are traditionally regarded as 'male' or 'female', not requiring high levels of education and have yet to be placed under heavy pressure to change (SOU, 2004:43, p.89; Gonäs, 2005).

Continuity seems to be the general pattern with regard to the gender distribution of unpaid work. Time-use studies have detected very little change in the division of labour between men and women (Lundberg, 2002; Statistics Sweden, 2003). Women still bear the primary responsibility for unpaid housework. As a result of their increasing participation in tertiary education, women in the labour force have higher educational levels than men (*Employment in Europe*, 2001). During the past decade, fertility rates declined steadily in all European countries. Today, the European fertility rate is among the lowest in the world (Ds, 2001:57).

Explanations of these changes can be found in the sharp decline in employment rates of young women, and rising education levels of women in general. Even for employed women, however, fertility rates were lower in the late 1990s than at the start of the decade, especially among women with temporary forms of employment. A precarious employment situation appears to be an explanation for the lower fertility rate (Gonäs and Wikman, 2002). At the opposite end of the age spectrum, increasing numbers of women leave the labour market due to long-term illness and early retirement. For many women, years of repetitive motions and heavy total workloads have caused strains leading to ill health and long-term sick leave (Kilbom and Messing, 1999).

Questions and objectives

For the most part, gender segregation in working life has been studied on either the societal, organizational or individual level. But those disparate analytical approaches have been combined in the multi-disciplinary project on which this discussion is based. One of the basic questions it addresses is the extent to which gender-based segregation patterns persist or take on new forms. Thus far, attempts to alter those patterns have not led to permanent changes (SOU, 2004:43; Gonäs and Lehto, 1999).

Research has yielded considerable knowledge about the lack of equal opportunity and, to some extent, the underlying reasons for this lack. But there have been few attempts to study the problem by combining the skills and knowledge of researchers within various fields of the social, behavioral and medical sciences. Our project has tried to do that.

The intended outcomes of the project included action-oriented research, and support for the development of increased gender equality and improved working conditions in business and non-profit organizations. The separate components were based on local conditions and development needs (Drejhammar, 1998; Gustavsen, 2001).

Based on these objectives the following questions have been formulated:

1. What changes have taken place in the labour market and at workplaces during the 1990s, and how have such changes affected gender-based patterns of segregation, working and living conditions, and health?
2. In what way does gender segregation in the labour market affect various types of employment, working conditions, means of influence *and* health/illness for women and men, respectively?
3. Within the framework of existing institutions and regulations, how can local actors influence gender segregation in the labour market and within organizations?

A regional approach

Focusing on a specific geographical region facilitates the study of individuals, organizations and society, including interactions between the various levels. It also provides a platform for development based on close cooperation with local and regional actors, including political decision makers, business leaders, and ordinary citizens who work and live in the region.

The region included the city of Norrköping and the neighbouring municipalities of Finspång and Söderköping and was chosen because it was a well-defined labour market region (Abbasian, 2000). Equally important to note was that we found a positive attitude towards development of equal opportunity, strong interest in the project, and good chances for a close fit between practice and research.

Work organization reorganized

One point of departure for this chapter is a scenario devised as part of the Swedish contribution to the UN population conference held in Bucharest in 1974. The scenario was entitled 'Work organization reorganized, and was first published in the report *The Bibliography of a People – Past and Future Population Changes in Sweden, Conditions and Consequences*. It was later revised and published in a Swedish version which is cited in the References (Guteland et al., 1975).

The scenario describes a post-industrial society with a dominant service sector, a stagnating and ageing population, and a time horizon of 25–30 years (Guteland et al., p. 161). It presents a picture of future working life in Sweden, around the year 2000. One reason that I have chosen to use this scenario as a starting point is that, like all scenarios, it is based on linking conditions and situations at different analytical levels. Another reason is that it assumes a need to redistribute both paid and unpaid work between men and women. The authors saw this as a necessary condition for meeting the needs of an ageing population and increasing the labour force participation of women.

Working life in 2000

According to the scenario, the size of the Swedish population would stabilize at the 1970 level, with a constant birth rate corresponding to a reproduction ratio of just less than one, or roughly 110 000 live births per year. Mortality is assumed to remain essentially unchanged, and the net effect of in- and out-migration is regarded as insignificant. In two alternative scenarios, the authors project the consequences of increased fertility and a large increase in immigration. Based on these demographic assumptions, the population would cease to grow within a period of twenty years.

The authors identified three problems:

1. A quantitative problem associated with the relationship between active and passive groups of the population.
2. A qualitative problem related to growing proportions of older age-groups in the labour force.
3. The possibilities of adapting people and activities in both time and space.

According to Guteland et al., these problems cannot be solved by traditional means, that is, with the measures available during the 1970s. It was especially important to implement changes within two areas: the organization of work, and the regional level and its organization. Specifically, this meant a new type of work organization where needed and:

1. an altered division of labour between men and women
2. the integration of new groups into working life
3. an increased supply of care services for a growing proportion of elderly persons
4. development of a full-employment policy toward a division of labour based on gender, age differences, and so on.

An important consequence of the demographic assumptions was that the structure of the population changed. There was no reduction of the population as a whole, but there were increases in the proportions of those requiring care, those unable to work, and women seeking work outside the home (Guteland et al., p. 184). The authors concluded that solutions to the problems noted above would require the reorganization of work:

> An increase in the gainful employment of women outside the home results in a change in the division of production in the home and outside the home, and thereby a redistribution

of work tasks between men and women. This has consequences for the organization of work, for example the introduction of flexible working hours for men. (Guteland et al., p. 185)

The foregoing quotation is interesting from several standpoints, it was very far-sighted, yet the authors did not to any great extent discuss how this was to be reached. They concluded that a new type of work organization was required to cope with the problems associated with the scenario's underlying assumptions. The first requirement was to change the division of labour between men and women.

Although it is somewhat unfair to compare old prognoses or visions of the future with current reality, the question naturally arises: How accurately did they assess the tenacity of gender segregation, both at home and in working life? Was their misjudgement due to lack of knowledge or to blind faith in the possibility of creating a new division of labour between the sexes within the space of thirty years?

The scenario stipulates *what* needs to be achieved, but not *how*. Rather, it takes the form of an analytical process consisting of five elements: demographic assumptions; population trends and their underlying conditions; consequences, including consistency testing and feedback; analysis of problems; and policy implications.

Work-related gender segregation was not regarded as especially problematical in this context. It was necessary to change that segregation in order to meet a steadily ageing population's need for care services, while taking into consideration the objectives of an egalitarian society with values favouring the equal right of men and women to education and gainful employment (Guteland et al., p. 175).

In the process of constructing a conceptual framework of a scenario, Guteland and his colleagues have described the relationship between individual and society as follows:

The individual's actions are constrained on the one hand by his or her abilities, on the other by a mixture of assets and restrictions existing in the material and social surroundings within reach. Taken together, these two categories of factors determine living conditions. (Guteland et al., p. 175)

Central to this discussion were the ideas about regarding activities within a local area as interconnected within a system of activities in time and space (Hägerstrand, 1986). Granted, there was also the belief that it was possible to influence the division of these activities and systems by political means. It was believed that planning and political decisions could influence the considerations of companies and individuals regarding the placement of businesses and other facilities. Today, the persistence of the division of labour between the sexes may be regarded as an obstacle to meeting the labour force requirements necessary to cope with the needs of an ageing population. A scenario which integrates various levels of analysis offers greater potential to understand the problems confronting modern society.

A multilevel approach

To be able to understand how gender segregation changes over time it is important to make studies on different analytical levels. The following discussion attempts to integrate various levels of analysis in order to illustrate the complexity of the phenomena we have been studying, and how they can change character depending on the level and perspective chosen. Gender segregation is analyzed with regard to the following levels and issues:

1. International – comparison of welfare state regimes.
2. National – employment policies.
3. Local – job and skill structures.
4. Organizational – recruitment strategies.
5. Individual – employment patterns.

This means that starting in the international comparisons of gender segregation in the labour market we can find both differences and similarities between countries belonging to different welfare state regimes. In the European context one of the objectives of the common European Employment Strategy (EES) is to increase employment levels and specifically the female employment levels (Council decision 2003/578/EC). Gender equality is one of the specific guidelines which the member states shall have as a priority. Not only does this specific guideline address gender gaps in employment rates and pay, but also sectorial and occupational segregation. The member states are also asked to take up the reconciliation of work and family in their national employment plans (NAPs). Going from the European level the chapter takes up the national employment policies from a gender perspective and continues by addressing how these polices have been adapted on the local labour market levels. To what extent do polices in practice adopt a gender perspective? What happens on the organizational level?

In her article, 'The Future of "Gender and Organizations": Connections and Boundaries', Joan Acker (1998) discusses how recent research on gender and organizations has broken the traditional boundaries between economics and the study of organizations. Those boundaries have been based on the concerns of the disciplines involved, not on the nature of the problems to be analyzed.

Studies of power and social relations cut across various disciplines and are not limited to the issue of gender, but also include issues of class and ethnic background (Acker, 1998). The qualifications of the single individual and his or her actions, organizational processes and the functioning of the labour market are connected. To be able to understand processes of segregation it is therefore necessary to engage in studies on different analytical levels; individual, organizational and societal levels.

There has been extensive research on gender segregation in the labour market, concerning how to measure it and the various forms it takes. The bibliography (*Women and Work*, 1999; Gonäs and Lehto, 1999) on gender segregation in the labour market summarizes the research within a European perspective. What clearly emerges from that summary is the great variety of research in this area. The theoretical assumptions are related to various levels, from over-arching issues and the functional processes of the labour market, to organizational issues and the individual's situation and opportunities.

One standpoint is that gender segregation in the labour market occurs and reoccurs through processes at several different levels. It has to do with the relationships between politics and the market, and between organizational principles and individual choices (Gonäs, 2005). Joan Acker analyses how women's subordinate status in working life is re-created in processes at the organizational level. She suggests that organizations can be regarded as processes and practices rather than as rational, well-defined systems (Acker, 1999). In order to analyze how gender is involved in various activities and complex processes, Acker identifies four different 'points of entry' to the subject:

1. *procedures and human activities* which lead to gender segregation and hierarchy
2. *ideas and symbols* that shape awareness so as to justify and legitimate existing gender relations
3. *interaction* between individuals and groups ('While doing the work of organizing, people are also "doing gender"')
4. *the internal mental processes of humans* by which they attempt to understand the gender-related expectations and opportunities of organizations (Acker, 1999).

These are processes that interact with each other and can be seen as taking place simultaneously, but their explanation has to be found on different analytical levels. A similar multi-faceted approach must be applied to the analysis of processes at the labour-market level, and the division of labour between the sexes at the individual level. I will begin at the societal level and review the results of an attempt to measure differences between the situation for women and men in the labour market in the European Union.

Comparison of welfare state regimes

From European research, it is clear that there are serious problems associated with the measurement of differences in the degree of gender segregation in various countries. The segregation index is widely used, but it is sensitive to classification errors, and it obscures simultaneous changes in the horizontal and vertical segregation dimensions (Rubery et al., 1999; Emerek, this volume).

At the same time, national politics and institutional conditions play important roles with regard to employment and economic compensation for work. International comparisons make it possible to analyze differences in the degree of gender segregation between countries whose labour markets and general welfare systems differ. Generally, it may be said that the higher the female employment rate, the greater the degree of segregation as measured by the most widely used international indexes (Emerek et al., 2001).

This type of comprehensive analysis provides the basis for political decisions within the framework of European labour market policy and EU Commission guidelines for member states. Those guidelines include recommendations for labour market policy in the various member states. Sweden has been repeatedly advised to reduce gender segregation in its labour market (EU Commission, 1999, 2000, 2001; Gonäs, 2004).

Assessing equal opportunity

A number of social and economic indicators can be used to assess the performance of the economy and the effects of various policies. Such indicators are usually combined to form a set of dimensions. For a benchmark study on equal opportunity in several European countries, three dimensions were selected: supply and demand factors; employment regime; and labour market/social policy (Plantenga and Hansen, 1999a and b; Gonäs, 2004).

The first of these dimensions was comprised of four indicators: economic growth and total employment; structural change; education and training; and attitudes towards the employment of women. The countries differed greatly with regard to GDP and employment growth. Ireland's GDP increased annually by an average rate of 8.2 percent during 1992–97, while the average rate for Sweden was 1.6 percent annually during the same period.

Using a shift-share analysis, we also found large differences in female employment trends during this period. Ireland experienced a net increase of 27.6 percent in female employment, while the Swedish level decreased by 6.0 percent (Gonäs, 1999; Plantenga and Hansen, 1999a, b).

The employment regime included the organization of the labour market, the tax system, the social insurance system, average working hours, and the wage-setting system.

The third and last dimension, labour-market/social policy, included the proportion of GDP used for active measures to promote employment and gender equality, childcare, and parental leave.

The study included Iceland and the seven EU member-states of Belgium, Germany, Spain, Ireland, The Netherlands, Austria and Sweden. Data were collected in 1992 and 1997. The eight countries were divided into three categories based on the degree of gender equality. The first group consisted of Sweden, Iceland and Austria. Sweden was most advanced with regard to childcare, an equal employment ratio and general attitudes toward gender equality. The second group consisted of Ireland, Belgium and Germany. Ireland had a rapidly increasing employment frequency among young women, who tended to continue working when they had children. Childcare and parental leave were largely non-existent. Neither can Germany be said to conduct a policy that facilitates the combination of work and family life; instead, women's employment rate was declining as the former East Germany's regulations had been discontinued, to be replaced by West Germany's more traditional forms of support. Belgium had a more favourable increase in employment among young women. Spain and The Netherlands comprised the third group. Neither had well-developed policies or legislation regarding childcare or parental leave.

Analyses like these are difficult; there are many details that cannot be accounted for. It is hard to detect any common pattern. There are many different institutional factors that affect gender differences in employment, income, working hours and paid/unpaid work. As long as the primary responsibility for providing care remains a private matter, the unequal division of unpaid labour leads to inequality in the paid labour market. But even in countries where care services are publicly financed and organized, women still do most of the unpaid work.

One of the important similarities between the countries in the study was the segregation patterns in paid and unpaid work. Even though there are national differences, the gender gaps in hours spent per week in unpaid child care were very large in all countries. Also the gap between women and men in leading positions were large when measuring the position of women and men in the labour market (Plantenga and Hansen, 1999a and b).

It was not possible to conclude from the benchmarking report that there has been any major convergence with regard to gender relations in the labour market. Deregulation, inadequate childcare, and little or no provision for parental leave indicated a lack of political support for women as wage-earners and family-providers.

Employment policies and national action plans

In response to the EU Commission and its recommendation that active measures be taken to reduce gender segregation in the Swedish labour market, the government asked the National Labour Market Board ('AMS') to develop an action plan for its area of responsibility. AMS has been addressing the issue for many years with various types of so-called 'break projects' (that is, whose purpose is to reduce gender segregation). These have been conducted since the late 1960s, with varying degrees of success (SOU, 2004:43).

In recent years, however, new methodological approaches have been developed which have been discussed and evaluated by both the government and the researcher community (Bergman and Schough, 2002; Westberg, 2003). Among these new approaches are methods for changing the work routines of local labour exchanges by applying knowledge of gender-related processes within organizations. The National Audit Bureau has carried out gender auditing in various segments of the labour market, and tools for mainstreaming were put in place long before guidelines on gender mainstreaming were formulated in national action plans from the side of the EU Commission. As a response to the recommendations of the EU Commission the Swedish government took action to reduce gender segregation in the labour market.

The terms of reference of the enquiry commission specified that it was to undertake a thorough investigation of gender-segregation trends in the Swedish labour market, include an international overview, and analyze the results of the various measures applied in efforts to reduce labour-market segregation. The commission's report was presented in the spring of 2004 (SOU, 2004:43).

As noted above, one of the reasons for decreasing gender segregation in the 1990s was a growing proportion of women in traditionally male jobs that demand higher education. It was more difficult to discern a similar trend for traditionally male jobs with lower educational demands. Men did not display the same level of interest in entering traditionally female occupations, regardless of educational requirements. The commission recommended that the government allocate economic resources to stimulate the interest of boys and men in the social services sector in order to meet its future labour demands. Another recommendation was for the National Education Agency to study the practical training of and the need for mentors. Statistics Sweden was urged to review its occupational classification system, and the National Labour Market Board to study the role of employers in reducing gender segregation. The Board was also urged to evaluate the educational guidance provided by local offices of the national employment service. Finally, the commission directed attention to the risk that, if women do not gain employment which is commensurate with their educational and other qualifications, Sweden could end up with a well-educated female proletariat that is over-qualified and underpaid.

Local labour markets

Returning to the region studied in our research project, the city of Norrköping has been dominated for decades by the textile, pulp and paper and engineering industries. During the past decade, the city developed into a more diverse industrial centre. The establishment of a branch of Linköping University in Norrköping ('Campus Norrköping') has had a positive effect on local development, including the growth of companies based on intellectual assets and advanced technology.

The population of Norrköping increased steadily during the late 1980s and early 1990s, but declined somewhat in the late 1990s. Today, the population of Norrköping exceeds 122 000.

Industry accounts for around 20 percent of employment, a higher proportion than for the county and the nation as a whole. Engineering and electronics, along with pulp and paper are now the largest industrial branches in Norrköping. The electronics branch has experienced rapid growth during past years, and been hard hit by the recession in the industry, not least through cutbacks at the Ericsson manufacturing plant.

Transformation of production

Swedish industry has been undergoing a process of transformation. This has resulted in several major changes, including a shrinking proportion of industrial production jobs, a more differentiated labour market, and a diverse business structure. In 1990, three sectors of the Norrköping economy – manufacturing, commerce and care services – accounted for roughly equal proportions of the daytime workforce, just under 25 percent each. Between 1990 and 1994, employment decreased in all three sectors by roughly 2000 workers each. Employment in the care sector continued to decline sharply through 1997; this was due to the fiscal problems of the local government, and a national economic policy requiring a balanced budget.

If the distributions of men and women over the economic sectors are analyzed separately, two very different employment patterns emerge (see Table 3.1 in Appendix). Among men, employment in the manufacturing and construction branches accounts for roughly 35 percent of the total; less than 5 percent are employed in care services.

Around 10 percent of all women in the labour force work in construction and industrial branches, while nearly 34 percent work in care services. The number of jobs cut from the care sector during the 1990s was the same as from the manufacturing sector. When labour shortages in the care sector became evident at the close of the 1990s, additional crises had already occurred in the manufacturing sector.

Thus, from the standpoint of crises and structural changes, it can be said that the public sector underwent changes during the 1990s that were at least as dramatic as those within the manufacturing sector. The sharp reduction of employment in the care sector during the 1990s was a new development for the Municipality of Norrköping. By the end of the decade, some 4 000 jobs had disappeared, which was equal to the number of jobs lost in the manufacturing sector during those ten years (see Grinups, 2001).

New and old jobs

Which jobs or occupations have arisen in recent years and what gender lable have they got? There has been an increase in private sector services, both new and traditional. Both qualified and less qualified labour is employed in relatively new fields such as market research, telephone sales and temporary-employment agencies; in terms of numbers, there is probably a greater proportion of less qualified labour in these branches. More traditional occupations are changing character, with shorter terms of employment and altered job descriptions. The changes are due not only to technological developments, but also to organizational restructuring.

The adjustments required of individuals affected by the changes that took place during the 1990s display a varied pattern. Many of those who lost their jobs are still unemployed. In Östergötland County, where Norrköping is located, the rate of unemployment in 2003 was 3.5 percent – the same as the national rate. In Norrköping it was somewhat higher at 4.4 percent (LAN, 2003). The proportion of those aged

16–64 who were unemployed and involved in labour market activities was 7–8 percent, which was significantly higher than in other municipalities of Östergötland County and in Sweden as a whole.

There are several explanations for this persistent problem. One is that educational requirements have increased for those seeking new jobs; the higher the educational level of the applicant, the easier it is to find work. But there are also a number of contradictory tendencies that are important to note.

Parallel processes

Regarding adaptation processes at the organizational level, one of our local studies disclosed that there was no agreement on the meaning of the concept, 'the new working life' (Gonäs and Knocke, 2004). The companies are reducing production where they cannot compete with low wage countries and have to concentrate on more knowledge intensive and advanced production. This means that information and communication technologies are to an increasing extent imbedded in all types of manufacturing processes. What seems to be important is the parallel processes of restructuring the production and at the same time starting up with new activities and products. The time frames and the intensities of restructuring become very limited. The introduction of new technology results in reduced needs for labour. As a consequence of the above mentioned processes, less qualified jobs have become fewer or have been moved to other workplaces in the local area or in other countries. This has aggravated the problems of women with limited education and individuals of both sexes with ethnic minority backgrounds.

Broader competence in terms of functional flexibility is emphasized in interviews as an element of the new working life in more general terms. This leads to a sorting of job applicants into categories of those who are capable of development or adaptation and those who do not fit in. The temporal dimension is important. Short lead times create pressure for rapid decisions, increased tempo and greater intensity, all of which leads to insecurity, increased sick leave and exhaustion.

Labour reserves and labour shortages are two concepts which illustrate these trends. The unemployed become a reserve for the labour market which can be called upon when local businesses take on new tasks, or which can be allocated to new areas and tasks for which there are labour shortages (Gonäs and Knocke, 2004). Diversity is understood in terms of gender (that is, women) and ethnicity. The concept is interpreted as referring to deviation from male hegemony and/or 'Swedishness'. Differences are used to justify inequality and labour-market segregation on the basis of gender and ethnicity.

It is important to say that the same results can not be said to appear in the public sector. During the crisis of the 1990s a large segment of the so-called low skilled occupational groups were made redundant. Largely female dominated occupations like assistant nurses in hospitals and assistant teachers in day care centres lost their jobs. In the aftermaths of the cutbacks of the 1990s in the health and care sectors a labour shortage appeared in these occupational groups. The employment reductions in these sectors were not related to new technology and global competition, but to the ambition to control the public deficit and reach a balanced economy, both locally and nationally. A result of the restructuring during the 1990s was a more differentiated labour market, where women came to take a greater part in the education sector and higher skilled jobs. But the price of this differentiation was higher unemployment levels and reduced overall employment levels for both women and men, mainly by cutbacks in low skill employment.

Individual career patterns

With the objective of getting information of the working and living conditions of the population in the region we made a large survey in the form of a questionnaire to a random sample of 10 000 inhabitants in our three municipalities in the region. The response rate was around 50 percent, and we have made extensive analyses of non-responses. It was more women than men who answered and older than younger, more well educated than low educated (Gonäs, 2005). The employment level decreased during the 1990s for both women and men, as was also the case nationally. One result of the crisis can be seen in Figure 3.1 and that is the gender gap in the employment profiles for the young age groups. Women have to a larger extent stayed in the educational system than the young men. Figure 3.2 illustrates the development over time for the female population that did not have an employment in the 1990s. The empirical data is income statistics linked to our survey data. Compared to men, women had a much faster increase in early retirement pensioning and long term sick leave than men. One of the main results from these data was the growth of the age related alternative support systems to regular employment. The labour market policy measures seemed to play a minor role for the single individual and instead it was early retirement pensioning and health insurance for those over 40 years of age and the educational system for the younger that came to be the support structure when regular employment was not an option (Gonäs, 2005).

Concluding observations

According to the personnel staff being interviewed, strategic recruitment was not seen as a specific instrument for changing the gender composition of the labour force (Knocke, Drejhammar, Gonäs and Isaksson, 2003). Public sector employers were more aware of the Equal Opportunity Act's stipulation that equal opportunity plans be prepared every year. The gap between rhetoric and practice was large in both public and private organizations. We found an awareness of the potential advantages of a more equal gender distribution in the workforces of high-tech industries and private service companies based on information and communications technology. In those branches, we found businesses that were actively searching for both male and female employees as complements to each other.

The development in the 1990s opened for both integration of women in new jobs and for a differentiated development where large groups lost their jobs and actually never returned to the labour market.

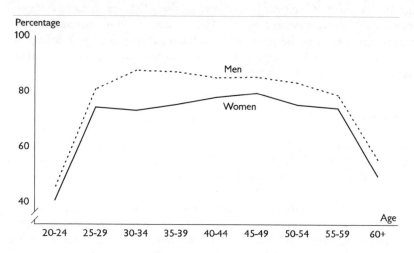

**Figure 3.1   Employed women and men in 2001 as percentage of the
                population in age groups from 20 to 64, data from the
                Östergötland survey**

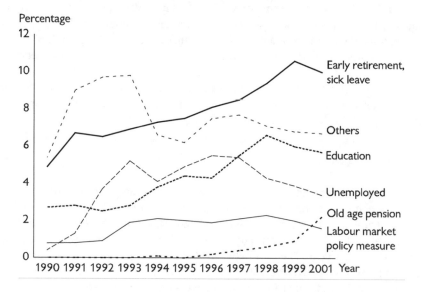

**Figure 3.2   Percentage of the female population in other labour market
                status 1990 to 2001, data from the Östergötland survey**

References

Abbasian, S. (2000), *Befolkning, arbetsmarknad och näringslivsutveckling i tre kommuner i Östergötland. En sammanställning av utvecklingen under 1990–talet*, Arbetslivsrapport nr 2000:12, Arbetslivsinstitutet, Stockholm.

Acker, J. (1998), 'The Future of "Gender and Organizations": Connections and Boundaries.' *Gender, Work and Organization*, vol. 5, pp. 195–206.

Acker, J. (1999), 'Gender and Organizations', in J. Saltzman Chafets (ed.), *Handbook of the Sociology of Gender*, Kluwer Academic/Plenum, Dordrecht, pp. 177–194.

Bergman, A. and C. Schough (2002), *Brytande handling. Förändringens villkor vid en arbetsförmedling*, Karlstad University Press, Karlstad.

Council decision 2003/578/EC, 'On Guidelines for the Employment Policies of the Member States', *Official Journal of the European Union* L 197/13.

Drejhammar, I-B. (1998), *Organisationsutveckling och jämställdhet – en studie i tre företag*, Lunds Universitet, Lund.

Ds, 2001:57. *Barnafödandet i fokus*, Governmental report, Ministry of Social Affairs, Stockholm.

Emerek, R., H. Figureiredo, M. P. González, L. Gonäs and J. Rubery (2001), 'Indicators on Gender Segregation', in J. Rubery, C. Fagan, D. Grimshaw, H. Figureiredo and M. Smith (eds), *Indicators on Gender Equality in the European Employment Strategy*, Report to the Equal Opportunities Unit, DG Employment, http://www.umist.ac.uk/management/ewerec/egge/egge.htm.

Employment in Europe, 2001, 2003. European Commission, Office for Official Publications of the European Communities, Luxembourg.

EU Commission, *Employment Guidelines, 1999, 2000, 2001*.

European Labour Force Survey, various years, EUROSTAT, European Commission, Office for Official Publications of the European Communities, Luxembourg.

Gonäs, L. (1999), *Benchmarking Equal Opportunities: The Swedish Example*, Report to the European Expert Group on Gender and Employment, National Institute for Working Life, Stockholm.

Gonäs, L. (2001), 'Varför studera könssegregationen? Ett jämförande perspektiv', in L. Gonäs, G. Lindgren and C. Bildt (eds), *Könssegregering i arbetslivet*, Arbetslivsinstitutet, Stockholm.

Gonäs, L. (2004), 'Gender Segregation and the European Employment Strategy: Levels and Divisions', *European Journal of Industrial Relations*, vol. 10, pp 139–159.

Gonäs, L. (2005), *På gränsen till genombrott*, Agora förlag, Stockholm.

Gonäs, L. and A. Lehto, (1999), 'Segregation of the Labour Market', in *Women and Work*, Report on Existing Research in the European Union, Employment and Social Affairs, Office for Official Publications of the European Communities, Luxembourg.

Gonäs, L. and A. Wikman (2002), *Föräldraskapets villkor på svensk arbetsmarknad*, Ds 2002: 56, Governmental Report, Ministry of Industry, Stockholm.

Gonäs L. and W. Knocke (2004), *Platsar mångfalden i det nya arbetslivet?*, Karlstad University Press, Karlstad.

Grinups, B. (2001), *Välfärd i Norrköping: Samtal med Norrköpingsbor. Slutrapport från projektet Välfärd – gamla och nya färdvägar möts 1999–2001*, Norrköpings kommun, Norrköping.

Gustavsen, B. (2001), 'Theory and Practice: the Mediating Discourse', in P. Resason and H. Bradbury (eds), *Handbook of Action Research*, Sage, London.

Guteland, G., I. Holmberg, T. Hägestrand, A. Karlqvist & B. Rundblad (1975), *Ett folks biografi. Befolkning och samhälle i Sverige från historia till framtid*, Publica, Stockholm.

Hägerstrand, T. (1986), 'Den geografiska traditionens kärnområde', in *Svensk Geografisk Årsbok*, vol. 62, pp. 38–43.

Kilbom, Å. and L. Gonäs (1999), *Kön och Arbete, ett forskningsprogram* (Gender and Work, A Research Program), Arbetslivsinstitutet, Stockholm.

Kilbom, Å. and K. Messing (1999), 'Värk och smärta ett kvinno problem? Arbetsrelaterade muskuloskelettala bevär bland kvinnor', in Å. Kilbom, K. Messing, C. Bild-Thorbjörnsson (eds), *Yrkesarbetande kvinnors hälsa*, National Institute for Working Life, Stockholm.

Knocke, W., I.-B. Drejhammar, L. Gonäs and K. Isaksson (2003), *Retorik och praktik i rekryteringsprocessen*, Arbetsliv i omvandling 2003:8, Arbetslivsinstitutet, Stockholm.

LAN (2003), *Sysselsättningsdata*, Material från Länsarbetsnämnden i Östergötland.

Lundberg, U. (2002), 'Has the Total Workload of Swedish Men and Women Become More Equal during the Last Ten Years?', *WWH 2002, Book of Abstracts*, WeS02:5, National Institute for Working Life, Stockholm.

Plantenga, J. and J. Hansen (1999a) *Benchmarking Equal Opportunities in the European Union*, Synthesis report based on eight European countries, Institute of Economics, Utrecht University, Utrecht.

Plantenga, J. and J. Hansen (1999b), 'Assessing Equal Opportunities in the European Union', *International Labour Review*, vol. 138, pp. 351–379.

Rubery, J., M. Smith and C. Fagan (1999), *Women's Employment in Europe: Trends and Prospects*, Routledge, London.

Statistics Sweden (2003), *Tid för vardagsliv, Kvinnors och mäns tidsanvändning 1990/1991 och 2000/2001, Rapport 1999*, Stockholm.

SOU, 2004:43, *Den könsuppdelade arbetsmarknaden. Betänkande av utredningen om den könssegregerade arbetsmarknaden*, Fritzes, Stockholm.

Westberg, H. (2003), *Att integrera och säkra jämställdhetsaspekten i det dagliga arbetet på arbetsförmedlingar och länsarbetsnämnden i Värmlands län*, Arbetslivsinstitutet, Stockholm.

Women and Work (1999), Report on Existing Research in the European Union, Published by Employment and Social Affairs, Office for Official Publications of the European Communities, Luxembourg.

Appendix

Table 3.1   Gainfully employed daytime labour force by gender and sector, year 2001 in the city of Norrköping

Economic sector	Percentage gainfully employed		
	Men	Women	Both sexes
Commerce & communications	26.6	16.9	22.0
Care services	4.5	33.8	18.5
Mining & manufacturing	23.7	8.9	16.6
Financial services	13.3	11.5	12.4
Education & research	4.9	11.5	8.1
Personal & cultural services	5.7	7.8	6.8
Construction	11.8	0.8	6.5
Public administration, etc.	5.0	7.2	6.1
Agriculture, forestry & fishing	2.3	0.6	1.5
Energy, water, waste	0.8	0.3	0.6
Other	1.3	0.6	0.9
Total	100	100	100

Sources: Statistics Sweden, Registerbaserad arbetsmarknadsstatistik; Municipality of Norrköping.

Chapter 4

Segregated Integration

Ann Bergman

Introduction

This is a chapter about gender segregation in work organizations. The first part deals with the problem area, the objective, the questions at issue, and the theoretical and analytical points of departure. The second and third parts present the findings of an empirical study and analyses of them. The chapter concludes with a summing-up discussion.

The analytical approach and design of the study

There is no great doubt about the fact that there is gender segregation in Swedish working life. There are a number of studies that illustrate in various ways the extremely persistent sorting and ranking of women and men (Abrahamsson, 2000; Nermo, 1999; Jonung, 1997). This chapter is based on yet another study. My objective is to try to understand the phenomenon of gender segregation – its complexity – and also to formulate some assumptions about the persistent character of gender segregation, that is to say its tendency to reproduce itself. A further aim is to contribute to a refinement of the equality debate that tends to single out the proportional relationship between women and men as both the obstacle and the solution to the problems of gender segregation. In other words, there are assumptions – not least political ones – that levelling out the proportion of women and men will contribute to undermining the segregation both in a horizontal and in a vertical sense. In my opinion, there are certain risks in adopting this view all too categorically, which does not mean that I consider proportional relationships uninteresting. Knowledge about proportions is of great importance for our understanding of gender segregation in working life, but this does not mean that we can equate proportional relationships with explanations. Particularly not if we regard gender segregation as a form of inequality.

The aim of this study is thus to provide knowledge about the complex phenomenon of gender segregation in the organizations of working life and about how it is reproduced. The first step in attaining this end is to study the various ways in which gender segregation can be manifested in a number of work organizations. The questions at issue in this case are: What is the distribution between women and men with regard to hierarchical positions, jobs and departments? How are the different types of gender segregation in the organization related to each other? In the next step the focus is not on the present picture but rather on how the extremely persistent phenomenon of gender segregation is reproduced. The questions to be answered in this case are: Are conditions for segregation or for integration created, and what occurs in such cases? In my efforts to answer these questions and offer the knowledge called for by its objective, I have structured the study round two basic components. One consists of a quantitative data material and the other of a hypothetical model of how gender segregation is reproduced. I will present the model next.

A hypothetical model of explanation

The model of explanation that has been used has been developed by weaving together theoretical and methodological assumptions (see Figure 4.1). This weave was not designed before the actual collection of material and data processing began, but after the material was collected and while the data was being processed. The model is thus a result of pendulating between theory and data. It functions as an explicit assumption about what gender segregation is and what happens when it is reproduced. Since gender segregation is a complex phenomenon and explanations are only partial and also fallible, my model is thus a simplification of the phenomenon, what it consists of and how it functions. This simplification is inspired by the theory of science tradition called critical realism (Danermark et al., 2002; Archer, 1995; Sayer, 1992, 2000; Bhaskar, 1979). However, I use the ideas of this tradition fairly pragmatically. Among other things, the realism view of causality and the character of society have made me identify a number of structures, mechanisms, actors and arenas that influence the manifestation of the phenomenon of gender segregation and its way of reproducing itself. The reason for my speaking in terms of conditions for the reproduction of gender segregation is that I am studying an existing social phenomenon – gender segregation – which by reason of already existing creates the conditions for its own reproduction. In other words, this is an analysis of how this reproduction may occur and not of why gender segregation exists at all (see Tilly, 1998; Young, 2003). I will now go through the components of the model.

First, three structures that I think are necessary for gender segregation in the organizations of working life are analytically identified on the basis of research in the field. These structures are gender, power and division of labour, which together contribute to creating the necessary conditions for a gender segregated working life. Thus, in my opinion, it is not possible to talk about gender as the decisive force in this respect. Gender is central to gender segregation as the structure is held up by the categories of women and men, who are what they are in relation to each other (Moi, 1997; Fraser, 1997; Tilly, 1998; Hacking, 1999; Young, 1990, 2003). Belonging to a social category, such as gender, in other words has repercussions on its members socially and culturally as well as materially. The conditions for women's and men's patterns of action and thought is also affected by other structures and contextual circumstances.

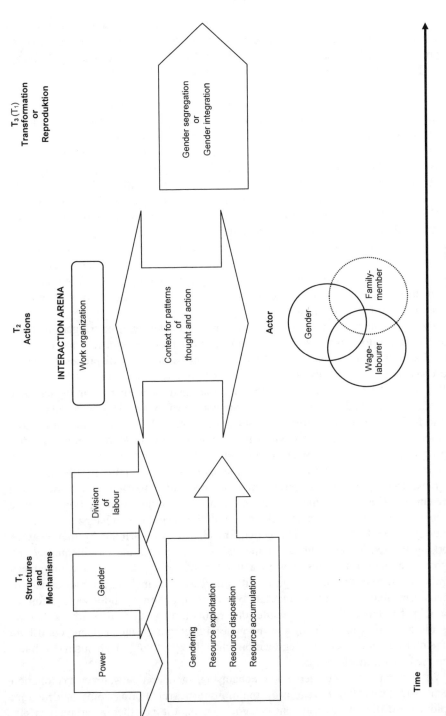

Figure 4.1   Analytical model over the process of gender segregation in working life

As far as the power structure is concerned, I treat it as a separate one. Power is seen here as both a potential and an exercised power to do things, make things happen or prevent them from happening (Isaac, 1987; Bhaskar, 1978; Harré, 1970; Clegg, 1989; Bunge, 1998). Power is thus not only 'power over' but also 'power to'. In many cases, however, people's potential 'power to' is reduced and cannot be exercised. This is in part due to the fact that the possibilities of certain categories are related to the limitations of other categories. As I have mentioned earlier, power in relation to gender contributes to gender power, while power in relation to the division of labour contributes to a hierarchization and stratification of society and working life. The division of labour, which is the third structure, facilitates segregation in working life by on the one hand differentiating and specializing tasks, jobs, departments, and so on, and on the other coordinating and integrating them (Sayer and Walker, 1992). The integration and combination of work and people in work organizations is usually vertical, in the form of different hierarchical levels.

My view is that together these three structures – in a capitalist society, in a number of work organization arenas and through women's and men's patterns of action and thought – contribute to reproducing gender segregation. What happens when this reproduction occurs is also connected with a number of mechanisms, some of which I have identified.

Social mechanisms are seen here as forms of background or triggering forces that contribute to making social phenomena what they are and to what they can do. Mechanisms are here regarded as activating parts of social processes and as the consequence of the dynamic interplay of structures and actors (Pawson and Tilley, 1997; Archer, 1995). It is in this interplay that mechanisms can be activated or not activated, and in that way affect the course of events. However, my goal is not to find the basic mechanism of gender segregation, but to show how a number of mechanisms, through their way of working, contribute to re-creating gender-segregating, and to some extent gender-integrating, conditions. Causality is seen here as relational and consequently in some respects cyclical (Bunge, 1996).

I use three general segregating mechanisms and a fourth specific gendering mechanism. The general mechanisms are those of resource exploitation, resource disposition and resource accumulation, and the specific mechanism is that of gendering (see Tilly, 1998). The general mechanisms contribute by their way of working to creating conditions for inequality and segregation. As inequality and segregation manifest themselves in a number of different ways and embrace a number of different social categories, it is necessary to include the mechanism or mechanisms that contribute to a certain type of segregation – gender segregation for example. The basic idea of the model that forms the basis of this study is that the specific gendering mechanism and the general segregation mechanisms contribute to the reproduction of gender segregation when the gendering mechanism combines with the general mechanisms.

With regard to the general mechanisms, gendered resource exploitation mechanisms lead to the re-creation of conditions for segregation as women and men are exploited in different ways and one category can exploit the other in certain respects.

Gendered resource disposition mechanisms contribute to re-creating conditions for gender segregation when women and men possess different resources and/or the resources they possess are valued differently. Gendered resource accumulation mechanisms re-create conditions for gender segregation when women's and men's possibilities to accumulate resources differ.

However, it is not only structures and mechanisms that are focused on in my model, but also arenas and actors. The arenas are three work organizations and the actors are the women and men employees who work in them. Since, in accordance with critical realism, I regard actors as the 'effective causes' of society, that is to say, acting is necessary for social occurrences, consideration of these actors is required (Archer, 1995; Danermark et al., 2002). This is done by treating them as different categories – as women or men and as wage earners. My inclusion of the economic dimension in the form of paid employment is connected with the fact that the contexts or arenas in which I am studying gender segregation and examining women's and men's conditions are characterized by the economic relations that constitute capitalism. Even though gender segregation is not dependent on capitalist society, this society shapes the context of the work organizations I am studying and thus also of the employees.

The study and the data material

The study is a critical comparative case study (Ragin, 1987; Blumer, 1988), where three different work organizations and their employees constitute the cases that the data material is intended to mirror. The data material is based on a quantitative total examination of these organizations and consists of data from two main sources: register data and questionnaire data from the three work organizations and their employees. The criteria for the selection of the three work organizations are that they must be relatively big and characterized by different gender compositions in the form of a predominance of women, a predominance of men, and a mixture of women and men.

Table 4.1   Organizations and the distribution of women and men

	Male-dominated Mill		Female-dominated Bank		Integrated University	
	Percent	Sum	Percent	Sum	Percent	Sum
Women	20	262	68	215	50	297
Men	80	1015	32	102	50	301
Total	100	1277	100	317	100	598

The result was three organizations in Värmland (a province in central Sweden): a male-dominated paper and pulp mill with 1 277 employees, a female-dominated bank with 315 employees, and an integrated university with 598 employees (see Table 4.1). When I speak in terms of a case study, it is the different segregation patterns of the three organizations that are the objects of my interest – not what specifically characterizes the way the organizations conduct their activities, the way they are organized, and so on. My efforts are also based on identifying a number of mechanisms and their consequences for the reproduction of gender segregation and not on statistical analyses of variables in the traditional sense. Neither do I try to generalize my findings in any other sense than analytically (see Crompton and Sanderson, 1990).

The collection of data took place during 1997, when I visited the different work organizations on repeated occasions and was able to look at registers and documents and distribute questionnaires. With regard to the register data there is no missing data, while the percentage of answers to the questionnaires varies between 72 and 84 percent. The register data used includes information about: the employee's job; hierarchical position; department, office or unit; age; sex; form of employment; period of employment; working hours; and pay. With the help of questionnaires I have obtained data about: the employee's level of education; job security; further training; overtime; business trips; work at home; influence on colleagues and immediate boss; career possibilities; opportunities for personal development; and aspirations with regard to career and personal development. I have also been able to connect the questionnaires with the registers and thus obtained a fairly comprehensive data set based on both objective and subjective data.

The data material has been treated with the help of simple descriptive statistics in the form of fairly comprehensive multivariate frequency and cross tables. The descriptions are a representation of different patterns of gender segregation in work organizations and of how segregating mechanisms can manifest themselves within the categories of women and men respectively. It is also with the help of theoretical reasoning that I discuss the conditions of structures and the possible presence of mechanisms in the different organizations and among the women and the men. In this paper I will focus upon the analytical threads which I find important for the knowledge of gender segregation instead of presenting the empirical patterns.[1]

Next I will discuss how I identified the segregation patterns and how they were manifested in the three organizations.

Patterns of gender segregation and integration in work organization

So, what kind of patterns of gender segregation exists in the work organizations? This part is aimed to show the complexity of gender segregation and integration when studied at an organizational level, including both horizontal and vertical dimensions of divisions of labour. In order to be able to identify different types and patterns of gender segregation, I have with the help of register data identified different forms of divisions of labour, which show *what* in the organization that is segregated – more precisely different jobs, hierarchical positions and departments.

---

[1]   Anyone interested in the result of the main study, see Bergman (2004).

I have also identified different types of gender composition, which show *how* the forms of division of labour are segregated – namely female-dominated, integrated and male-dominated. To define whether an organization, job and so on are integrated or not I have used the quantitative definition of equality which is used in Swedish gender equality politics. An equitable distribution of women and men is a group composed of women to men of 40–60 percent (INT). If women constitute more than 60 percent the group is female-dominated (WD), if it is the men that constitute more than 60 percent then the group is male-dominated (MD). The different forms of division of labour and the different gender compositions together constitute what I call types of segregation, for example female-dominated jobs or departments.

Traces of integration

The findings show that there is marked gender segregation in all three work organizations. In other words, mixing women and men is the exception rather than the rule both with regard to how great a proportion of positions, jobs and departments are integrated, and with regard to the proportion of women and men to be found within these integrated domains. Concerning the proportions of hierarchical positions, jobs and departments that are integrated the following patterns are shown: In the male-dominated Mill 8 percent of the jobs and 11 percent of the departments are integrated, the rest are either female- or male-dominated. There is only one hierarchical level of seven that are integrated and that is middle white collar worker level. In the female-dominated Bank 19 percent of the jobs and 15 percent of the departments are integrated. The rest of the jobs and departments are segregated in either direction. There are two hierarchical levels of six that are integrated, the lower managerial level and the lower middle white collar level. In the integrated University 14 percent of the jobs and 25 percent of the departments are integrated. One hierarchical level of six are integrated, namely the higher white collar level. These patterns provide evidence that the different types of division of labour in the organizations in a very obvious way are gender-typed. Most of the hierarchical positions, jobs and departments are segregated or gender-typed in either direction (see Bradley, 1989). To organize work is to divide and rank different tasks and so on, but also to coordinate them. The data shows that this differentiation and coordination process very much are modified by gender structure. As long as work divides in a gendered way – in other words are gender-typed – we can presuppose that segregating mechanisms are activated.

Even if integrated domains exist in the organization, this does not mean that we cannot find segregation within them. For example, in none of the three organizations the integrated domains contain the same share of women and of men. In the Mill it is more likely for women than for men to work in an integrated hierarchical position, a job or a department. In the Bank and University the opposite pattern is noticeable, in other words it is the men that to a greater extent then the women are found in integrated domains. This pattern is more extensive in the Bank then in the University. Comparing the organizations shows that the greater the proportion of men is in the organization, the more likely it is that women are to be found in integrated domains

than men and vice versa. So, a closer investigation of integrated domains show that
we still can find traces of segregation since the share of women and men in these
domains differ in all three organizations.

The data further show that integration in one domain does not necessarily mean
integration in another. Relating the different types of segregation to each other reveals
that in the Mill a majority of women and men in integrated hierarchical positions have
jobs that are dominated by their own sex. In the Bank and in the University women
and men in integrated hierarchical positions to some extent have integrated jobs; on
the other hand the majority of them work in a department that are dominated by their
own sex. There are hardly any examples of women and men situated in a position
where they meet integration in *all three* dimensions – hierarchy, job and department.
In the Bank no one of the 317 employees work in an integrated position when all
three dimensions are considered. In the Mill there are two women and three men out
of all 1 277 employees that work in this type of position, which is less than 1 percent
of all employees. At the University with 598 employees there are 30 women and 26
men in positions that are integrated in all three dimensions, which means 9 percent
altogether. In other words: we have to be careful when we are talking about gender
integration in working life if we only consider one of these dimensions. Segregation
within integration is in other words an obvious pattern.

The findings also show that when job type is related to hierarchy, female-
dominated jobs are clustered in the lower regions of the hierarchy and to some extent
up to the middle level in all three organizations. Male-dominated jobs, on the other
hand, are mainly at the upper levels, except in the Mill where they are to be found
at the two workers' levels. We can therefore assume that jobs constitute a significant
breakpoint in the reproduction of segregation, in which both differentiating and
stratifying forces are present and activated. In this connection it may be worth noting
that there is a certain degree of mutual transfer effect between jobs and the people
who do the jobs, which contributes to reproducing gender-segregating conditions.
The status of a certain job can spread to the people who have it (Cockburn, 1985).
The status of the social category that predominates in the performance of a certain
job can, in turn, spread to the job. If, for example, women predominate in a certain
type of job, this may function as an obstacle to men selecting or being selected for
these jobs.

Patterns of segregation and of crossing gender borders

I have above tried to show that integration is not a very widespread phenomenon
in my empirical material, no matter what type of organization considered. Next I
will present some of the results that focus on the segregated parts, which means the
domains that are either male-dominated or female-dominated. Let us look at how
the gender pressure manifests itself in terms of where women and men are found in
the three organizations. Are they mainly in a same-sex domain or do they break into
the opposite-sex domains? In Table 4.2 we can see that in the male-dominated Mill
a massive majority of the men are found in male-dominated hierarchical positions,

jobs or departments. Only to a very limited extent are men working in female-dominated areas. The women on the contrary show another pattern. Even though also they tend to gather in female-dominated domains, they don't do it in the same obvious way as men in male-dominated domains. Looking at those crossing gender borders there is quite a great share of the women that work in a male-dominated hierarchical position. The share is considerably smaller when it comes to jobs and departments. The table shows that it is more likely for women than for men to work in a domain where they are the minority.

Table 4.2   Organization and segregation type: Distribution in per cent within the category of women and men respectively

	Mill		Bank		University	
	Women	**Men**	**Women**	**Men**	**Women**	**Men**
Position						
WD	28	2	61	15	49	16
INT	8	3	38	70	45	68
MD	64	95	1	25	6	16
Sum %	100	100	100	100	100	100
Job						
WD	60	3	85	25	53	4
INT	16	4	8	19	33	38
MD	24	93	7	56	14	58
Sum %	100	100	100	100	100	100
Depart.						
WD	45	4	85	51	55	12
INT	28	7	12	24	23	24
MD	27	89	3	25	22	64
Sum %	100	100	100	100	100	100
N	262	1015	215	102	297	301

In the Bank a majority of the women are clustered in positions, jobs and departments that are dominated by their own sex and only a couple of percent of them are found in male-dominated domains. The men in the Bank do not show any specific pattern by mainly working in male- or female-dominated domain. They do not work in male-dominated hierarchical positions and departments in an extensive way, while a little bit more than 50 percent work in male-dominated jobs. On the other hand even if men to some extent can be found in female-dominated domains it is not a big share of them, with the exception for female-dominated departments where about 50 percent of the men work. In the Bank it is the women who predominantly are crowded into same-sex domains, while the men to a greater extent are more likely to be found in opposite-sex domains. Men crossing gender borders is far more common, but it is still not the general pattern for women or men.

In the integrated University there is yet another pattern. Approximately half of each category of women and men work in a hierarchical position, job or department dominated by their own sex. There is an exception and that is along the hierarchical dimension where 16 percent of the men are found in male-dominated positions. This shows that there are reasons to talk about the University as an organization where gender-borders are being kept intact by both women's and men's locations. This pattern becomes even more obvious when looking at the share of women and men found in domains dominated by the opposite sex. Table 4.2 shows that breaking the gender-border is not a widespread pattern for either women or men. Further, we can see that it is somewhat more likely that a woman cross a gender-border than a man.

It is evident that gender borders can be identified in all three organizations. Women's and men's locations within these segregated domains are likely to reproduce patterns of thought and of action as a result of doing different things in different departments and on different hierarchical levels. This differentiation in where, with what and with whom women and men work, and thereby also interact, reproduces segregation as an – in many ways – unintended consequence; a consequence that can be thought of as a structurally conditioned process where durability of segregation goes on through situated everyday praxis.

An important aspect of gender segregation in organizations is therefore the different forms of internal categorization, that is, the different forms of divisions of work that exist in the organizations (Tilly, 1998). They constitute the internal organizational categories and units that are matched with external social categories – such as gender – when people are recruited for a job. This matching process affects both the external gender categories and the internal job categories and in many cases this influence leads to gender-bound patterns being taken over, incorporated and thus maintained. In other words, I consider the actual work tasks – those that are put together for different jobs – as the hub of this process. Jobs are part of a number of other contexts, however, such as hierarchical, departmental, organizational and trade contexts, for example. Thus job segregation contributes not only to differentiation but also to stratification.

Due to the fact that the differences between women and men are institutionalized in the horizontal and vertical patterns of work distribution of the organization and therefore in the economic structure of society, this contributes to the reproduction of gender-segregating conditions through disparate socio-economic conditions and the maintenance of a status difference between women and men.

Women and men and their conditions in working life

This section is devoted to women and men as genders and as wage earners, and to how as such they contribute to reproducing gender-segregating conditions in certain respects and to undermining them in others. The section aims to answer the last of the questions at issue: How is gender segregation reproduced in work organizations, are gendered mechanisms of resource exploitation, resource disposition and resource accumulation present? The analysis of the material is based on how the mechanisms can be assumed to have a segregating effect, if they are present in the empirical material and if they manifest gender-typed patterns. In the presentation, the material is not divided according to the organizations in the same way as above; instead the different mechanisms are in focus. Next I will shortly recapitulate the mechanisms at issue and present the hypotheses that I have been working with.

Mechanisms and hypotheses

As mentioned earlier gendered resource exploitation mechanisms lead to the re-creation of conditions for segregation if women and men are exploited in different ways. Variables used are monthly salary, form of employment, security of employment, working hours, overtime, and business journeys. Gender resource disposition mechanisms contribute to re-creating conditions for gender segregation if women and men possess different resources and/or the resources they possess are valued differently. Variables used are age, period of employment, level of education and control/influence in the work group. Gendered resource accumulation mechanisms re-create conditions for gender segregation if women's and men's possibilities to accumulate resources differ. Variables used are career possibilities, skill development possibilities and staff training.

In order to answer my questions, I use three hypotheses. The first concerns the assumption that there exists a *general difference* between women and men, regardless of hierarchical positions, types of job or types of department. Here the women and men are compared with respect to various factors connected with all three different segregation mechanisms. The second hypothesis focuses on the domains with equal proportions of men and women, and is based on the assumption that there is *segregated integration*, which does not necessarily mean that women and men have the same conditions but rather the opposite. The third hypothesis, *men's domains stand out*, is based on the assumption that men's domains in organizations, that is, domains where men have higher hierarchical positions and where there are male-dominated jobs and departments, entail better conditions for both women and men in comparison with women and men in integrated and female-dominated domains.

With the help of the first two hypotheses I can investigate whether there are differences between women and men within the same hierarchical positions, types of job and types of department in general and in integrated types in particular, and in this way identify the segregating mechanisms' gendering presence or absence. In the third case it is more a question of investigating whether gender segregation is reproduced due to the fact that men's domains stand out in relation to the other domains, that is, if it is better. If the hypotheses are valid, conditions for segregation are re-created. If the hypotheses are false, possibilities for integration are created.

How conditions of segregation are re-created

Starting with the investigation of the hypotheses in relation to the mechanism of resource exploitation, the findings show that women and men tend to be exploited differently, independently of which hierarchical position, type of department or type of job they are located in. Women's wages are lower than men's and they have more insecure forms of employment than men. The hypotheses concerning a general difference and about a segregated integration are accordingly confirmed. This means that conditions for segregation are created in all types of segregation, even in the integrated ones. The material also shows that men's domains do not necessarily stand out as regards exploitation for men, but to some extent for women. Men's conditions tend to be more stable in this case, independently of what type of segregation they work in. It can be pointed out, however, that segregating conditions are re-created, since resource exploitation are more marked for women in men's domains compared with women in other domains.

The production of goods and services are put together with different categories of workers through the organization of work. There is a need for a diversity of employees, some with higher status and better conditions than others. The categories of women and men are both examples of categories that are exploited, but in different ways. In one way we could say that women are more exploitable than men since the mechanism of exploitation is gendered and re-creates conditions where women are kept some distance from men.

In the discussion about resource exploitation I analytically treat both women and men as resources that the organization exploit in different ways. Next I will present the findings in the material concerning the resource dispositions of women and men to see if the mechanisms are gendered to some extent or not.

The results show that women and men – no matter what type of hierarchical position, job or department studied – exhibit a similar pattern with regard to experience resources such as age and period of employment, but not with regard to educational resources and action resources as control/influence in the work group. In the latter case men to a greater extent than women have educational resources and action resources at their disposal. This means that the hypotheses general difference and segregated integration are verified in some respects, but not in all. In other words, integrating conditions are created as regards experience resources in the different types of segregation, while segregating conditions are re-created as regards educational and action resources. The men's domains do not stand out for either women or men with regard to experience resources, and exhibit ambiguous patterns with regard to educational and action resources. In other words, here conditions are created for both segregation and integration.

Women and men tend to show the same characteristics with regard to age and period of employment, which can be understood as they have similar conditions concerning life- and work experience resources. It is not that one category consequently is older or has worked for a longer time than the other. On the other hand the material shows that with regard to educational level and control/influence in the work group, women and men differ to the favour of men. A possible consequence of this pattern of resource disposition is that women are likely to suffer from lack of status, power and respect in relation to men, no matter what type of segregation type they are to be found in – female-dominated, male-dominated or integrated. Belonging to a minority or a majority or a mix does not change the gendered resource disposition mechanisms of education or control/influence.

Finally, mechanisms for resource accumulation are to be considered. They tend to re-create segregation if they are gendered and therefore are contributory causes of keeping the distance between women and men by difference in possibilities to accumulate valuable resources. The data show that mechanisms for resource accumulation exhibit – with only a few exceptions – a gender-typed pattern regardless of hierarchical position, type of job or type of department. Women get less personnel training than men. They also have less opportunity to make a career and to develop their skills within their job than men. Thus there is a general gender difference which confirms the hypothesis with reference to general difference. In the integrated domains there is an obvious dissimilarity between women and men concerning to what extent they have the opportunity to accumulate resources. The result shows that the hypothesis segregated integration is verified. In other words, the resource accumulation of women and men contributes to the re-creation of conditions for segregation in all different segregation types in general and in the integrated ones in particular. When it comes to the last hypothesis – men's domains stand out – the data show that the possibilities of resource accumulation does not stand out to any great degree in the men's domains compared to women's domains and the integrated ones. However, it is evident that it stands out more for the women than for the men. Women in men's domains are more likely to be able to accumulate resources than other women. This means that there is not always a negative thing to be a minority or a positive thing to be a majority. It depends on the actual conditions.

All in all, the results show that conditions for segregation and integration exist at the same time. However, the predominant tendency is that the segregating mechanisms combine with the gendering mechanisms regardless of hierarchical position, type of job or type of department. In other words, there is no great doubt that in the material there are predominant actual differences between the women and men with regard to how they are exploited, the resources they have at their disposal, and their chances to accumulate resources. This difference is not only generated by how gender, power and division of labour structures melt together in work organizations, it also contributes to maintaining these structures through situated women's and men's conditioned patterns of thought and action.

The findings also show that gender segregation in working life is connected with how the structures of gender, power and division of labour work – not separately, but through the way they are related to each other. Since these three structures are part of my way of defining gender segregation, it is not only a question of differentiation but also one of stratification – and it thus constitutes a form of inequality. I think it is necessary to understand gender segregation and inequality in relation to each other and I will give arguments in support of this below.

Segregation and inequality

The definition of the concept of segregation as a form of separation or distinction indicates that segregation does not necessarily entail stratification. This study has shown, however, that this assumption does not have any empirical support with regard to gender segregation, which has consequences for some of the more common ways of presenting gender segregation in working life in both social science and in politics. Two of these ways are illustrated in Figure 4.2. In the first case it is the gender-power relationship – stratification – that contributes to the women and men being in different places and doing different things – differentiation. In the second case it is the separation – the differentiation – between the gender categories in social life and/or working life that is decisive for the unequal power relationship – stratification – between women and men. In the first case it is assumed that if the power of the category of men over the category of women is undermined, it will lead to women (and men) being able to freely cross the gender boundaries in different areas. In the second case it is more a question of trying to make women and men mix in as many areas as possible, since lack of differentiation will undermine men's power (Hirdman, 1988).

I will now discuss some of the reasons why the approaches fall short when it comes to understanding the problems of gender segregation. In the first approach – where gender stratification is assumed to precede and lead to gender differentiation – many of the political measures are a question of attempts to even out the power differences between women and men by redistributing various forms of resources and positions (Fraser, 1997). In this approach there is a tendency to take it for granted that the power has been realized due to the fact that the access to resources and positions is different for women and men, which contributes in turn to the fact that they gather in different areas of working life – are differentiated – and thus have different chances to realize their capacities. This approach is in many respects important for our understanding of gender segregation in working life, as it points to the importance of the unequal distribution of opportunities and of stratified positioning. At the same time differentiation in working life is given subordinate importance – or rather, it becomes a consequence of a number of factors, including gender and power structures. I have pointed out earlier that differentiation and co-ordination, that is, the division of labour, is a structure of its own with its own causal forces (Sayer and Walker, 1992). This means that it affects the gender and power structures, which means that the division of labour both influences and is part of the stratification, and not only a consequence thereof.

The second approach – in which differentiation is assumed to lead to stratification – is clearly realized in the political goals that aim to work towards equalizing the proportions of women and men in the different areas of society. As I have shown repeatedly, equal proportions of women and men – in jobs, departments and hierarchical positions – do not necessarily mean that women and men have the same conditions. Equal proportions of women and men do not prevent power structures determining the conditions for how women and men act. In other words, we cannot assume that mixing women and men necessarily constitutes a form of win–win situation for both women and men. This material shows that the opposite may be the case, that is, that in many cases it is in integrated jobs, departments and hierarchical positions that the gendering segregation mechanisms appear the most clearly. Neither does the integrated University stand out as an organization in which stratification based on gender is absent. Proportional majorities, minorities and mixed cases are principally quantitative units, which do not say anything about the real conditions within and between these units. In certain respects the predominance of one's own sex is associated with better conditions and in others not. The predominance of women has proved to be characterized by bad conditions for the women in these types of segregation. At the same time, the study shows that it is in the female-dominated departments that women are able to attain higher positions. Differentiation here means possibilities for a certain hierarchical integration. Or, formulated in other words, the integration of women occurs mainly within the framework of segregation. Since equality politics mostly focus on the proportional relationship between women and men, it is important, in the light of the findings that have emerged from this study, to point out what such a focus may overlook.

Even though both approaches give us valuable insights into the problems of gender segregation, I think that in both cases we tend to get caught in either-or thinking. The important thing is not to decide what comes first and what is most decisive for gender segregation – stratification or differentiation. Instead I argue in favour of the importance of seeing the involved structures in relation to each other and with a mutual influence on each other. My way of looking at gender segregation is illustrated in Figure 4.3.

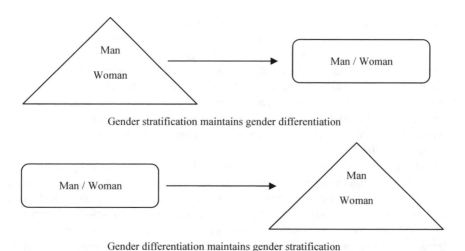

Gender stratification maintains gender differentiation

Gender differentiation maintains gender stratification

Figure 4.2   Different ways of looking at the relation between gender differentiation and gender stratification

If the approach applied in this study is found to be fruitful, studies of gender segregation should include consideration of the structures of gender, power and the division of labour, and how they combine to influence the organization of our working life. Through this routine interaction, this structural weave contributes to certain mechanisms tending to be activated in such a way and in such contexts that persistent patterns of segregation and inequality are maintained. I am of the opinion that the organization of conditions for acting must be changed for gender segregation in working life to be affected. It is difficult for changes that only address proportional relationships or the capacities or abilities of individual women and men – and not the organizational contexts that surround them – to have any great impact.

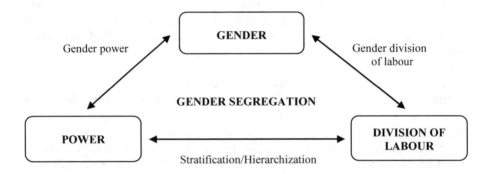

Figure 4.3   Necessary structures for the reproduction of gender segregation in work organizations

With regard to the three organizations included in the study, the result shows that they are to a great extent structured in such a way that gender-segregating and gender unequal conditions are reproduced. The patterns are broken in some cases. The question is whether they are the result of how the work is organized, of the efforts of individuals or accidental circumstances. Patterns are broken for a number of reasons, but the achievement of durable breaks demands a change in the organization of both society and working life itself. When segregation is a voluntary or accidental separation and not generated by different conditions – then segregation is not the same as inequality.

    Last but not least, the main result of the study is that integration by numbers is not the same as integration by conditions. In other words, gender equality in working life is not necessarily the outcome of an equivalent number of women and men. There is a lot of segregation in terms of qualitative conditions within quantitative integration, and some qualitative integration in quantitative segregation. Since segregation sometimes takes place within integration and vice versa, an analysis of women's and men's working conditions is crucial for our understanding of the reproduction and transformation of it.

References

Abrahamsson, L. (2000), *Att återställa ordningen. Könsmönster och förändring i arbetsorganisationer*, Boréa, Umeå.

Archer, M. (1995), *Realist Social Theory: The Morphogenetic Approach*, Cambridge University Press, Cambridge.

Bergman, A. (2004), *Segregerad integrering. Mönster av könssegregering i arbetslivet*, Karlstad University Press, Karlstad.

Bhaskar, R. (1978), *A Realist Theory of Science*, Harvester Press, Brighton.

Bhaskar, R. (1979), *The Possibility of Naturalism*, Harvester Press, Brighton.

Blumer, M. (1988), 'Some Reflections upon Research in Organizations', in A. Bryman (ed.), *Doing Research in Organizations*, Routledge, London.

Bradley, H. (1989), *Men's Work, Women's Work: A Sociological History of the Sexual Division of Labour in Employment*, Polity Press, Cambridge.

Bryman, A. (1989), *Research Methods and Organization Studies*, Routledge, London.

Bunge, M. (1996), *Finding Philosophy in Social Science*, Yale University Press, New Haven.

Bunge, M. (1998), *Social Science under Debate: A Philosophical Perspective*, University of Toronto Press, Toronto.

Clegg, S. (1989), *Frameworks of Power*, Sage, London.

Cockburn, C. (1985), *Machinery of Dominance: Women, Men and Technological Know-How*, Pluto Press, London.

Crompton, R. and K. Sanderson (1990), *Gendered Jobs and Social Change*, Unwin Hyman, London.

Danermark, B., M. Ekström, L. Jakobsen and J. Ch. Karlsson (2002), *Explaining Society: Critical Realism in the Social Sciences*, Routledge, London.

Fraser, N. (1997), *Justice Interruptus: Critical Reflections on the 'Postsocialist' Condition*, Routledge, London.

Hacking, I. (1999), *The Social Construction of What?*, Harvard University Press, Cambridge.

Harré, R. (1970), 'Powers', *British Journal for the Philosophy of Science*, no. 21.

Hirdman, Y. (1988), 'Genussystemet – reflexioner kring kvinnors sociala underordning', *Kvinnovetenskaplig tidskrift*, no 3/1998.

Isaac, J. (1987), *Power and Marxist Theory*, Cornell University Press, Ithaca.

Jónasdóttir, A. (1994), *Why Women Are Oppressed*, Temple University Press, Philadelphia.

Jonung, C. (1997), 'Yrkessegregering mellan kvinnor och män', in I. Persson and E. Wadensjö (eds), *Glastak och glasväggar? Den könssegregerade arbetsmarknaden*, SOU, 1997:137, Fritzes, Stockholm.

Moi, T. (1997), 'Vad är en kvinna? Kön och genus i feministisk teori', *Res Publica*, no. 35/36.

Nermo, M. (1999), *Structured by Gender: Patterns of Sex Segregation in the Swedish Labour Market: Historical and Cross-National Comparisons*, Swedish Institute for Social Research, Stockholm.

Pawson, R. and N. Tilley (1997), *Realistic Evaluation*, Sage, London.

Ragin, C. (1987), *The Comparative Method: Moving Beyond the Qualitative and Quantitative Strategies*, University of California Press, Berkeley, CA.

Sayer, A. (1992), *Method in Social Science: A Realist Approach*, Routledge, London

Sayer, A. (2000), *Realism and Social Science*, Sage, London.

Sayer, A. and R. Walker (1992), *The New Social Economy: Reworking the Division of Labor*, Blackwell, Oxford.

Tilly, C. (1998), *Durable Inequality*, University of California Press, Berkeley, CA.

Young, I. M. (1990), *Justice and the Politics of Difference*, Princeton University Press, New Jersey.

Young, I. M. (2003), 'Lived Body vs. Gender. Reflections on Social Structure and Subjectivity', in M. Proudfoot (ed.). *The Philosophy of Body*, Blackwell, Oxford.

Chapter 5

Measuring Gender Segregation

Ruth Emerek

Introduction

Gender division of work in households has been the norm in years without any great outspoken concern – except from feminists – and regarded as a matter of private agreement within households. Gender division of paid work has by contrast become a more and more important issue in public debate and politics. This is reflected in an enormous amount of literature within the last 20 years on segregation and how to measure segregation (see among others Jenson et al., 1988; Walby, 1990; Rees, 1992; Blackburn et al., 1993; Walby 1997; Gonäs et al., 1999; Rubery et al., 1999; Gonäs et al., 2001; Blackburn et al., 2002; Charles, 2003; and Löfström, 2004 for discussion and further references).

The objective of this chapter is to present and discuss various measures of this concept – from simple more graphical to more complex measures based on calculation. The discussion of different measures is illustrated by data from Denmark and from EU15.

Gender segregation

Gender segregation of the labour market means originally that women and men work in different sectors (horizontal segregation) and hold jobs with different occupational status (vertical segregation). Sylvia Walby reports how a male union in the UK earlier succeeded in a strategy of excluding women from its job areas. When this exclusion strategy failed (in the middle of the Second World War), the strategy was replaced by a segregation strategy, where women were only admitted to certain areas of work as well as to separate sections of the union (Walby, 1990). Segregation in other areas of the labour market in the UK and other countries is not necessarily a result of a process as deliberate – although they may be the result of power struggles as well as various forms of discrimination or even forms of protection (Wikander et al., 1995). Segregation may however also be due to skills and education and linked to differences in women's and men's choice of education and career path.

Consequently segregation must be seen as a result of various factors, as well as the development where segregation in the pure form (with occupational areas exclusively for women or men) is broken down and gradually replaced with female or male dominated areas. Today few areas in the labour market are totally male or female dominated. Nevertheless 'segregation' is still used as a synonym for women's and men's unequal distribution across occupations and sectors. Latest available Danish data (from January 2003) show that less than 0.005 percent of men in employment hold jobs where the share of women is zero, and less than 0.03 percent of all women in employment hold jobs where the share of men is zero.[1] At the same time Denmark, which has one of the highest employment rates for women, comes out as having one of the most segregated labour markets in Europe, when segregation is measured by some of the various developed measures. And indeed, women and men still are unequally distributed over the various jobs in the Danish labour market – as even a very rough categorization in sectors and occupational status as quoted in Table 5.1 reveals.

Table 5.1   The female share of employment by occupational status and sector, Denmark January 2003

Horizontal segregation: Sector										In total	Persons in total
Vertical segregation: Occupational status	(1) %	(2) %	(3) %	(4) %	(5) %	(6) %	(7) %	(8) %	(9) %	%	In 1000
Self employed	9.4	20.4	17.9	3.9	30.3	8.2	31.0	53.3	50.3	**25.6**	176.0
Assisting spouses	97.1	93.1	100.0	95.5	85.9	94.2	89.3	90.2	81.7	**92.8**	9.3
Top managers	11.1	12.5	7.3	6.3	20.2	18.0	17.2	43.3	0.0	**25.2**	60.1
Employees – upper level	28.0	24.9	15.0	10.3	36.3	22.5	28.8	55.6	28.6	**45.6**	330.02
Employees – medium level	33.7	41.7	31.4	26.6	39.6	29.3	47.8	81.3	9.1	**61.4**	418.3
Employees – basic level	22.5	28.0	26.4	8.6	49.3	36.9	64.1	76.0	30.6	**49.3**	1081.4
Other employees	27.6	34.2	10.3	2.1	35.5	7.8	51.4	53.9	15.4	**36.3**	267.4
Employees, not specified	25.9	53.6	34.2	24.7	50.0	26.7	44.7	60.4	21.4	**47.3**	310.3
The female share of employment	**22.4**	**31.9**	**23.7**	**9.5**	**44.3**	**27.2**	**45.8**	**68.7**	**50.0**	**47.2**	
Persons in total (in 1000)	85.3	423.2	13.7	165.4	472.8	170.4	359.3	952.1	10.6		2652.8

Note: Data stems from the Register Based Statistics (January 2003) including all Danes. Employed persons (aged 16-66 years old) are divided by gender, sector (9 categories) and occupational status (8 levels).
      Sectors are: (1) Agriculture, fishing and quarrying. (2) Manufacturing. (3) Electricity, gas and water supply. (4) Construction. (5) Wholesale and retail trade. Hotels, restaurants. (6) Transport, storage and communication. (7) Financial intermediation, business activity. (8) Public and personal services. (9) Activity not stated.
Source: Statistikbanken, Statistics Denmark.

---

[1]   This is based on a disaggregation of the work force in 111 sectors and eight levels of occupational status. A more disaggregated categorization may reveal higher percentages.

Although there have been big structural changes in the labour markets, the main categories in national statistics are still the same as 'always' – and do not reflect the change in occupational structure and the change in women's employment. This means that the number of persons in the various sectors vary considerably. As an example: Women form 47.2 percent of the persons in employment in Denmark, and are overrepresented in the area of 'Public and personal services', which cover over one third of all employed, and where the female share amounts to more than two thirds – with an even higher overrepresentation in this sector in employment on a medium and basic level. Women are furthermore overrepresented in the small category of assisting spouses (which counts for less than 1 percent of employed and where women form almost all employed) and underrepresented among self employed and top managers in all sectors.

The table reveals that the female share of employment may vary considerably in occupational status within sectors (which is hardly surprising) and also among sectors within the same occupational status. The female share of top managers in the female dominated sector 'Public and personal services' is more than twice the share in other sectors in Denmark. This pinpoints the fact already given in the original concept of segregation, that segregation should be studied for jobs – that is a combination of occupational status and sectors. This should also be considered in the attempts of finding relevant measurements, which – though quantitative – in few figures reflect the difference in women's and men's employment. In fact the very different distributions of occupational status within sectors just exemplify that segregation in jobs may be very different from the segregation in sectors. Theoretically the female share of the various sectors and of the various occupational statuses may be equal (to the overall female share of employment) and thus indicates no segregation at the same time as the labour market is very highly segregated in relation to jobs.

A graphical approach

A simple calculation of the cumulative distribution of women and men in employment with regard to the female share of the various jobs may be a first step in revealing differences. The Danish labour market – though not totally segregated – still has areas, which are clearly female or male dominated. This is shown by the distribution in Figure 5.1 of women and men in employment as functions of the female share of employment on a subdivision of sectors into more categories (111) along with the same subdivision of sectors combined with occupational status (8 categories).[2]

---

[2] The calculations include only jobs (that is here the combination of a sector and an occupational status) with at least one person in all years in the period 1997–2003, which reduces the number of different jobs to 861.

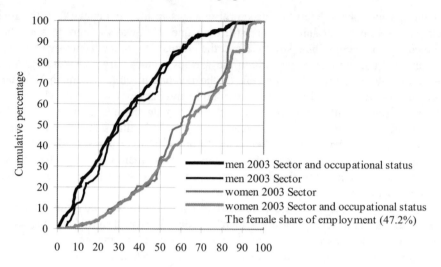

Figure 5.1   The cumulative distribution of employed men and women after the female share of employment in sectors as well as in sectors and occupational status, Denmark 2003

Note: Data stems from the Register Based Statistics (January 2003) including all Danes. Employed persons (aged 16–66 years old) are divided by gender, sector (111 categories) and occupational status (eight levels).

Source: Statistikbanken, Statistics Denmark.

The curves for sectors alone indicate less differentiation in employment between women and men than the curves for sectors combined with occupational status. However, all curves reveal a highly segregated labour market. Half of all men in employment hold jobs in sectors with a female share lower than 30 percent – and only a little over 10 percent of all women in employment work in these sectors. On the other hand: Half of all women in employment hold jobs in sectors with a female share over 60 percent and where only around 10 percent of all employed men hold jobs. In fact, to indicate an equal and less segregated distribution of employment, the curves for women as well as for men should be lower than the actual curves for women until the actual female share of employment (which in this case is 47.2 percent), and afterward the curves should be above the actual curves for men.

Segregation can also be illustrated in a histogram, where the female share of jobs is grouped in five categories inspired by the work of Kolehmainen (1999) and Tyrkkö and Wesberg (2001):

- 'male dominated' jobs, where the female share of jobs is less than 20 percent
- 'medium male dominated' jobs where the female share of jobs is 20 or more but less than 40 percent

- 'mixed gendered' jobs, where the female share of jobs is 40 to 60 percent
- 'medium female dominated' jobs where the female share of jobs is more than 60 and less or equal 80 percent
- 'female dominated' jobs where the female share of jobs is more than 80 percent.

The number of categories is always up to discussion as well as the cutting points between categories. For simplicity – to show the principle – only five categories are used as in the previously mentioned work. Figure 5.2 (based on the subdivision of sectors into 111 categories combined with occupational status in eight categories) shows the results from Denmark in 1997 and 2003.

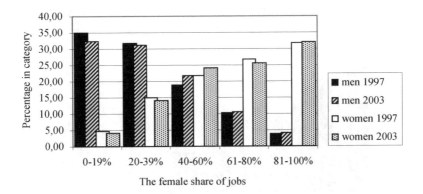

Figure 5.2   The distribution of employed men and women in 'male dominated', 'medium male dominated', 'mixed gendered', 'medium female dominated' and 'female dominated' jobs, Denmark 1997 and 2003

Note: There is a data break and it is difficult to compare with data earlier than 1997. Furthermore there are minor corrections and changes from 2002 to 2003. The task here is however to illustrate possibilities for analysis of segregation – not to give totally precise results from Denmark. For further comments to data, see note to Figure 5.1.
Source: Statistikbanken, Statistics Denmark.

The figure reveals that in 1997 and 2003:

- more than 30 percent of all men in employment hold 'male dominated' jobs
- more than 30 percent of all men in employment hold 'medium male dominated' jobs
- less than 25 percent of men and women in employment work in mixed gendered jobs, where 40-60 percent of their colleagues have the same gender
- more than 25 percent of all women in employment hold 'medium female dominated' jobs

- more than 30 percent of all women in employment hold 'female dominated' jobs.

Categories and change

The categorization also makes it possible to study the directions of change and the movement of jobs – towards 'feminization' or 'masculinization' over a period – in this case 1997–2003. Figure 5.2 indicated a slight movement towards desegregation as the percentage of employed men and women in 'male dominated' and 'medium male dominated' jobs has decreased over the period while the percent of employed men and women in 'mixed gendered' jobs has increased. This is however a result of a process of jobs moving in different directions. Figure 5.3 shows the distributions of jobs in 1997 and 2003 divided by the female share of jobs in the five categories.

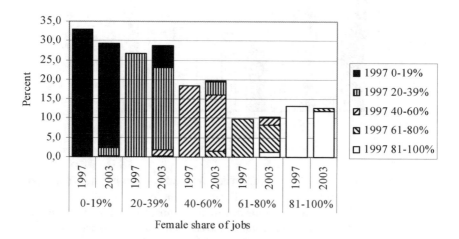

Figure 5.3   The distribution of jobs in 'male dominated', 'medium male dominated', 'mixed gendered', 'medium female dominated' and 'female dominated' jobs, Denmark 1997 and 2003

Note: The origin of the categories in 1997 is shown for the categories in 2003. For further comments to data, see note to Figure 5.1 and 5.2.
Source: Statistikbanken, Statistics Denmark.

Some movements point to less segregation. Part of all jobs in 1997 in the 'male dominated' and 'medium male dominated' categories have moved to less male dominated categories in 2003, and part of the 'female dominated' and 'medium female dominated' jobs in 1997 have become less female dominated in 2003. However, almost as many movements point to more segregation, part of all 'mixed gendered' jobs have moved equally in the male dominated or female dominated direction, part of 'medium male dominated' jobs have become 'male dominated' and part of 'medium female dominated' jobs have become 'female dominated'. The simple differences in Figure 5.2 thus cover great fluctuations between categories over the period, and they are not just a result of an overall movement toward less segregation and a more equal female share of all jobs.

These measurements do not account for differences as to how many persons hold the various jobs. A job with few persons may easily 'change' category – it may take only a few persons. As the traditional male sectors are specified in detail whereas female sectors as health and care are compounded in broad categories, it is easier for male dominated jobs to 'change' category. Therefore, by studying movements between job categories alone one may give a biased picture of the development of gender segregation. In Figure 5.4 the movements from and to the five categories have been weighted by the number of persons in the various jobs at the start and at the end of the period respectively.

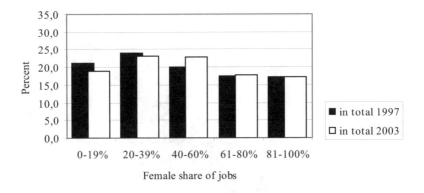

Figure 5.4   The distribution of persons in employment in 'male dominated', 'medium male dominated', 'mixed gendered', 'medium female dominated' and 'female dominated' jobs, Denmark 1997 and 2003

Note: For comments to data, see note to Figure 5.1 and 5.2.
Source: Statistikbanken, Statistics Denmark.

The figure reveals that less persons work in 'male dominated' and 'medium male dominated' jobs and more persons work in 'mixed gendered' and 'medium female dominated' jobs in 2003, which instead of desegregation may point to a 'demasculinization' of jobs.

What has been seen, as a form of desegregation – especially from male dominated jobs – may thus also partly be a result of a declining number of persons in male dominated jobs. A categorization based on a very unequal distribution of the number of persons in the various jobs may – as illustrated in this case – give biased findings. Therefore it is hardly recommendable to make the categorization of jobs (after the female and male share) the only object for the analysis of the development of segregation.

Furthermore – in general – by dividing jobs in categories to study movements *between* categories, movements *within* categories become invisible. It is thus a choice – the fewer categories (to make the result easy to comprehend and report), the more potential invisible movements within the categories.

Regression models to study change over time

All information on the female share of jobs can be utilized in the study of the increase or decrease of the female/male share of jobs, when the female share of jobs one year is mapped on the female share of jobs for a previous year as in Figure 5.5.

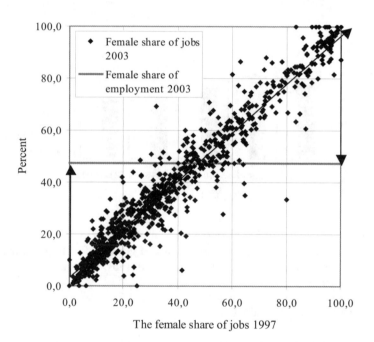

Figure 5.5   The distribution of the female share of a job in 2003 mapped as a function of the female share of the job in 1997

Note: Data stems from the Register Based Statistics (January 2003) including all Danes. Employed persons (aged 16–66 years old) are divided by gender, sector (111 categories) and occupational status (eight levels).
Source: Statistikbanken, Statistics Denmark.

The figure indicates a slight movement in form of a regress from 1997 to 2003 towards more gender mixed jobs – in other words a more equal share of jobs. Regression analysis of the female share of jobs in 1998, 1999, 2000, 2001, 2002 and 2003 as a function of the female share of jobs in 1997 shows an increasing regress – that is, the sharing of jobs is gradually becoming more and more equal over the period 1997–2003 (Table 5.2, section A). With no development the constant would have been zero and the slope one. The constant is however growing significantly over the short period (from about 0.7 to about 3.0) while the slope is dropping significantly from 0.987 to 0.958 – a clear indication of a gradual development in a slow speed towards a more equal female share of jobs. With this speed it will however take 100 years before the 'line' has moved to women's share of employment – that is to total equality.

Still, as mentioned earlier, the female share of a job may easily change within jobs which few persons hold. When the different numbers of persons within the various jobs are counted for – the desegregation is still significant – it will however take place at an even slower speed (Table 5.2, section B).

Table 5.2   The result of a regression analysis of the female share of jobs in 1998, 1999, …, 2003 as function of the female share of jobs in 1997, Denmark

Model for		A: Occupations				B: Occupation weighted by number of employed			
		B	Std. Error	Sig.	Adj. R-sq.	B	Std. Error	Sig.	Adj. R-sq.
1998	(Constant)	0.693	0.006	0.000	0.989	0.472	0.003	0.000	0.993
	Female share in 97	0.987	0.000	0.000		0.990	0.000	0.000	
1999	(Constant)	1.832	0.007	0.000	0.985	1.159	0.003	0.000	0.991
	Female share in 97	0.974	0.000	0.000		0.983	0.000	0.000	
2000	(Constant)	2.307	0.008	0.000	0.979	1.547	0.004	0.000	0.986
	Female share in 97	0.969	0.000	0.000		0.978	0.000	0.000	
2001	(Constant)	2.449	0.010	0.000	0.969	1.687	0.005	0.000	0.977
	Female share in 97	0.968	0.000	0.000		0.977	0.000	0.000	
2002	(Constant)	3.033	0.011	0.000	0.964	1.994	0.005	0.000	0.973
	Female share in 97	0.958	0.000	0.000		0.970	0.000	0.000	
2003	(Constant)	2.953	0.012	0.000	0.961	1.774	0.006	0.000	0.971
	Female share in 97	0.958	0.000	0.000		0.972	0.000	0.000	

Note: Data stems from the Register Based Statistics (January 2003) including all Danes. Employed persons (aged 16–66 years old) are divided by gender, sector (111 categories) and occupational status (eight levels). The calculations include only jobs (that is here the combination of a sector and an occupational status) with at least one person in all years in the period 1997–2003, which reduces the number of different jobs to 861.
Source: Statistikbanken, Statistics Denmark.

A new regression on the estimated parameters will give a more precise picture of the development. Controlling for various factors can of course also sophisticate this way of measuring development in segregation.

To study and reveal changes by comparisons of the female or male share of jobs over time or by the transitions between more or less fine categories of male and female dominated jobs over time is without a doubt useful – especially when the occupational structure is relatively stable. It is, however, still an open question as to how this form of measurement can be made useful in a broader context – and for example, be used in comparing gender segregation between countries because of differences in the occupational structures and in the scale of women's employment.

Traditional measures

Traditional measures to compare segregation over time and between countries do not normally use a longitudinal approach. They are based on annual data and mostly relatively simple indices, which can relatively easily be understood. The most commonly used indices are:

- the Index of dissimilarity (ID)
- the Moir and Selby-Smith segregation indicator (MSS) also called WE Index
- the standardized or Karmel and MacLachlan Index (IP).[3]

The *ID-index* is half the sum of the absolute difference in women and men's distribution across occupations or across sectors. The ID-index equals zero in case of complete equality (where women's employment is distributed similarly to men's across categories, for example, occupations or sectors) and 100 percent in the case of complete dissimilarity (where women and men are in totally different categories).

The *MSS-index* is the sum of the absolute difference in women's distribution and the total distribution of persons in employment across occupations or across sectors. The MSS-index equals zero in case of complete equality, and is equal to twice the male share of employment – in the case of complete dissimilarity. This index may thus exceed 100 percent.

The *IP-index* is the sum of the average absolute difference between women's and men's actual distribution compared to a theoretical distribution based on equality like the total distribution across occupations or sectors. The IP-index equals zero in the case of complete equality, and is equal to twice the male share of employment multiplied by the female share of employment in the case of complete dissimilarity.

---

[3]   Mathematical expressions for the indices are placed in the Appendix.

All three indices are based on the understanding that segregation means different distributions of women and men across the occupational categories, and the more equal the distribution across occupations for women and men, the less the segregation. All three indices are interrelated. The ID-index is dependent on the distribution of occupations and thus indirectly on the scale of women's employment. As the MSS-index and the IP-index are just modifications of the ID-index, they are also indirectly dependent on the scale of women's employment, even though they adjust for the female employment rate.

The indices may, however, point in different directions for the same development in women's and men's employment. If, for instance, the female share of employment increases towards 50 percent, while the distribution of women's and men's employment across categories remains stable, the ID-index will show no difference, the MSS-index will decrease (because the male share of employment will fall) resulting in lower measure of segregation, and the IP-index will increase (as 'the male share of employment multiplied by the female share of employment' will increase toward 50 percent), resulting in higher measure of segregation.[4] The case in which the female share of employment increases, while the distribution of women's and men's employment across categories remains stable, is hardly likely in reality. It is however important, when interpreting the results of an investigation based on an index for comparisons over time and countries, to know that the index may point in an erroneous direction.

Table 5.3 based on data from Denmark shows that all three indices – measured at different levels of categorization – point in the same direction even though the female share of employment is increasing. The table shows by all indices and all three categorizations that segregation is declining in Denmark as the former analyses also demonstrated. The table reveals, however, also that all three segregation indices are dependent on the categorization, the better (that is the more comprehensive) the categorization, the higher the measure of segregation for all indices. This indicates that the index of segregation not only measures the segregation, but also the sensitivity and level of the categorization.

The ID-index is the only proper index among the three indices (with 100 percent as a maximum). However the ID-index contains another problem, as it does not depend on the female or male share of employment. This is partly accounted for in the MSS-index and even more in the IP-index. This section will consequently concentrate on the IP-index, which is further interesting as the European Commission uses it as the index to monitor the development of the gender segregated labour market and to compare gender segregation in the labour market between the EU-countries.

The Employment and Social Affairs DG in the European Commission uses two indicators for segregation (Emerek et al., 2001):

---

4   See Emerek et al. (2001) for a more comprehensive introduction and discussion of these indices.

- IP-Index of gender segregation in occupations. The data source is the Labour Force Survey (LFS), ISCO classification of occupations.
- IP-Index of gender segregation in sectors. The data source is the Labour Force Survey, NACE classification of sectors.

Table 5.3   The ID-index, the MSS-index and the IP-index measured at different levels of categorization, Denmark 1997–2003

		1997 %	1998 %	1999 %	2000 %	2001 %	2002 %	2003 %
Sectors (9 categories) and occupational status (8 categories)								
	ID	37.2	36.7	36.2	35.9	35.6	35.4	35.6
	MSS	40.1	39.5	38.7	38.2	37.7	37.4	37.6
	IP	18.5	18.2	18.0	17.9	17.7	17.6	17.8
Sectors (111 categories)								
	ID	45.2	45.0	44.7	44.4	44.2	44.1	44.2
	MSS	48.7	48.4	47.8	47.2	46.9	46.6	46.7
	IP	22.4	22.4	22.2	22.1	22.0	22.0	22.1
Sectors (111 categories) and occupational status (8 categories)								
	ID	48.4	48.0	47.4	47.1	46.6	46.2	46.3
	MSS	52.2	51.6	50.7	50.1	49.4	48.9	48.9
	IP	24.1	23.9	23.6	23.4	23.2	23.0	23.1
The female share of employment		46.1	46.2	46.5	46.8	46.9	47.1	47.2

Note: See note to Figure 5.2.
Sources: Statistikbanken, Statistics Denmark.

The NACE classification is very broad (with 61 categories) and includes fewer categories than the ISCO classification (111 categories) (Eurostat, 1996). The IP-index gives a higher figure for gender segregation in occupation than for sectors, which also may be due to the number and sensitivity of categories. The EU-average is 25 percent for occupational segregation and 18 for sector segregation. The IP-index has the advantage of a relatively simple calculation but at the same time the disadvantages and problems that a change in the IP-index may be due to a change in dissimilarity or to a change in women's employment rate – possibly to a combination of the two.

The graphical presentation of the IP-indices in Figure 5.6 shows a positive connection between the IP-indices and women's employment rate. One way of accounting for this is controlling for women's employment rate when comparing indices over time and between countries.

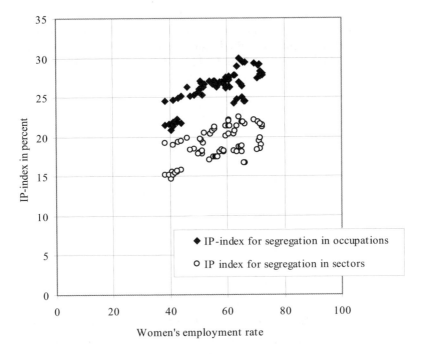

Figure 5.6   IP-indices for occupation and sector respectively as function of women's employment rate: Countries in EU15 (except Luxembourg), annual data for the period 1999–2003

Source: European Commission's Indicators for monitoring the European Guidelines.

The EU-commission's data on indicators for monitoring the Employment Guidelines allows a comparison over 5 years (1999–2003) of all EU-15 countries (except Luxembourg) of the occupational and sector segregation controlled for women's employment rate. The results of linear regression models with these variables (in Table 5.4) show that both the IP-index for occupational and sector segregation is positively correlated with women's employment rate, though it seems to influence the occupational segregation to a greater extent than the sector segregation. The most interesting result is found in the model for occupational segregation (section A). When women's employment rate is accounted for, Austria, Belgium, Germany, Spain, Finland, France, Ireland and Portugal have higher values for segregation than Denmark and Sweden, which normally top the occupational IP-index together with Finland as the average for 1999–2003 also shows. The values for Denmark and Sweden are not even significantly different from the EU-15 average.

The model shows a declining tendency for the occupational segregation over the period. This is not the case for sector segregation (where there is no significant dependency of the year) and the result for sector segregation is not in the same way distorted among countries.

Table 5.4   **The IP-index for occupational and sector segregation as a function of year (1999–2003), country and women's employment rate (compared to the Lisbon target for 2010 of 60 percent) and the average of the IP-index for occupational and sector segregation in the period 1999–2003**

| | Section A: IP-Index for occupational segregation | | | | Section B: IP-Index for sector segregation | | | |
| | as dependent variable | | | Average 99-03 | as dependent variable | | | Average 99-03 |
	B	Std. Error	Sig.		B	Std. Error	Sig.	
(Constant)	26.229	0.076	0.000		17.992	0.046	0.000	
Year from 2000	-0.118	0.010	0.000					
Austria	1.231	0.086	0.000	27.5	2.271	0.060	0.000	20.3
Belgium	1.657	0.062	0.000	26.1	0.734	0.049	0.000	18.2
Germany	1.079	0.063	0.000	26.9	0.278	0.049	0.000	18.2
Denmark	-0.100	0.195	0.608	28.2	0.383	0.117	0.001	19.0
Greece	-1.145	0.155	0.000	21.5	-1.661	0.096	0.000	15.3
Spain	2.360	0.146	0.000	25.1	2.318	0.090	0.000	19.3
Finland	2.420	0.125	0.000	29.5	3.596	0.079	0.000	21.9
France	1.399	0.048	0.000	26.7	-0.374	0.044	0.000	17.4
Ireland	1.803	0.047	0.000	26.9	3.073	0.043	0.000	20.8
Italy	-0.602	0.167	0.000	21.8	-1.605	0.102	0.000	15.3
Netherlands	-2.370	0.122	0.000	24.6	-0.684	0.078	0.000	17.6
Portugal	0.610	0.081	0.000	26.8	3.628	0.057	0.000	21.6
Sweden	0.109	0.194	0.573	28.4	3.032	0.116	0.000	21.6
United Kingdom	-0.452	0.125	0.000	26.6	0.475	0.079	0.000	18.7
Women's employment rate minus 60%	0.191	0.011	0.000		0.055	0.007	0.000	

Note: The baseline for the model is the EU15 average; Luxembourg is not included due to lack of data. The adjusted R-square is 96.8 percent for the model with occupational segregation and 97.0 percent for the model with sector segregation. The year is left out in the model for sector segregation, as it is not significant.
Source: European Commissions Indicators for monitoring the European Guidelines.

The regression analysis may control for more factors – for example the size of the service sector, as a large-scale involvement of women in employment generally results in a higher percentage of employment in the service sector.

Concluding remarks

This chapter has been yet another demonstration of the problems of measuring segregation. It is not a new statement that none of the traditional indices provide satisfactory measures of gender segregation over time and across countries. However the measuring by these indices may be slightly improved just by adding an extra index – namely the cross section of sector and occupation – to the separate indices for sector and occupation. This will to a greater extent make it possible to monitor the interaction of horizontal and vertical segregation. Still, this is not a solution to the measuring problems in the long run. Using the indices as measures to compare over time and across countries presupposes a relatively constant and equal female employment rate as well as a stable and homogeneous occupational structure – conditions not possible to fulfil in the long run and between all countries.

The question is what to do? Firstly, it is necessary to be aware of the problems in measuring segregation – and in fact it may be better to use the traditional relatively simple measures, for which problems and pitfalls are already known, than less transparent and more complicated measures.

Secondly, better (more homogeneous and equal sized) categories must be asked for in the EU and national statistics. It is hardly worth the effort to develop new measures as long as the categories are as biased towards the traditional male dominated labour market as they are at present – or make new measures to offset the antiquated categorization.

Finally, new measures should be developed to reveal – in a proper way – longitudinal dynamic and change as well as cross-country differences. At present we do not have to develop new measures that are easy to calculate – but rather measures easy to interpret and understand.

References

Blackburn, R., J. Brown, B. Brooks and J. Jarman (2002), 'Explaining Gender Segregation', *The British Journal of Sociology*, vol. 53, pp. 513–536.

Blackburn, M., J. Jarman, and S. Siltanen (1993), 'The Analysis of Occupational Gender Segregation over Time and Place: Some Considerations of Measurement and Some New Evidence', *Work, Employment and Society*, vol. 7, pp. 335–357.

Charles, M. (2003), 'Deciphering Sex Segregation', *Acta Sociologica*, vol. 46, pp. 267–287.

Emerek, R., H. Figueredo, M. P. Gonzales, L. Gonäs and J. Rubery (2001), 'Indicators on Gender Segregation', in J. Rubery, C. Fagan, D. Grimshaw, H. Figueiredo and M. Smith (eds), *Indicators on Gender Equality in the European Employment Strategy: European Expert Group on Gender and Employment*, Report to the Equal Opportunities Unit, DG Employment, http://www.umist.ac.uk/management/ewerc/egge/egge.htm.

EUROSTAT (1996), *The European Union Labour Force Survey, Methods and Definitions*.

Gonäs, L., G. Lindgren and C. Bildt (2001), *Könssegregeringen i Arbetslivet*, Arbetslivsinstitutet, Stockholm.

Gonäs, L., J. Plantega and J. Rubery (1999), *Den Könsuppdelade Arbetsmarknaden – ett Europeisk Perspektiv*, Arbetslivsinstitutet, Stockholm.

Kolehmainen, S. (1999), *Women's and Men's Work: Labour Market Segregation in Finland 1970–1990*, Research reports 227, Statistics Finland, Helsinki.

Jenson, J., E. Hagen and C. Reddy (eds) (1988), *Feminization of the Labour Force – Paradoxes and Promises*, Polity Press, Cambridge.

Löfström, Å. (2004), *Den könsuppdelade arbetsmarknaden*, SOU, 2004:43, Stockholm.

Rees, T. (1992), *Women and the Labour Market*, Routledge, London.

Rubery, J., M. Smith and C. Fagan (1999), *Women's Employment in Europe: Trends and Prospects*, Routledge, London.

Tyrkkö, A. and H. Westberg (2001), *Förskjutning i segregationsmönster på yrkesnivå*, Arbetsliv i omvandling, Arbetslivsinstitutet, Stockholm.

Walby, S. (1990), *Theorizing Patriarchy*, Blackwell, London.

Walby, S. (1997), *Gender Transformations*, Routledge, London.

Wikander, U., A. Kessler-Harris and J. Lewis (eds) (1995), *Protecting Women: Labor Legislation in Europe, the United States, and Australia, 1880–1920*, University of Illinois Press, Champaign, IL.

Data from:

European Commission: *Indicators for Monitoring the Employment Guidelines, 2004–2005 Compendium.*

Statistics Denmark, Statistikbanken, http://www.statistikbanken.dk.

Appendix: The ID, MSS and IP-index

The *index of dissimilarity* (ID) is defined as:

$$D = \tfrac{1}{2}\sum_i \left| \frac{M_i}{M} - \frac{F_i}{F} \right|$$

The *Moir and Selby-Smith indicator* (MSS-index) also called the WE-Index is defined as:

$$MSS = \sum_i \left| \frac{F_i}{F} - \frac{N_i}{N} \right|$$

By calculations it can be shown (Emerek et al., 2001) that the MSS-index can be reformulated as a function of the ID-index

$$MSS = \frac{M}{N}\sum_i \left| \frac{M_i}{M} - \frac{F_i}{F} \right| = 2\cdot\frac{M}{N}\cdot D$$

The *standardised or Karmel and MacLachlan-index* (IP) is defined as:

$$P = \frac{1}{N}\sum_i \tfrac{1}{2}\left(\left| M_i - \frac{N_i}{N}\cdot M \right| + \left| F_i - \frac{N_i}{N}\cdot F \right| \right)$$

By calculations it can be shown (Emerek et al., 2001) that there is a relation between the IP, the MMS and the ID-index:

$$P = \frac{F}{N}\sum_i \left| \frac{N_i}{N} - \frac{F_i}{F} \right| = \frac{F}{N}\cdot MSS = 2\cdot\frac{M}{N}\cdot\frac{F}{N}\cdot D$$

Where:
- M represents the total number of males in employment
- M_i the number of males in occupation i
- F the total number of females in employment
- F_i the number of females in occupation i
- N the total number in employment
- N_i the total number in occupation i.

Chapter 6

The New Economy and the Work Life Balance: Conceptual Explorations and a Case Study of New Media

Diane Perrons

Introduction

Given the diverse nature, varied understandings and different claims made about the new economy, this chapter seeks to explore how one sector, new media, has materialized in one particular location – Brighton and Hove, focusing on the gender differentiated nature of opportunities and risks, work and working hours and the impact on work life balance.

The chapter divides into three sections. The first explores some of the varied conceptualizations of the new economy and outlines some of the potential risks and opportunities that have been identified in the literature. The second outlines the view put forward by government and politicians, including the UK's Women's Unit, that the new economy, especially the development of communication and information technologies and in particular the Internet, which potentially extends the spatial and temporal range of paid work, provides new opportunities for people with caring responsibilities, and potentially a means of reducing gender inequality. The main section evaluates this expectation by reference to a qualitative study of the new media sector in Brighton and Hove, which has become a new media hub. It does so by exploring gender differentiated patterns of ownership, management and earnings; working practices, in particular long hours, flexible working patterns and homeworking, and considers the extent to which these working patterns are compatible with a work life balance, especially when caring responsibilities are involved. The chapter concludes by contesting some of the ideas about the new economy and makes some suggestions for redressing gender imbalance that, so far, seems to be being reproduced in this new area of activity.

The new economy, new media and the organization of work

The new economy is a concept that has recently entered academic and media discourse and although widely used has several meanings with differing implications for the well-being of the economy, individual and social welfare. Optimistically the term has been used to refer to the unprecedented coexistence of economic growth and a booming stock market with low inflation, tight labour markets and low wage pressures (Greenspan, 1998). More substantively it has been used to depict 'a new technological paradigm centred around micro electronics-based information/ communication technologies, and genetic engineering' (Castells, 2000:9). The development of the Internet, in particular, is said to have profound implications for the organization of economic activity and for increasing productivity (Castells, 2001). Other analyses focus more circumspectly, on the changing character of work associated with technological change, deregulation and globalization (Sennett, 1998; Beck, 2000; Carnoy, 2000) and the new social inequalities that seem to be accompanying these processes. Ulrich Beck (2000) argues that work at all levels is characterized by insecurity and increasing inequality. Similarly, Richard Sennett (1998) maintains that new, insecure and increasingly fragmented forms of work are leading to an imbalance between the values required for a successful working life and those required for a stable family leading to the 'Corrosion of Character'. Fernando Flores and John Gray (2000:24) speak of the 'death of the career' and argue that lifelong identities are giving way to 'brief habits' and 'the lives of wired people are more like collections of short stories than the narrative of a bourgeois novel'. The empirical support for these claims is however more varied. Interestingly, Danny Quah (1996, 2001) and Robert Reich (2001) in different ways link the positive and negative dimensions analytically and argue that they form part of an emerging digital divide. That is, they argue that some of the essential characteristics of the knowledge-based economy, which contribute to economic growth, also increase economic inequality (Perrons, 2004). Reich (2001) and Martin Carnoy (2000) also emphasize that the new economy puts increasing pressure on maintaining a work life balance, and on social sustainability, but otherwise less attention has been given to questions of reproduction and the gendered nature of emerging inequalities in the new economy, an omission noted by Castells (2001)[1] and something this chapter seeks to explore.

Perhaps more is said about the 'new economy' and the lives and livelihoods of people working within it than is actually known and there may be a tendency to generalize from the little that is known especially within popular writings (see for example Reeves, 2001 in which a very optimistic and one sided view of the future of work is developed). Thus, detailed, comparative, empirical work is necessary in order to investigate the varied forms taken by the new economy and how it is experienced in practice. Kevin Doogan (2001) has made an explicit empirical critique of the insecurity thesis and this chapter also seeks to make a contribution to the debate by reporting on a qualitative analysis of the experiences of women and men working in the new media sector in Brighton and Hove.

---

[1]   Castells (2001:7) makes a pledge to remedy this omission viz 'I have vowed to myself (and to the reader) to continue working on this topic (gender and the Internet) and have it ready for a possible second edition of this book' (Internet Galaxy). (my insertions)

In this brief review of work on the new economy emphasis is placed on explanations which foreground long lasting, substantive changes, that is, the potential offered by new information and commuting technologies and new working arrangements in terms of time and contracts, rather than those that rest on nominal economic variables, such as inflation free growth, as the sustainability of the new economy on these criteria has already been questioned as economic growth in the USA began to slow down in the middle of 2001.

Thus thinking of the new economy as characterized by the increasing use of information and computing technologies, and the Internet, it is clear that new ways of organizing the production, distribution and exchange of existing goods as well as entirely new goods and services have come into being. The distribution and exchange of goods via the Internet is generally referred to as E-commerce and takes place between businesses and consumers (B2C), a well known example of which would be Amazon.com which supplies books, videos and CDs, and transactions between firms or businesses (B2B) which so far are quantitatively more significant (OECD, 2000) and have been said to lead to new forms of business organization. Castells (2001) argues for example that the Internet has allowed the potential of networked forms of organization within and between firms to be realized. Existing services such as training, marketing, advertising and public relations are also increasingly being provided through the Internet, becoming e-training, e-marketing and e-pr, usually in addition to traditional means of provision through CD Roms, videos and brochures. The Internet also facilitates the development of new interactive services including digital TV, games and interaction with virtual worlds, for example with a pop group.[2] In turn, these new services, products and methods of distribution generate new forms of knowledge-based employment ranging from web based graphic design, web system/database management, video installations through to programming. One outcome is a range of new activities and jobs now commonly referred to as new media, which do not fit neatly into existing industrial sectors or occupational categories.

This conceptualization of the new economy conforms to media images, which emphasize ICT and high status employment and also forms the main subject of this chapter. Nevertheless, it is important to recognize that these activities also generate and depend on a range of lower level jobs in distribution and consumer services. E-commerce, designed and managed by the higher-level workers, generates low status employment in warehousing and delivery.[3] Some work is displaced from conventional retailers and banks to call centres and some is transferred to consumers

---

[2]   For example the Gorillaz, a virtual pop group designed by Damon Albarn of Blur, had a top ten hit in June 2001 and also a top selling CD. It is possible to visit the site, talk interactively to the virtual band members and spray graffiti on the walls of their virtual flat.

[3]   This is encapsulated in a recent advert for Consignia in which Elton John selects a whole range of expensive goods from the Internet, then expresses frustration that they are only virtual, but the door then opens and a large group of very happy looking, (but in reality low paid) postal workers appear with the physical parcels.

who manage their own transactions directly via the Internet. Furthermore, given the long hours worked by knowledge-workers (see IER/IFF, 2001) there has been an expansion of jobs in the personal care and consumer services sector to cater for their needs (see Perrons, 2004). Thus, the new economy is characterized by a duality or digital divide, which in practice may build upon and possibly reinforce existing social divisions of class, gender, race and ethnicity. Middle class, well-educated and white men are likely to be over represented in high level 'self programmable' (Castells, 2000) jobs, while women, ethnic minorities and people from lower social classes are more likely to be found in the generic, lower paid jobs, in delivery and personal services such as office cleaning, personal fitness, catering and care. There is however some similarity in the contractual structure and temporal demands of employment, if not in lifestyles and levels of pay, between high and low level workers that create problems for managing work life balance.

New working patterns and the work life balance

With the possibilities offered by ICT, increasing deregulation and associated moves towards the 24/7 society, the temporal range of working hours has expanded leading to an expansion of flexible and long working hours (Harkness, 1999; Presser, 1999; Rubery, Smith and Fagan, 1998; IER/IFF, 2001; Twomey, 2001). For example, the recent IER/IFF (2001) survey found that 11 percent of workplaces in the UK (covering 19 percent of the employees) operated 24 hours a day 7 days a week and 11 percent of employees, amongst whom fathers were especially prevalent, were working 60 or more hours a week. There was also a connection between flexibility and long hours in that the former were sometimes allowed simply to permit the latter, that is the demands of the workplace were so intense that people were 'allowed' to work on Saturdays and Sundays and take work home, a practice which has been facilitated by ICT and internet access which enables continual connection between work and home through mobile phones and email.[4] This can be construed positively as a means of extending the range of locations from which paid work can be carried out, more negatively as a means of work invading the home or indeed elements of both. The Department for Employment and Education (DfEE, 2000a and 2000b) emphasizes the business case for flexibility, termed work life balance, and provides illustrations of how it can increase productivity, reduce absenteeism, improve staff commitment, increase retention rates and so reduce employer costs. Indeed within this perspective flexible working seems to be more concerned with accommodating life to rather demanding and unquestioned working hours rather than one of reorganizing work to allow time for domestic and caring responsibilities. The IER/IFF survey (2001) found that while some forms of flexible working were permitted, especially work at weekends and during unsocial hours, only a tiny minority of employers provided other forms of flexibility such as job shares or forms

---

[4]   Overall in the IER/IFF survey 15 percent of employees worked on Sunday and 12.5 percent on Saturday and Sunday.

of leave additional to statutory requirements. Neither did many provide any direct assistance with childcare (2 percent provided a workplace crèche and 3 percent financial assistance) yet 26 percent of workplaces provided workplace counselling/ stress management. They suggest that employers are prepared to pay to alleviate their employees' stress but less willing to provide facilities that might prevent it in the first place' (IER/IFF, 2001: 25). It is important to recognize however that even when available, the take up rate of family leave related arrangements is low (DfEE, 2000a) possibly because of stigmatization. Thus, flexible working patterns have opened up opportunities for a wide range of people, including carers, to take paid employment, even though employers often retain control over the parameters of flexibility (Dex and McCulloch, 1997; Breedveld, 1998; Figart and Mutari, 1998; Rubery, Smith and Fagan, 1998; Perrons, 1999).

New working patterns have eroded the boundaries and collective rhythms of working life and the concept and reality of a fixed working day has declined for many people. The process is also cumulative. As working hours become more varied, people will expect services to be available at a wider range of times. Further, as the boundaries of the working day have become more opaque, many salaried workers are expected to work long hours to demonstrate commitment (Hochschild, 1997; McDowell, 1997; Doyle and Reeves, 2001; Fagan, 2001) and to match the working hours of different time zones. The main reason given by employees for long hours is 'to get the work done' but the IER/IFF survey (2001) found that 70 percent of those working over 60 hours enjoyed their work compared to 57 percent in the survey as a whole. Entrepreneurs and freelancers similarly work long hours to get the work done, but also because of the unpredictable nature and flow of work together with tight deadlines and in some cases endorsing the findings of the IER/IFF survey, because of intrinsic work satisfaction, which means that the boundaries between work and life become blurred (see Massey, 1996; IER/IFF, 2001; Reeves, 2001 and the case study below). This blurring can also be explained by the fact that knowledge work depends on human rather than fixed capital and so is characterized by bursts of activity followed by fallow periods and thus does not fit easily into a 9–5 structure (Gershuny, 2000). Consequently knowledge based societies are said to be moving to a postindustrial time regime (Doyle and Reeves, 2001; Fagan, 2001; Gershuny, 2000).

Richard Reeves (2001) argues that concern over long working hours is misplaced because they often reflect worker preferences. He argues that time at work increasingly involves doing interesting things in attractive physical and social environments and so may be preferred to watching a TV soap, carrying out domestic work or looking after children. In part following the ideas of Arlie Hochschild (1997) Reeves argues that:

> While the workplace is growing in attractiveness for many people home, or 'life' is looking a bit gloomy. For dual-earner couples with children, life outside work is one of fixed timetables (childcare), conflict (whose turn is it to pick up the kids?), low-skill work (cooking, cleaning nappy disposal) and thankless masters and mistresses (the kids). As

work enters the post-industrial era, home life has become industrial. (Reeves, 2001, p. 128)

There may be some truth in this illustration for some people, or on occasions for many but Reeves (2001) pays little attention to the terms and conditions of employment for those who might provide childcare and domestic services or 'life-style fixers' (Denny, 2001) or whether they similarly would welcome increased working hours. Furthermore, Reeves (2001) seems to overlook the complex nature of care work. Although the domestic division of labour may be a source of conflict (Beck, 2000) or the outcome of complex processes of intra household negotiation (see Jarvis, 1999), this should not negate the multifaceted nature of care work, or its potential for positive utility (Perrons, 2000). Michael Rose (1999) for example, found that domestic workers, including cleaners and dinner ladies had the highest levels of job satisfaction. Good quality care may also bring positive social benefits (see Folbre and Nelson, 2000; Folbre, 2001). If however the gender division of domestic labour and child care is systematically uneven, which it currently is in the UK (Murgatroyd and Neuburger, 1997) and if longer working hours are generalized, then time or the willingness to work long hours will form a new means of gender differentiation, just as other differences, such as qualifications and formal opportunities are becoming more equal. That is, even though some people may enjoy their paid work, it should not automatically be assumed that they dislike reproductive work but rather that the demands of the long hours culture in the context of a society with a social deficit in child and elder care provision, often forces a choice between jobs with career possibilities and those that can be combined with caring for at least one parent, typically the mother.

A further strand of thought in discussions of the new economy is insecurity and risk in both work and home life. Dealing only with the former in this chapter, workers at both ends of the jobs hierarchy have been said to have been affected by increasing insecurity (Beck, 2000; Sennett, 1998; Flores and Gray, 2000) but there is also extensive debate about whether there is any evidence for their claims in relation to the UK (Doogan, 2001; Heery and Salmon, 1999). At the aggregate level only a small proportion of new jobs in the UK during the 1990s were full time and permanent (Gregg and Wadsworth, 1999), giving some support for the insecurity thesis but counter evidence suggests that there has been little change in the average length of time that people stay with any individual employer: average job duration for men was 10.5 years in the 1970s and now 9.5 years and for women there has been little aggregate change (Green, Felstead and Burchell, 2000). Furthermore there has been an increase in long-term employment (defined as employees who have been in 'current employment' for ten years or more) from 34.6 percent to 36.7 percent for men and from 21.2 percent to 28.5 percent for women between 1992 and 1999. These increases were found across growing and declining, public and private, traditional and new sectors and across all occupations, and was greater in the higher skilled, managerial and professional groups than in elementary and lower skilled occupations (Doogan, 2001, p. 423). Doogan (2001) explains the paradox of increasing long term employment and the high perception of insecurity among employees, varying between 28 percent to 53 percent (MORI, 2000 cited by Doogan, 2001), to 'manufactured insecurity' generated by the government introducing market discipline into a growing range of jobs, partly through privatization. This manufactured insecurity may have lowered wage demands (see IPPR, 2000) and thus contributed to inflation free growth and possibly to an unwillingness to risk changing jobs, thereby accounting for the increase in long term employment. Whatever the explanation, not all elements in society ever had a career so writers emphasizing increasing insecurity are perhaps overstating the extent of change. Furthermore, in new media temporary or contract work can also be a positive choice, as it provides an opportunity for individuals to continually update their skills, knowledge and pay as they move from project to project and firm to firm (Ó'Riain, 2000). However, this security is very contingent on tight and expanding labour markets and leaves unanswered broader questions of caring and social reproduction or social sustainability (Carnoy, 2000).

The range of the developments associated with the new economy is immense and the ramifications difficult to assess. It is important to emphasize however that these developments have not happened because of new technologies but rather because of the ways in which technological developments occur within a capitalist and increasingly global economy. The processes shaping these changes are those which motivate the decision makers in the large corporations and nation states and on the individual and social response. Similarly, the capacity of people to organize their own work biographies and plan their lifetime finances continues to vary now, as in the past, with individual and social factors. The former include responsibilities and opportunities outside as well as within the workplace and these remain highly structured by individual characteristics including gender, ethnicity, race, social class, educational background, age and stage in life course as well as individual preferences. Social factors include the level of development, the welfare regime and prevailing labour market regulations, company size and status. Thus although everyone is affected by and to a lesser degree affects these developments, they are experienced in different ways and to different degrees depending on their existing individual and social positions. Therefore, these issues require empirical investigation, as there will be considerable variation in outcomes. Before presenting the findings of the case study however, the current state of gender inequality in the UK is outlined together with some indication of official thinking about how the new economy might contribute to increasing gender equality while maintaining a work life balance.

The new economy potential for redressing gender imbalances

Gender inequalities in employment in the UK have narrowed in that more women, (73 percent) more mothers with dependent children (69 percent) and more mothers with very young children (under five) (58 percent in 2000 compared to 48 percent in 1990) are economically active than ever before while male activity rates continue to decline from 88 percent to 84 percent during the 1990s. The figures above together with the fact that in the age group 25–39 the gap between the female (75 percent) and male (94 percent) activity rates is at its highest (Twomey, 2001) indicate that children still constrain women's participation rate and although there has been some convergence between women and men, gender inequalities in terms of hours of work, segregation and earnings remain (Rubery, Smith and Fagan, 1998; Thair and Risdon, 1999; Twomey, 2001; Bower, 2001). On the most favourable measure, hourly earnings, women remain at 80 percent of the male level but only receive 60 percent of male average earnings (EOC, 2000). A study projecting lifetime incomes identified a very wide gender gap, 'the female forfeit', even for those women without children (Rake, 2000). Furthermore, women are overrepresented in part time employment, which often represents the private solution to the low levels of childcare in the UK and indeed the increase in women's activity rate is associated with the increase (12 percent) in part time work between 1990 and 2000 compared with a 4 percent increase in full time employment (Twomey, 2001).

There is an extensive range of recent literature on the position of women in the labour market (Crompton, 1997; Walby, 1997; Rubery, Smith and Fagan, 1998; Bradley, 1999; Thair and Risdon, 1999; McDowell, 2001 to name a few) and some studies of women in various sectors associated with the new economy (Baines, 1999; Stanworth, 2000) but to my knowledge less detailed analysis of the implications of ICT on women's employment overall. Nevertheless the Women's Unit of the UK government has argued that ICT represents 'one of the biggest opportunities for women in the 21st century to earn more, have more flexible working practices and adapt their current business or try a business start-up'. Thus, they maintain that 'self-employment and enterprise offer women a real alternative means of earning good income and achieving greater flexibility in their working lives' (Women's Unit, 2000). That is given the way that contemporary technologies extend the range of working opportunities both temporally and spatially they potentially provide a means of opening up new opportunities for paid work and thereby potentially redress current gender inequalities. As the case study below illustrates there is some substance to this view, but the flexibility offered by ICT for new working patterns could also be seen as a way of allowing government and employers to sidestep any responsibility for facilitating work life balance by passing the responsibility entirely to the individual (woman) by allowing her to adjust her life around paid work (see also Hardill and Graham, 2001).

Entrepreneurs, homeworkers and freelancers can manage their own routines, even if they always cannot control the quantity of work. In some ways they may realize the vision of the 'electronic cottage' (Toffler, 1980) although the problems of social isolation, family tensions also have to be recognized (Phizacklea and Wolkowitz, 1995; Huws, 1996; Baruch, 2000) leading to the contrasting image of the 'electronic cage' (Zimmerman cited by Baines, 1999, p. 20). Women also face constraints; although they are beginning to become more qualified than men as measured by the number of graduates, they have a long historic deficit to overcome. Furthermore they are under-represented on ICT courses and the proportion working in IT has fallen. Women also have greater difficulty in obtaining access to capital and the Women's

Unit have been holding workshops to identify ways of overcoming these constraints. The purpose of the empirical investigation discussed below is to illuminate some aspects of new economy, to outline the differential opportunities and constraints experienced by women and men in this sector and to consider the implications for managing work life balance.

Opportunities and constraints for women and men in the new media sector in Brighton and Hove

Brighton and Hove: 'The Place to Be'

Brighton and Hove on the South Coast of England with a population of 255 800 (ONS, 2001) has been socially constructed as 'The Place to Be' and become the 'focal point for creative industries in Europe' (Brighton and Hove Council, 1999). It has always been a very vibrant place where *'eyebrows are more often pierced rather than raised at eccentric behaviour'* (Brighton and Hove Council, 1999) and it attracts celebrities, media, arts people as well as tourists. It is also a divided town, with more restaurants but also more people sleeping rough per head than anywhere outside London and of 354 council areas in the UK it is the 94th poorest (ONS, 2001; Edwards, 2000). Thus while marketing itself as the 'Place to be' it is simultaneously applying for and receiving funds targeted at the poorest areas under a variety of regeneration programmes nationally and from the European Union.

Brighton and Hove was chosen for this study because it is said to constitute a 'new media hub' and in fact reflects the varied dimensions of the new economy within a relatively small location (see also Tang, 1999; Pratt, 2000). It has at least 200 new media companies with a further 170 companies in East Sussex – the surrounding county.[5] Most of the companies are very small but it is this type of company that corresponds to the opportunities for women identified by the Women's Unit. However, the research findings suggest that although the new media sector provides opportunities for women, significant gender divisions remain.

The results reported come from a wider study of the local labour market in the context of the new economy, deregulation, equity and representation. Initially, seven in-depth interviews were carried out with women who attended the Women in the New Economy seminar in Sussex sponsored by the Women's Unit in July 2000. From these, key issues were identified and fifty further interviews lasting between 45 and 75 minutes, based around a structured questionnaire, were carried out with owners, managers and some employees of small firms and micro enterprises.[6]

---

[5]   This data comes from the Wired Sussex data base – this database is regularly updated, registration is voluntary and free – so is likely to be an under rather than overstatement. In total about 3000 people are employed with a turnover of about £300m.

[6]   The firms were identified from the Wired Sussex database and invited to participate in the study by email. A 25 percent response rate was obtained.

Gender composition, size of companies and earnings

New media is an emerging sector comprising of wholly new companies, which have developed in response to new needs as well as existing companies that have restructured their operations to make use of contemporary technologies. Of the companies participating in the survey, 63 percent had been in existence for less than three years, while 14 percent were over five and a further 11 percent over ten years old. The majority (70 percent, n = 38) are owned and managed by men, despite the fact that the original interviewees were women attending the Women in the New Economy conference. Just over half of the total are limited companies (38 percent female and 63 percent male) and 20 percent (43 percent female and 11 percent male) are one-person firms. Measured by direct employment the majority of the companies in the survey were small, 50 percent having no direct employees and 25 percent not even employing freelancers on an occasional basis (see Figure 6.1). Companies owned by women tended to have a smaller number of employees of either kind than men but the difference was not statistically significant (see Figure 6.1).

Women are also overrepresented among the smaller companies as measured by turnover. Only one wholly owned female company, compared to 14 owned by men had a turnover of above £500 000 and the two female companies in the £250 000 to £500 000 category were co-owned with their male partners (see Figure 6.2). When divided into two broad categories – above and below £50 000 – this gender difference is statistically significant.[7]

There was a significant association in the data between earnings and turnover,[8] but in the case of small companies, and especially sole traders, earnings are difficult to evaluate. The owner can receive earnings, dividends or re-invest profits in the company, Indeed, accountants often advise owners that it is tax efficient to pay themselves only the minimum wage. With these qualifications in mind, women in general earned less than men.[9] Taking earnings and turnover together it is clear that the majority of people in this sector do not conform to the media image of high earners even though they were mainly graduates and worked long hours (see below). For people on low earnings especially, a further problem arises from their irregularity:

> I earn less than £10 000 p.a. Sometimes there is a whole month with no earnings – the big companies in particular are very slow at paying out. (Woman, aged 35–44, web page designer, caring responsibilities, herself major role, ID 1)

---

[7]   For calculations about company size I have changed the gender of one company from female to male because the interviewee was neither the owner nor manager. Chi square was significant at the 5 percent level.

[8]   Chi-Square was significant at the 1 percent level.

[9]   For example 58 percent of women (n = 10) earned less than £15 000 p.a. compared to 43 percent of men (n = 16) and 22 percent of men (n = 8) above £50 000 compared to 11.8 percent (n = 2) women, but the differences were not statistically significant.

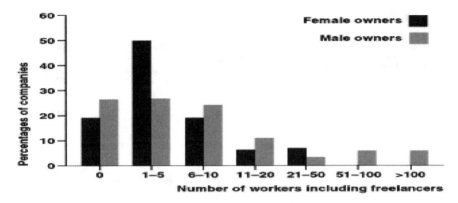

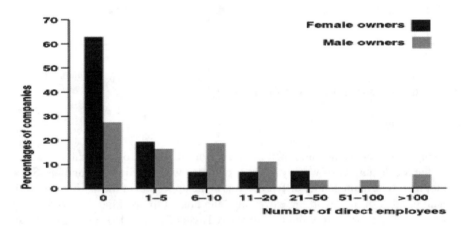

Figure 6.1   Company size and gender

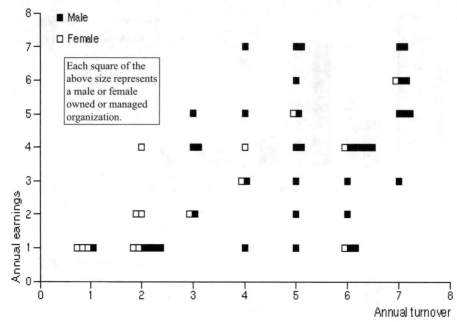

Figure 6.2   Gender, turnover and earnings

Gender, caring responsibilities and working hours

Working hours for women and men in this sector are varied, often flexible but also long, the mean number of weekly hours for women was 46 (SD = 16) and 48 (SD = 17) for men. The main gender difference was at the upper end of the distribution with a small number of men working extremely long hours (six working over 70 hours a week compared to only one woman who worked over 65 hours). However, the median (45) and mode (55) for women were higher than for men 45 and 40 respectively, probably because men were more likely to be managers of larger companies with more standard working hours, while women were more likely to be sole traders or owners with more varied working patterns. Some women and men worked part-time hours but for different reasons. For the men this was either because their new media activity was a second job (this was also the case for one of the women), or because they had been unable to get more work. For women domestic responsibilities were more likely to curtail their hours (see Figure 6.3). Women were statistically more likely (at the 5 percent level) to have a major responsibility for childcare. Overall working hours were long and were either increasing or remaining the same as was the pressure of work, only a minority 12 percent and 9 percent respectively reporting trends in the reverse direction. It is necessary however to point out that the data rests on self-reporting – there is no independent corroboration and being 'busy' forms part of the identity of a successful operator in new media (see Reich, 2001).

There are four main reasons why people work long hours in this sector: the unpredictable nature and flow of work; uncertainty associated with a business start up (see also Baines and Wheelock, 2000); the need to continually update skills and knowledge, and the intrinsic satisfaction derived from the work itself.

In new media, many products and services are 'bespoke', but clients are often uncertain about what they want or what to expect and frequently change their specifications as the project develops. Over a third of interviewees autonomously identified this lack of clear boundaries around project content and corresponding uncertainty about the volume of work, as a major source of strain especially because deadlines were often inflexible – for example, the launch date for a web site. As many of the companies were new and building their reputations they wanted to produce high quality products, and often did not charge for all of the amendments made. They also considered themselves to be at the cutting edge of new software developments and were intellectually interested in exploring new possibilities. Thus the hours of unpaid work could be seen as a form of 'physic income' (Baines, 1999) or self-exploitation or indeed a combination of the two. Furthermore, there was a reluctance to turn down work, similarly to all new start-ups, because of uncertainty about future contracts.

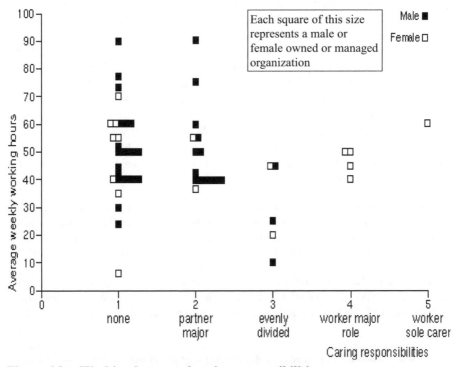

Figure 6.3   Working hours and caring responsibilities

For owners and sole traders, working long hours was often seen as temporary, and a form of investment in the company and their own future as illustrated in the sentiments below which were repeated many times:

> I am working long hours now (110 a week) but this will not be forever. I want to earn a lot now so that I can *do* things later on – like travelling. (His emphasis, man, aged 25–34, specialist web programmer, no caring responsibilities, ID 7)

> At present I am building the company up, – the harder I work the more I enjoy it. As a Director, at present, the company's interests come first.' (Man, aged 25–34, project manager and localiser, on average working 74 hours a week no caring responsibilities, ID 13)

> Well, I'm in a start up role at present and we have been expanding a lot so I'm still trying to get structures in place. Last week I worked about 70 hours but this will go down. I aim to work standard hours. I do aim to 'get a life'. But work is part of life – I enjoy it. The company is covered by the Working Time Directive and they agree with it. (Woman, aged 25–34, manager, no caring responsibilities, ID 39)

Many of those unhappy with the current volume of work had considered expanding the number of employees or utilizing freelancers more intensively. Freelancers form an important part of this sector, not only do they help companies manage the fluctuations in the flow of work, but also allow companies, especially the smaller ones, to draw upon a much wider range of skills than their size would permit, in accordance with the changing nature of their work. One of the larger companies, which had experienced dramatic expansion immediately prior to the survey, subsequently 'let go' half of its staff, but then within two days was advertising for freelancers.[10] Indeed uncertainty was an important reason why others were reluctant to expand. Besides having to finance extra office space to accommodate new workers and ensuring a sufficient flow of work there were also problems of monitoring quality, given that there was little formal accreditation for skills in this sector and concern that growing beyond a 'reasonable size' would lead a loss of control and a qualitative change in their working lives:

> We plan to expand to about the size of 25–30. After that we would have to think carefully about the costs and benefits of further expansion. If we expanded too much it would change the atmosphere. We might set up another company instead. (Man, aged 25–34, database design and management, caring responsibilities, partner major role, ID 15)

This perspective confirms the image of new independent operators as a 'cross between employer and day labourer, self exploiter and boss on their own account… with the objective of moulding their own lives rather than conquering world markets'

---

10 Information from an academic and entrepreneur in the new media sector obtained in the follow up survey and verified by the company concerned. The role of freelancers is being explored in further research.

(Beck, 2000, pp. 54–55; see also Baines, 1999 for a similar finding in the case of media freelancers). Having control over their work was important, as explained below by a respondent, previously earning £100 000 p.a. with a London company, now paying himself only 25 percent above the minimum wage (having allowed for dividends):

> Well it's like prostitution isn't it. I set up my own company so that I have freedom and can control what work I do. (Man, aged 25–34, E-commerce developer, no caring responsibilities, ID 53)

This comment reflects the findings of Rose (1999) from the wider scale analysis of SCELI data in relation to work satisfaction, that although there was a positive association between job skills and job satisfaction, the more significant association was found between own skills and job satisfaction. Specifically, the least satisfied workers were high skilled workers in low skilled jobs. In the case of Brighton and Hove, job dissatisfaction arising from the nature of the work or the wider context in which it was offered were important reasons for new media people to set up on their own (see also the comment from ID 35 below). Indeed for the ordinary employee there may be an inverse relation between firm size and job satisfaction, in that work in the larger firms was more likely to become formulaic and less challenging. In several cases, there was also desire to escape from office politics and from male power structures. Having been independent one female respondent found that:

> After a while you can't go back – you think why should I be doing this for them and they aren't doing it very well anyway. Power has to be earned by respect for competencies – not imposed. The IT world is still a very male world and some men have difficulty in treating women as equal. (Woman, aged 35–44, Internet PR, caring responsibilities, partner major role, ID 12)

For this woman working independently enabled her to escape the glass ceiling, which she had continued to experience in the new economy (see Stanworth, 2000).

For employees, the situation of long working hours was more problematical and employees were often treated in a rather paternalistic way. Employers, just as owners, faced unpredictable volumes of work and tight deadlines and although they could, and in fact often did, take on temporary or freelance workers, this could not always be done at short notice, so existing employees found themselves working extremely long hours. One company as a matter of policy required employees to voluntarily opt out of the EU Working Time Directive, but if employees did work long hours they were compensated by time off in lieu and also by special bonuses:

> If they 'throw an all nighter' (work through the night) I pay for them to have a 'stressbuster – at the Grand' – one or half day special massage and health treatment at a major hotel. (Man, aged 25–34, project manager and localizer, no caring responsibilities, ID 13)

Another small company provided a free breakfast at 8.30 a.m. because:

It encourages people to be here on time and so we can start work fairly promptly at 9 a.m. (Man, aged 35–44, manager and internet marketer, some caring responsibilities, ID 43)

Thus echoing the concierge strategy of Microsoft (Chaudhuri, 2000). This company also held various social events such as long weekends away and a company football team (male only), but was also in conflict with employees over the implications of the EU Working Time Directive for paid holiday. In fact, there was a curious mixture of concern for employees' well being on the one hand, but an unwillingness to endorse regulations to enhance employees' rights on the other.

Time is especially important in new media, where skills and knowledge need continual updating and networking is necessary to find out about contemporary developments and to acquire work. The vast majority of companies stated that they provided time at work for employees to engage in self-learning via magazines and the Internet. Some also had informal systems of work shadowing and workshops for exchanging ideas. Single operators would clearly have to provide this time for themselves. Some employees also saw their time with an organization as a period in which to acquire new skills prior to setting up on their own:

I have always worked long hours – it is self-imposed, I have a tendency to be a workaholic. When I worked for an organisation, I was trying to gather work experience. I would stay late to work with the software experimenting etc. At home I would no longer want to see a computer – I tried to incorporate study hours into the working environment but it was difficult – you were often so busy – working every minute. Different projects would dovetail with one another, it was like a continuous production line – I wanted to get away from feeling a cog in a process, I wanted more autonomy. (Man, aged 25–34, web design and multi media, caring responsibilities evenly divided, ID 35)

Work life balance

The most striking finding was that the vast majority of people surveyed liked their work, with (80 percent) strongly agreeing or agreeing with the statement that 'generally speaking I am very satisfied with the nature of my work'. Gender differences were not very marked except that the 10 percent that disagreed with this perspective were all male. The following quotations encapsulate this perspective:

I enjoy work – the barriers between work and non work are very blurred. (Woman, aged 35–44, web designer, caring responsibilities, partner major role, ID 12)

Work and life merge – work is my hobby, work is myth. (Man, aged 45–54, web designer, no caring responsibilities, ID 9)

Work excitement and pressure are opposite sides of the same coin. (Man, aged 35–44, Internet consultancy and web designer, caring responsibilities, partner major role, ID 24)

People clearly enjoyed and were 'personally very much involved in their work' (75 percent strongly agreeing or agreeing with this view and 90 percent thinking about work when they were not there (see Figure 6.4) even though work was very demanding, 57 percent strongly agreeing or agreeing with the statement: 'I am often too tired when I get home from work to do other things' and 64 percent often taking work home. Responses were more divided over the question of work life balance with just under 50 percent agreeing or strongly agreeing with the statement that 'my work takes up time beyond a reasonable working day that I would rather spend on other activities' and the same proportion strongly agreeing or agreeing (54 percent men and 47 percent of women) with the statement that 'generally speaking I am very satisfied with my work life balance'.

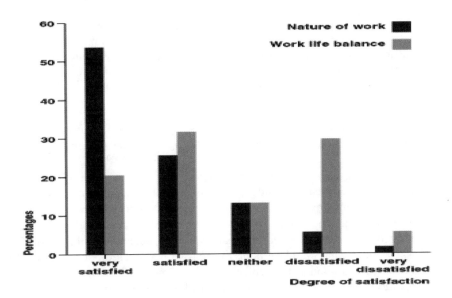

Figure 6.4   Work satisfaction and work life balance

One third of men and 40 percent of women were however dissatisfied and either disagreed or strongly disagreed with this statement, as did just over 40 percent of people with pre-teen children living at home. The reasons underlying the negative response differed between women and men. A higher proportion of men than women were dissatisfied with the amount of time they spent at work (too much) and in the home (too little). Similarly, people, women and men, without caring responsibilities expressed concern that they were perhaps becoming rather one dimensional and spent too much time working. Those with pre-teen children living at home, women and men, basically felt time starved and often felt very torn between the competing demands on their time, wanting to have more time to spend at work and at home as the women below explain:

I have to cut down work in the school holidays because I cannot do that much when the kids are around. I feel very torn. (Woman, aged 35–44, web page designer, caring responsibilities, major role, ID 1)

I only managed to take one day off with my daughter during the whole of her summer holidays. (Woman, aged 35–44, web designer, caring responsibilities, partner major role, ID 12)

Another man with three young children regularly spent the time between six and eight in the evening having dinner with and helping his children with homework, but this was just about the only time, other than a few hours on Sunday and sleeping that he spent away from his computer:

All I do is work, I have no concept of not working. The job rules me – I started as a programmer but I am now a manager, litigation, marketer. All the pressure is on me and I don't pass it on. I don't have holidays or any social life. I absolutely hate it. (Man, aged 25–34, E commerce and web application, caring responsibilities, partner major role, ID 14)

This particular individual might well fit the description of working in an electronic cage (Zimmerman, 1983 cited by Baines, 1999, p. 20) rather than the electronic cottage.

All of which provides some empirical support for a renegotiation of the gender division of labour between paid and unpaid work. Another woman, a single parent running her own company and working on average 60 hours a week, when asked what happened if her school-aged child was unwell replied, 'I am sodded big time' (woman, aged 35, Internet PR, caring responsibilities, sole responsibility, ID 54). When asked about what could be done to improve her situation she replied, 'I'd like to find myself a good wife', which provides some confirmation for the ideas of Reeves (2001) about the relative preferences between paid work and childcare and domestic services, although in this case, and probably more generally too, these preferences are shaped by perceived financial constraints. This person was however an owner/manager and had considerable flexibility and was able to take the child into the office when all other arrangements failed.

Flexible working

Flexible working and home working, neither of which affected the volume of work, were practised to organize working time around domestic responsibilities, or vice versa. Working in the evening, at night and during the weekend was also inevitable, in cases where the number of hours worked exceeded a standard week. Only a minority of people in the survey regularly worked standard hours and women were less likely to do so than men. Over two thirds regularly worked flexible hours and only 2 percent never did so. Nearly 60 percent of people regularly worked evenings and 35 percent did so sometimes and just under a quarter of people reported that they regularly worked at night (between 10 p.m. and 6 a.m. in the morning). Relative to their representation in the survey, women expressed a slightly higher tendency to regularly work in the evening and a lower tendency to work at night than men. However, the proportion saying that they worked at night sometimes was relatively higher than for men. Nearly half of the people reported that they regularly worked on a Saturday and Sunday with only 25 percent never doing so, figures considerably higher than the IER/IFF (2001) survey reported earlier.

Just over 40 percent of the sample had pre-teen children living with them, but only 20 percent had an evenly divided, a major role or total responsibility for their care (see Figure 6.2). None of the respondents had responsibility for elder care. Where the partner of the interviewee had major responsibility for childcare, which was more likely the case for men rather than women, working hours followed a similar pattern to those with no caring responsibilities, corresponding to the general tendency in the UK for fathers to work very long hours (Harkness, 1999; IER/IFF, 2001). Of the fourteen people who worked over 50 hours a week five had dependent children living with them including two women, one a single parent and sole carer and one whose partner took major responsibility for care. What is striking is the lack of caring responsibilities overall, which can not be explained by age as the majority (80 percent) were between 25 and 44 (38 percent between 25 and 34 and 42 percent between 35 and 44 years) the primary childrearing ages, which raises doubts about the extent to which this sector facilitates work life balance. Indeed recognizing the incompatibility one manager argued:

> We have no intentions of starting a family until we can get to grips with the business. (Man, aged 35–44, project manager, no caring responsibilities, ID 10)

For those with senior positions or running their own companies even when the hours of work are long the pattern can be arranged so as to enable them to spend some time with their children as one respondent explained:

> I would like to be able to spend more time with the children. Being an MD (managing director) however enables me to work flexible hours so I can go to school events. (Man, aged 35–44, new media productions, caring responsibilities, partner major role, ID 36)

For some people, especially mothers, being able to work flexibly was critical given the continuing low level of publicly provided and high cost of private childcare in the UK, despite recent initiatives:

> During school holidays it's a bit tricky, but otherwise after dropping kids to school, I do 0.5 hours housework and then work through until I pick the children up at 3 p.m. Then I will work in the evening, sometimes at night and usually one of the weekend days. (Woman, aged 35–44, web page designer, caring responsibilities, major role, ID 1)

But even so she went on to point out that:

The school hours limit my day – it ruins concentration. I would like something like an au pair to pick up children from school. The children go to an after school club (open until 6 p.m.) on two days a week but it does not always work and it costs quite a lot – £8 for the two children for each session. (Woman, aged 35–44, web page designer, caring responsibilities, major role, ID 1)

Home working and work life balance

Of those working from home either some or all of the time (63 percent), most (58 percent) felt that it enabled them to combine work and family life. Some were extremely positive in this respect and the proportion of women expressing this view was greater than men; 55 percent of women who worked from home viewed homeworking positively in this respect compared to 44 percent of men. One respondent was particularly enthusiastic:

It's wonderful! (her emphasis) As I own and run my own business in the home, my work/life balance could not really be improved. I have the flexibility I need which is why I set up the business in the first place. (Woman, aged 35–44, web design and specialist software, caring responsibilities, major role, ID 46)

Another respondent (similar to ID 1 above) commented on the way school hours can interrupt the flow of thought but also pointed out the value of children:

You just get motoring on a project and you have to pick them up. On the other hand sometimes the enforced break is needed. I enjoy looking after them – I don't resent it.

He went on to say:

I don't mind if they (the children) come in the office. I sometimes work there while they play – children do not need a high input all of the time, they just like you to be there. People in the West worry too much. I think children like to see you working and being with you – the notion of a special period of childhood is a particularly Western concept. (Man, aged 25–34, web design and multi media, caring responsibilities, evenly divided, ID 35)

This comment was unusual, but unfortunately partners were not interviewed in this study so there is no independent corroboration of this rather positive view of combining paid work with caring. More often mixed responses and tensions between home and work were reported together with strategies for overcoming them:

You need to create a workspace, then working at home is enjoyable. If the job is difficult then being at home can be difficult – if she cries and my partner is looking after her it's hard to concentrate and not to interfere. Otherwise at present I enjoy the flexibility because I can take her to the park etc and be around. (Woman, aged 25–34, web designer, caring responsibilities, major role, ID 28)

Home work does create some tensions with the children but I don't feel isolated – I have increased the number of contacts through the web. (Man, aged 45–54, consultant and trainer, caring responsibilities, partner major role, ID 31)

This comment also reflects the way in which the web itself has become an important medium for social contact, and in some cases virtual connections were consolidated through physical meetings. For example there is a locally based electronic email list through which members exchange technical, discuss local and national events and organize physical social gatherings. One respondent actually met her current partner via a chat room. Only a tiny minority appeared to depend on the Internet as the primary means of social (virtual) contact.

Homeworking also created tensions:

I work from home, so am continually kicked out of the office and accused of ignoring my family and being a workaholic and preferring the computer to real people. It's too easy to just go in for 30 minutes and spend 3 or 4 hours without noticing the time slipping away. (Woman, aged 35–44, Internet PR, caring responsibilities, partner major role, ID 12)

Overall the findings indicate that the experience of homeworking is varied and is probably influenced by the precise nature of the work being done as well as the gendered politics of the household (see Baines, 1999). There were also tensions for the homeworkers themselves, as they could never really escape from work even when they wanted to:

Even when I *do* have some spare time, I sometimes find it difficult to relax in my home as I associate it with work and the PC and the 'to do' list always beckoning. (Woman, aged 25–34, web designer and writer, no caring responsibilities, ID 34)

After working at home I was a wreck …it is not healthy there are enough pressures at home already – it is much better now – when I close the door I can forget work. I would never do it again – not as a business – I worked longer hours at home because it is quite compulsive – you are constantly reminded of work, – you could never escape it. (Man, aged 25–34, web designer, no direct caring responsibilities, ID 18)

Some respondents also reported that home working was positive from the point of view of managing a work life balance but had negative effects in terms of the work itself:

The main problem with working from home is both social and work isolation – there is no one to bounce ideas off. Otherwise working from home enables me to combine work and family life and have a higher net income than if I worked elsewhere. There are tensions though and I can't always concentrate when there are piles of washing lying around for example. (Woman, aged 35–44, web designer, caring responsibilities, major role, ID 1)

Other respondents reported that although much could be done through the internet, face to face meetings were vital both to convince potential clients of their own merits, considered difficult from the home, and so that they too could assess whether they could trust their potential clients, which is crucial considering that the products or services supplied are often customer specific:

> I moved into the studio because I needed a space to meet clients – I could not meet them in my flat because it was too small. Face to face contact still matters so I need a space in which to meet clients so as to convince them that you can do the job. (Man, aged 25–34, specialist web programmer, no caring responsibilities, ID 7)

Other home workers met clients in the numerous cafes or hotel restaurants in the town, thereby facilitating the necessary face to face contact without disclosing the actual size of the company. Contemporary telephone technology was also used to divert calls or provide an answering service that also provides a professional image for small organizations.

This study really confirms that there are mixed responses to homeworking, and whether it enables people to manage their work/life balance is really contingent on their overall context (see Baines, 1999). The key difference between this sector and other forms of homeworking is that potentially incomes are higher as the new technologies allow single operators to operate very efficiently in highly professional ways from home as one woman explained:

> The Internet – this is just what I was waiting for. I can now run my own business from home and have much more flexibility and control over my work than when I was a freelancer. (Woman, aged 35–44, web designer, caring responsibilities, partner major role, ID 12)

Conclusions

The new media sector in Brighton and Hove provides a small-scale illustration of the way some aspects of the new economy materialize in practice. This research is based on 55 interviews in an emerging and varied sector, which is highly volatile, so further research is necessary before any definitive statements can be made about the opportunities and constraints it provides (see Batt, Christopherson, Rightor and Jaarsveld, 2001 for work on the new media in the US).

Two of the findings, at least, conflict the theoretical work on the new economy, which emphasizes insecurity, isolation and community fragmentation (Beck, 2000; Sennett, 1998). With a small number of exceptions, both men and women owners, managers and self-employed had few concerns about job security, or their ability to acquire work. It has to be emphasized however, that the survey was conducted mainly in the Autumn of 2000, that is after the first burst of the dot.com boom but before the onset of the first recession of the 21st century, since when the job market has been much more volatile and there have been job losses in Brighton and Hove, especially in some of the fast growing companies, and freelancers, who probably bear the cost of the fluctuations, were not the focus of the study, though the distinctions between freelancers and sole traders in this sector are rather blurred. At the time of the survey, the problem was more likely to be over work arising from its unpredictable nature and flow, and the former was often seen as an exciting intellectual challenge. There was also a strong sense of community, in terms of the physical location, Brighton and Hove, and in terms of physical, virtual, social and business locally based networks, thus casting some doubt on the ideas of insecurity and fragmentation that have been associated with the new economy. There was also little concern with questions of health and safety, despite long hours spent at the computer.

The research provides mixed support for the expectations of the Women's Unit that ICT will provide new opportunities for women to earn more and have more flexible working practices. The use of ICT which forms a vital part of the new media sector has expanded the temporal and spatial range of paid work and thereby provided the necessary flexibility and time sovereignty to enable people to combine interesting, enjoyable, intellectually challenging and highly satisfying work with family life. Indeed the survey included some people who fully encapsulated the positive image of teleworking in the global economy, for example a woman working from her front room and sub contracting some of her work to a programmer in India. Furthermore, some women found that this was the only way of entering this sector as their age (perceived to be too old at the age of 35 to 40) and lack of formal qualifications meant that they had been unable to obtain work as employees. Nevertheless serious tensions between work and life remained for half of the sample overall and a higher percentage among those with major or sole caring responsibilities who were disproportionately women. The reasons for dissatisfaction varied; a higher proportion of men wanted to have more time to spend at home and women expressed a strong desire for more time for both. Furthermore, the sector is characterized by gender imbalance with women being underrepresented overall and overrepresented in the smaller firms measured either by turnover or by the number of employees. The sector is characterized by high qualifications but from a wide variety of disciplinary backgrounds so the main constraints seem to lie with finance and especially time. Some provisional explanations are given below but more research on this issue is required as well as on the extent of and reasons for gender imbalance in the sector more generally and especially among employees.

There was some suggestion of gender bias in lending practices by banks and venture capitalists. One company in particular emphasized the significance of assistance from a business angel, known through past business contacts, who had been far more effective in terms of offering the required level of funding while allowing the firm autonomy over its use. Certainly, the women owners of larger companies were in the older age group and had finance from a previous working life. Some short to medium term financial support for equipment and especially income to sustain a livelihood during the early phases of development would be helpful. Many people and especially women had failed to obtain bank loans and venture capitalists were often not interested, as the projects were considered too small or financially insufficiently attractive. Moreover the entrepreneurs, micro businesses were sometimes viewed with suspicion, as some prioritized personal objectives for making a reasonable standard of living in an enjoyable way rather than rapid growth. Earnings overall appear comparatively low and especially for women, considering the hours worked, their qualifications and experience but these are quite hard to assess, especially in the case of independent operators. In terms of time, women worked fewer hours, earned less than men and were more likely to have sole or major responsibility for childcare, although only a small proportion in the survey had any direct responsibility for care and this is not explained by age and thus casts some doubt on the compatibility between work in this sector and family life.

Thus although ICT permits greater flexibility in working hours and locations which potentially allows those with caring responsibilities access to paid work, an important starting point for redressing gender inequalities, the traditional constraint of time arising from the uneven division of domestic work and caring remains. This finding echoes previous work and suggests that it is necessary to look beyond the work place to wider systems of social support for caring and to ways of resolving inequalities in time use between women and men to resolve persistent gender inequalities in work and to provide a better work life balance for men as well as women. That is, although technology provides new opportunities it is introduced within existing social structures and unless these are challenged it is likely that they will simply allow life to be squeezed around the growing demands of the work and gender inequality, albeit in new forms, will remain.

References

Baines, S. (1999), 'Servicing the Media: Freelancing, Teleworking and Enterprising Careers', *New Technology, Work and Employment*, vol. 14, pp. 18–31.

Baines, S. and J. Wheelock (2000), 'Work and Employment in Small Businesses: Perpetuating and Challenging Gender Traditions', *Gender, Work and Organization*, vol. 7, pp. 45–56.

Baruch, Y. (2000), 'Teleworking: Benefits and Pitfalls as Perceived by Professionals and Managers', *New Technology, Work and Employment*, vol. 15, pp. 334–49.

Batt, R., S. Christopherson, N. Rightor, and D. Van Jaarsveld (2001), *Networking: Work Patterns and Workforce Policies for the New Media Industries*, Economic Policy Institute, Washington.

Beck, U. (2000), *The Brave New World of Work*, Polity Press, Cambridge.

Bower, C. (2001), 'Trends in Female Employment', *Labour Market Trends*, vol. 109, pp. 107–119.

Bradley, H. (1999), *Gender and Power in the Work Place: Analysing the Impact of Economic Change*, Macmillan, London.

Breedveld, K. (1998), 'The Double Myth of Flexibilisation: Trends in Scattered Work Hours and Differences in Time-Sovereignty', *Time and Society*, vol. 7, pp. 129–143.

Brighton and Hove Council (1999), *The Place to Be*, Brighton and Hove Council, Brighton.

Carnoy, M. (2000), *Sustaining the New Economy: Work, Family, and Community in the Information Age*, Russell Sage Foundation, New York.

Castells, M. (2000), 'Materials for an Exploratory Theory of the Network Society', *British Journal of Sociology*, vol. 51, pp. 5–24.

Castells, M. (2001), *The Internet Galaxy: Reflections on the Internet, Business and Society*, Oxford University Press, Oxford.

Chaudhuri, A. (2000), 'Work Unlimited', *Guardian*, August 30.

Crompton, R. (1997), *Women and Work in Modern Britain*, Oxford University Press, Oxford.

Denny, C. (2001), 'Lifestyle Fixers Take the Strain for City Workers', *Guardian*, 16/07, p. 5.

Dex, S. and A. McCulloch (1997), *Flexible Employment: The Future of Britain's Jobs*, Macmillan, London.

DfEE (2000a), *Creating a Work-Life Balance: A Good Practice Guide for Employers*, DfEE, London.

DfEE (2000b), *Changing Patterns in a Changing World: Work Life Balance Feedback*, DfEE, London.

Doogan, K. (2001), 'Insecurity and Long-Term Employment', *Work, Employment and Society*, vol. 15, pp. 419–441.

Doyle, J. and R. Reeves (2001), *Time Out: The Case for Time Sovereignty*, The Industrial Society, London.

Edwards, G. (ed.) (2000), *Region in Figures: London*, Office for National Statistics, HMSO, London.

Equal Opportunities Commission (2000), *Women and Men in Britain 1999/2000 Pay and Income*, EOC, Manchester.

Fagan, C. (2001), 'Time, Money and the Gender Order: Work Orientations and Working-Time Preferences in Britain', *Gender, Work and Organization*, vol. 8, pp. 239–266.

Figart, D. and E. Mutari (1998), 'Degendering Work Time in Comparative Perspective: Alternative Policy Frameworks', *Review of Social Economy*, vol. LVI, pp. 460–480.

Flores, F. and J. Gray (2000), *Entrepreneurship and the Wired Life: Work in the Wake of Careers*, Demos, London.

Folbre, N. (2001), *The Invisible Heart: Economics and Family Values*, New York Press, New York.

Folbre, N. and J. Nelson (2000), 'For Love or Money – Or both?', *Journal of Economic Perspectives*, vol. 14, pp. 123–140.

Gershuny, J. (2000), *Changing Times: Work and Leisure in Post-Industrial Society*, Oxford University Press, Oxford.

Green, F., A. Felstead and B. Burchell (2000), 'Job Insecurity and the Difficulty of Regaining Employment: An Empirical Study of Unemployment Expectations', *Oxford Bulletin of Economics and Statistics*, December 62, (Special Issue), pp. 857–885.

Greenspan, A. (1998), 'Is There a New Economy?', *California Management Review*, vol. 41, pp. 74–85.

Gregg, P. and J. Wadsworth (1999), 'Job Tenure 1975–98', in P. Gregg and J. Wadsworth (eds), *The State of Working Britain*, Manchester University Press, Manchester, pp. 109–126.

Hardill, I. and D. Graham (2001), 'The Tyranny of Time: Balancing Work and Home in Dual-Career Households', Paper presented at the *Regional Transitions: European Regions and the Challenges of Development, Integration and Enlargement – International Conference of the Regional Studies Association*, University of Gdansk, Poland.

Harkness, S. (1999), 'Working 9 to 5?', in P. Gregg and J Wadsworth (eds), *The State of Working Britain*, Manchester University Press, Manchester, pp. 90–108.

Heery, E. and J. Salmon (eds) (1999), *The Insecure Workforce*, Routledge, London.

Hochschild, A. (1997), *The Time Bind*, Metropolitan Books, New York.

Huws, U. (1996), *Teleworking and Gender*, Institute of Employment Studies, Brighton.

IER/IFF (2001), *Work-Life Balance 2000: Baseline Study of Work-Life Balance in Great Britain*, Institute of Employment Research, Warwick.

IPPR (2000), 'Future of Work Findings of a Series of Focus Groups with People in Low Paid Jobs', Funded by the Reed Academy of Enterprise Institute for Public Policy Research, 30–32 Southampton Street.

Jarvis, H. (1999), 'The Tangled Webs We Weave: Household Strategies to Co-ordinate Home and Work', *Work, Employment and Society*, vol. 13, pp. 225–247.

McDowell, L. (1997), *Capital Culture: Gender at Work in the City*, Blackwell, London.

McDowell, L. (2001), 'Father and Ford Revisited: Gender, Class and Employment Change in the New Millennium', *Transactions of the Institute of British Geographers*, vol. 26, pp. 448–465.

Massey, D. (1996), 'Masculinity, Dualisms and High Technology', in N. Duncan (ed.), *Bodyspace*, Routledge, London, pp. 109–126.

Murgatroyd, L. and H. Neuburger (1997), 'A Household Satellite Account for the UK', *Economic Trends*, no. 527, pp. 63–71.

OECD (2000), 'E-Commerce: Impacts and Policy Challenges', *Economic Outlook*, June, No. 67, Volume 2000, Issue 1, Organisation for Economic Co-operation and Development, Paris.

ONS (2001), *Neighbourhood Statistics*, ONS website.

Ó'Riain, S. (2000), in Michael Burawoy, Joseph A. Blum, Sheba George, Zsuzsa Gille, Teresa Gowan, Lynne Haney, Maren Klawiter, Steve H. Lopez, Sean Riain and Millie Thayer (eds), *Global Ethnography Forces, Connections and Imaginations in a Postmodern World*, University of California Press, Berkeley.

Perrons, D. (1999), 'Flexible Working Patterns and Equal Opportunities in the European Union: Conflict or Compatibility?', *European Journal of Women's Studies*, vol. 6, pp. 391–418.

Perrons, D. (2000), 'Care Paid Work and Leisure: Rounding the Triangle', *Feminist Economics*, vol. 6, pp. 105–114.

Perrons, D. (2004), *Globalization and Social Change: People and Places in a Divided World*, Routledge, London.

Phizacklea, A. and C. Wolkowitz (1995), *Homeworking Women: Gender, Racism and Class at Work*, Sage, London.

Pratt, A. C. (2000), 'New Media, the New Economy and New Spaces', *Geoforum*, vol. 31, pp. 425–436.

Presser, H. (1999), 'Toward a 24-Hour Economy', *Science*, vol. 284, pp. 1777–1779.

Quah, D. (1996), *The Invisible Hand and the Weightless Economy*, Centre for Economic Performance, Occasional paper No. 12, LSE, London.

Quah, D. (2001), *Technology Dissemination and Economic Growth, Some Lessons for the New Economy*, Public lecture University of Hong Kong (available from the author's website).

Rake, K. (ed.) (2000), *Women's Incomes over the Lifetime*, The Stationery Office, London.

Reeves, R. (2001), *Happy Mondays: Putting the Pleasure Back into Work*, Momentum, London.

Reich, R. (2001), *The Future of Success Work and Life in the New Economy*, Heinemann, London.

Rose, M. (1999), *Employee Skill, Occupation, and Work Involvement*, ESRC Future of Work Research Programme Employee Skill, Occupation and Work Involvement Working Paper 1: Work Centrality, Work Careers and Household: Let's Ask for Numbers, University of Bath.

Rubery, J., M. Smith and C. Fagan (1998), 'National Working-Time Regimes and Equal Opportunities', *Feminist Economics*, vol. 4, pp. 103–126.

Sennett, R. (1998), *The Corrosion of Character*, WW Norton and Company, London.

Stanworth, C. (2000), 'Women and Work in the Information Age', *Gender, Work and Organisation*, vol. 7, pp. 20–32.

Tang, P. (1999), 'The Southeast England High-Tech Corridor: Not Quite Silicon Valley Yet', in H-J. Braczyk, G. Fuchs and H-G. Wolf (eds), *Multimedia and Regional Restructuring*, Routledge, London, pp. 218–238.

Thair, T. and A. Risdon (1999), 'Women in the Labour Market: Results from the Spring 1998 LFS', *Labour Market Trends*, March, pp. 103–114.

Toffler, A. (1980), *The Third Wave*, William Morrow, New York.

Twomey, B. (2001), 'Women in the Labour Market: Results from the Spring 2000 LFS', *Labour Market Trends*, vol. 109, pp. 73–124.

Walby, S. (1997), *Gender Transformations*, Routledge, London.

Women's Unit (2000), *More Choice for Women in the New Economy: The Facts*, Cabinet Office, London.

Zimmerman, J. (1983), *The Technological Woman: Interfacing with Tomorrow*, Praeger, New York.

Chapter 7

Life Modes and Gender in the Swedish Public-Health Sector

Liselotte Jakobsen

Introduction

This chapter discusses a follow up study of assistant nurses working in the Swedish public-health sector. I suggest that the mechanisms underlying the events that took place could in large measure be understood as representing the interplay between the practices and ideologies of *socio-structural life modes* in modern Western society, in this particular case the worker life mode, the housewife life mode and the career life mode.

One core process comprised the so-called *neoculturation* of the housewife life mode existing among the nurses. Most nurses experienced substantial difficulties in maintaining what they felt to be satisfactory everyday lives in the face of workplace reorganization, and they also partly succeeded in doing this. This however, benefited the employer, who was able to continuously exploit this female work force. This was found to be the case, where existing gender relationships were reproduced in changing settings, both at work and in the family.

Background

The background is the Swedish public sector reorganization of the 1990s. The reorganization introduced market-oriented organizational models so as to improve service effectiveness and quality. Money was to be saved through staffing reductions, while the qualifications of remaining staff were to be raised. This meant that many assistant nurses were given notice, and that their jobs were transformed into nurses' jobs. As a result, approximately two-thirds of assistant nurses lost their jobs, entirely or partially. We conducted a case study to examine the possible consequences of such extensive cut-back in the largest women's occupation in the country. Twenty assistant nurses, 18 women and two men, were followed up for between five and eight years from when they were given notice.

Results

The nurses were interviewed twice. The first set of interviews showed, somewhat surprisingly, that at that time, most were still working in their occupation in the public sector, and that they had been doing so for years, sometimes even in the same workplace.

However, part time employment and temporary employment had increased gradually and considerably in the studied group, and there was considerable deterioration in the terms of employment. In practice, assistant nurses had gradually become a flexible work force that the employer could use where and when needed. While this benefited employers, nurses lost predictability and control of everyday life, and many also experienced economic hardships.

The nurses also felt badly treated by their employers: they were worried about the future and expressed anxiety as to how reorganization had affected the situation of the patients. Yet the majority wanted to continue in their occupations, firmly believing that things would change. Only one of them, a man, had left for another job. Three younger women had begun various educational programmes, while the other man and one more woman were thinking of doing so.

When new interviews were carried out three and a half years later, conditions in the public-health sector had changed rather dramatically. The organization had been slimmed down, and it was beginning to be difficult to get enough personnel: it was difficult to fill new nurses' positions and even assistant nurses were sometimes difficult to recruit.

The interviews revealed that nurses who in the first interview had been planning to leave nursing – among them the two men – were about to do this and were on their way to new jobs.

We also found that all 14 female nurses who wanted to stay in their jobs had done so. Moreover, they had done this while improving their working conditions: most were permanently employed, and most had achieved the working hours they wanted. They had bided their time in the critical years, and in many ways now appeared to have won. Was this, however, so?

In a way it was, as they had secured the everyday life they wanted. However, they complained of the heavy working pressure. They also reported that conditions for the patients had become even worse. They were very critical of what they called 'the whole system', and could see no improvements in terms of effectiveness or quality; rather the opposite was true. They still, however, wanted to continue being assistant nurses.

How should we understand these events? The data suggest that gender, socio-economic background, age, and the local labour market were all factors that had at least some influence on what took place, but this understanding is not unproblematic.

The most surprising thing is perhaps that the 14 women, about half of them in their 30s, wanted to remain assistant nurses. Although they were very disappointed with their employer, thought that 'the system' was incomprehensible and degenerating, and believed that care quality was declining, they wished and managed to keep working in their occupation and even improve their terms of employment. They had, however, worked hard to achieve this for several years and under difficult conditions.

I suggest that structural life mode analysis might shed some light on what actually took place in these processes and why. The basic mechanisms underlying the external sequence of events and the experience of the nurses could largely be understood as interplay between the practices and ideologies of various socio-structural life modes in modern society, in this case the housewife, worker and career life modes.

Structural life mode analysis

Life mode analysis, as a specific approach in the social sciences, first emerged in Denmark in the 1980s (Højrup, 1983, 1989, 2003; Christensen, 1987) and later developed in Sweden (Jakobsen, 1999; Jakobsen and Karlsson, 1993).

Modern Western society and its social life modes could be considered as two sides of the same coin. Life modes are *structurally positioned social practices* through which people gain the means of existence and human existence itself. One could also conceive of a life mode as a collective practice whereby people contribute in some way to society, so as to gain access to necessary means of existence and to become fully human. The contribution is the *means* of the life mode, while the reason for contributing is the *goal* of the life mode. However, the goal and the means vary depending on the structural positions. At the same time, surrounding society is dependent on the contribution of the various life modes. Thus a life mode is a goal–means structured practice, built up so that it continuously (re)produces its own *external conditions* of existence.

The *internal condition of existence* of each life mode practice is a specific corresponding *ideology* – a worldview. Different practices demand different cognitive equipment, if people living a particular life mode are to orient themselves and for everyday life to function in a reasonably practical and meaningful way given current conditions. This worldview is often unconscious, saying little about how life *ought* to be, commenting rather on how life *is*. It gives rise to qualitatively differing meanings for important everyday concepts such as 'work', 'leisure time', 'home', 'family', 'love', 'freedom', 'justice', and 'solidarity', and differing conceptions of what is a 'normal' and 'good' everyday life. What is conceived of as 'good' or 'natural' in one life mode might stand out as 'bad' or 'not quite normal' in another, as the life modes form various everyday cultures in one and the same population. However, when we share a language these conceptual distinctions are rarely recognized. The words we have in common conceal them, so people who live different life modes tend to misunderstand and misinterpret each other rather systematically. The recognition of such *sociocentrism* existing between the life modes is crucial to life mode analysis.

It is crucial, however, to realize that structural life modes and actual people are discrete phenomena. Life modes tend to be important mechanisms underlying far-reaching and systematic variations in patterns of action and beliefs in the population.

People, however, can move between life modes. This movement *may* coincide with overarching changes in the life modes of society resulting from historical processes, in which case we are usually dealing with very long-term changes. In the short term, movement between life modes is likely to cause changes for the individuals, who in such cases will be living mixed life modes – as is the case in Sweden for most women and quite a few men. I shall return to this matter later.

These structural influences impinge on people by shaping the situations in which they find themselves, but it is people who reproduce, modify, or transform the structures through their actions, and who have the power of choice. However, there are different *opportunity costs* attached to making the same choices in different social positions, just as there are different reasons for making different choices in different social positions. This means that the choices are structurally *conditioned*, though they are not structurally determined (see Archer, 1995). Many different mechanisms can be involved when people make choices; similarly various empirical events also involve multiple mechanisms. Empirical research determines which particular mechanisms are germane in a given context (Danermark et al., 2002).

So far life mode analysis has distinguished ten life modes, which are supposed to exist in variants in all modern western societies that engage in both simple and capitalist modes of production. The former gives rise to *the independent life mode* and the latter to *the investor life mode* and *the capitalist life mode*. The capitalist mode of production also subsumes *the worker life mode* and *the career life mode*.

Because of the existing gender order, these life modes are fundamentally *male* – although women frequently live them – but at least three of them are coupled to a genuine and supporting *female* life mode. The independent life mode is connected with *the assistance life mode*, the worker life mode with *the housewife life mode*, and the career life mode with *the backing up woman life mode*. We can assume that there are also female life modes related to the investor and capitalist life modes, but so far there has been very little research into this.

Another way to express this is to say that each life mode is based on a certain combination of *work form* and what I refer to as *love form*, that is, a position in the social gender order.

Work forms and love forms

The concept of work form used in this analysis stems from an investigation of conceptual problems in working life science (for example Karlsson, 1994, 2004). In this context work could be summarized as 'acting in the sphere of necessity'. People work to the extent that their doing is based on external necessity, to which they must submit in order to secure their existence. One and the same activity could be work or non-work, depending on whether it is exercised in this sphere or not. The essence of this line of argument lies in the notion of work as primarily constituted by internal social relationships, not by certain activities. A work form is a specific way of socially structuring 'the sphere of necessity' in a society, and there can be a whole set of different such forms. Every work form is a social structure in itself, with specific mechanisms.

The names of the life modes themselves say a great deal about the work forms on which particular life modes are based. What is less obvious is the nature of the associated love form, which is part of this base, and makes some work forms – hence also life modes – structurally male and others female. These love forms tend to be rendered invisible by a process of 'naturalization' – just as the whole social gender order has traditionally been overlooked.

The concept of 'love form' has been deduced from a 'feminist basic theory' (Jónasdóttir, 1994). In line with this theory, the concept of 'love form' rests on the assumed existence of a relatively autonomous and *material socio-sexual structure of production*, the production of *life and human existence as such*, alongside the *socio-economic structure of production* – that is, the production of the *means of existence*. While the economic mode of production is based on people's work power and on the structures and conditions of work in society, the socio-sexual mode of production is based on people's *love power* and forms the conditions under which love is practised in society.

This socio-sexual structure of production has its own specific qualities, powers, and mechanisms. Most notably, it structures people's ability to empower each other both as individuals and as a species. The socio-sexual structure of contemporary Western society means that women and men enter into a specific relationship of exploitation, a relationship through which men tend to exploit women's love power, converting it into individual and collective power over which women lose control.

I have postulated this to be the internal social relationship existing between two structural positions, comprising two *love forms*. The love form structurally 'designated' for men I call the *love form of the empowered*, and the one structurally assigned to women I call the *love form of the empowerers*. Each of these love forms is regarded as comprising a specific practice and a corresponding ideology. The determining traits of these practices and ideologies are initially defined as follows: In the love form of the empowered there is the *practice of appropriation* and an *instrumental and performance-oriented ideology* – one has goals 'for oneself' in terms of one's own interests, personal development, and so on. In the female love form, the love form of the empowerers, there is instead a *practice of caring*, and a *caring-, need-, and relationship-oriented ideology*. One's goals are manifest in *others* – in other people's wellbeing and personal development – and it is crucial that wellbeing and personal development should take place on the terms of 'the other's' underlying assumptions.

There additionally seems to be different concepts of time in the male and female love form respectively. In the male love form time tends to be experienced as 'my time', to be used according to one's own interests and priorities. In contrast, in the female love form time tends to be 'others' time': it is a question of being at hand and prepared for other people's needs, on these people's underlying assumptions.

Together with the work forms of economic production these love forms lay the basis for a number of qualitatively different life modes, some structurally male and others structurally female, which establish quite different conditions for people's everyday lives and their possibilities of securing the means of existence and of attaining full humanity (Jakobsen, 1999; Jónasdóttir, 1994).

The life modes of modern Western society

Male life modes, then, are all based on the love form of the empowered combined with various work forms localized directly in economic production. They thus belong primarily to the social organization for the production of the *means of existence*, as they are oriented towards working life and the economy.

Female life modes are all based on the love form of the empowerers, combined with work forms that do *not* build on positions in, or directly related to, economic production. The work forms here are instead oriented toward the production of *human life* – human existence – *as such* and are related to the work forms in economic production via *marriage* (or corresponding forms of cohabitation). This means that instead of the orientation toward working life and the economy found in the male life modes, here we have an orientation toward people, as physical as well as existential beings, and an orientation toward human relationships.

Female life modes also all treat home and family as the basic field of work and responsibility. Therefore, in all female life modes the home- and family sphere contains both the goals of and the means to achieve a good everyday life, although the various life modes differ as to how home and family should be created: this is relative to what the man in the family could use in *his* life mode.

I will next describe the six life modes that are best known today: the worker life mode, housewife life mode, career life mode, backing-up woman life mode, independent life mode and assistance life mode. It is vital, however, to remember that these descriptions concern material and cultural social structures: individuals can move between life modes, they can live more than one life mode, women can live male life modes, men can live female life modes, and so on – structural life modes and concrete individuals are quite discrete phenomena.

The worker life mode

The worker life mode combines the love form of the empowered with the work form of traditional wage work. This practice has four characteristics: the worker does not own the means of production, the worker sells the right to use and control his labour power during a certain period, the buyer – the employer – is responsible for how the labour power is used (the worker's position being subordinated in the hierarchy of the work organization), and this part of the labour market does not contain any career ladders.

Wage labour is thus distinct not only in time but also in its internal structure and constitution from all other activities and contexts. The world view of the worker life mode is correspondingly divided into two separate spheres: on the one hand wage labour, on the other hand the rest of life, that is, leisure time. There is a sharp contrast between 'work' and 'non-work'. What you do for others (the wage work) becomes work, what you do for yourself (which *might* include the family) becomes non-work – time free from work. Work becomes the sphere of means, duties and external necessity; leisure time becomes the sphere of goals, freedom, and internal satisfaction. This does not mean that the worker could not feel happy at work, enjoy tasks, and be skilled and engaged, but it does mean that there is a limit to how much work is allowed to intrude on the rest of the worker's life.

Wage work, then, is a means of achieving a possibly wide range of goals, but these goals are always located in leisure time. Because of the love form that is part of the life mode, the worker can choose to what to devote himself when off work: he is empowered, and his leisure time is 'his own'.

The housewife life mode

The housewife life mode emerges from the institution of the homemaker, and is based on a combination of the empowering love form and the housewife's work form. At least in Sweden it is probably the empirically most widespread of the female life modes.

Structurally, this life mode presupposes marriage to a man with traditional wage work. Marriage guarantees, formalistically anyway, that a homemaker obtains support and certain other rights in exchange for contributing to home and family. But the fact that female life modes are based on the personal relationship of living with a man has specific effects in the case of the housewife. Although it is a shared characteristic of female life modes that working hours and working tasks are loosely defined, fluid, and depend on the work form of the man, it is a distinguishing quality of housewives' work that it is structurally totally separate from either direct or indirect relationship with economic production in society. Unlike women married to men who live other life modes, the housewife in the worker's family has no way of actively influencing or controlling the income on which she bases her life. The man's wage earnings are not determined in relation to anything that she could help to produce: they are determined through labour market negotiations – far beyond the reach of anything she can affect.

These structural conditions mean that the housewife's goals and means become located entirely within home and family, where they tend to melt together without being confined to any particular activities or time – the housewife's time belongs to 'others'.

The ideology of the housewife life mode contains no sharp division in terms of either structure or time between work and leisure activities. Everything a housewife does can appear to be meaningful, useable, and valuable to home and family, whether it be cooking, baking, cleaning, furnishing, sewing, knitting, playing with the children, or keeping her husband company.

The crucial point in the housewife's practice, however, is that she and her husband have very different relationships to the wage on which they both base their existence. The man is a wage earner and has an income whether he has a wife or not; the housewife's work and the family are of no significance to his means of support – the wage work. The housewife, however, is wholly dependent on this personal relationship with the wage-earning man. The structural conditions in this case mean that the housewife's practice, in order to function as means in her life mode, must comprise things that could be included in her husband's goals, in his life in the sphere outside work. And since the structure of the wage work does not point to anything specific to which leisure time should be devoted, and since the worker, but not the housewife, is comfortably off, so the individual man decides about his leisure time himself. These are the structural 'arrangements' that make the reproduction of the empowered love form – where time is 'my time' – possible within the worker life mode. It also means that the housewife will have to make do with having a very indirect and uncertain influence on her means of existence and goals.

Until recently the structural conditions of the housewife practice were, generally, guaranteed by a number of social circumstances that made it almost impossible for married women, especially those with children, to work outside the home. The housewife seldom had any good alternatives, if any, to her work form. Today such alternatives are available, but in many cases the opportunity costs for choosing them are still high.

However, the entire complex can produce two quite different outcomes. One is that the man's leisure time becomes mainly devoted to activities that lie entirely *outside* the family, such as sports and politics. The other possibility is that the man's leisure-time goals may be such that they can be realized *within* the home and family context. While one or the other of these outcomes is structurally inevitable, it is almost always coincidences that end up settling the actual outcome; the housewife's possibility of achieving her life goals depends on such coincidences.

It is common for housewives to feel that parts of their activity, housework for example, are means to an end – things done so as to achieve other goals (for example family life within the framework home, where 'home' represents something more then merely a place to live). Harmonious family life is often prominent among a housewife's life goals, but most characteristic of the housewife life mode is that a good life presupposes a unity of home and family, where *all* family members feel good.

The career life mode

In the career life mode, the love form of the empowered is combined with a work form we can call 'career work'. This is also wage work, but different in kind from the traditional one. Having a career means that what you sell and get paid for on the labour market is not time but work performed. The 'goods' on this part of the labour market are specific personal skills and qualifications to handle functions such as management, marketing, product development, research; participants in this mode in fact sell a sort of 'personal unicity'. The labour market is structured in such a way as to present more or less complete career ladders to be climbed, and promotion from one job to another is expected: you commence on a relatively low rung of the ladder and attain promotion by exhibiting ability. It is a matter of continuously developing a competitive personal unicity.

In the ideology of this life mode, the goals of life are located in work, while leisure time tends to appear as a means to reach these goals. There is no such idea – as in the ideology of the worker life mode – that you should not think about work tasks after a certain time of day, or that things done outside normal working hours are of no significance to work. This is so, because the important distinction in the career life mode is between work of a routine character and one's own engaging work. The higher one climbs in the hierarchy, the more engaging one's work becomes. Work becomes a challenge, something to be responsible for, to develop, and – not least – through which to develop oneself. Jobs further down the ladder, not to mention jobs in the worker life mode, do not demand such responsibility and engagement, but are instead marked by routine.

This distinction corresponds to the split between work and leisure time in the worker life mode. There the great divide is between two spheres of life, between work and leisure time; in the career life mode the divide exists *within* work, between routine and engaging work. The aim of life becomes not just engaging work; a good life in the career life mode means constantly developing one's 'personal unicity' in and through work. Usually this requires that one changes working tasks, and also place of work.

Leisure time could be put to the service of work, in several ways. This could, for example, be done through leisure-time education, undertaken to qualify oneself for higher positions, through working in one's leisure time or through representation at home or outside the home. Hence representability and respectability are important. One's entire life style is significant to one's career possibilities: the right type of home, brand of car, style of clothing, relationships, interests, and type of family are all important. When needed, some leisure time must also be used for recreation, but this has not, as is the case in the worker life mode, much to do with recreation as an end in itself. Instead it is a question of 'recharging the batteries', so one can get back to work with renewed and fresh engagement.

The life of the career man, then, is build around work, and his efforts in this can hardly be too great. But since the career life mode is based on the love form of the empowered, it must have access to a supporting, empowering life mode – the backing-up woman life mode.

The backing-up woman life mode

Career work, as well as traditional wage work, is connected with the general expansion of wage work. Hence career work also is based on a split between 'working life' and 'private life', where working life presupposes another practice, responsible for private life.

In line with gender relations and the gender division of work, from the outset the career practice developed into a male practice; therefore a complementary female practice of homemaking also arose in connection with the career life mode. However, since the career practice is based on a different social relationship than is traditional wage work – the career man does not sell abstract 'work power' during certain hours of the day, but rather sells personal unicity – the conditions of the complementary homemaking practice here are different. Here, the sphere of home and family is related to the man's life mode. Unlike the housewife, the backing-up woman has relationships of her own to that which constitutes her own support, that is, the man's career work; she has a certain, some times even a considerable, amount of influence on this.

This is so because, contrary to the situation in the worker life mode, the career life mode requires direct backing-up in relation to the career work. The backing-up woman participates in producing the things her husband sells and gets paid for, namely his competence, commitment, representability, and respectability. On the whole, she helps in building a suitable milieu – in relation to the career – for the career man. This also includes removing things that might damage or harm the career: the man must be able to work at home without disturbance, rest when needed, and engage in other sorts of recreation and stimulation. No other family demands should be made on the career man than what are appropriate in view of the career.

In return the backing-up woman gains access to the necessary conditions for her specific practice – a certain income level and social context – so that she, in a personally and economically independent way, can devote herself to her own interests and commitments. The backing-up woman, then, also has both means and goals in the home- and family sphere, and typically these will concern aesthetic/artistic activity of some kind, and there are many ways, in which such activity could serve the man's career. Depending on the sort of employment the husband holds, the career could require anything from a wide range of tasks to a single function. If it is necessary for the career man's position to invite business contacts home, then it must be a goal within the woman's practice to furnish a fashionable home, prepare gastronomically pleasing dinners, try out new dishes, arrange the table attractively and so on. The practice could also include taking an interest in subjects such as literature, art, music and dance, so as to be able to make interesting conversations, or being proficient in handicrafts, or music, or engaging in charity or other kinds of social activity. All of this presents to the husband's colleagues and to the outside world a certain image, which demands acknowledgement and respect – an atmosphere of personal unicity – which should be associated with the family name, and which is most useful to the career.

In fortunate cases, the career practice and the backing-up woman practice relate to each other as teamwork. The spouses are each other's means to their respective goals – his in work, hers in her personal interests and commitments. But this symbiosis functions only as long as her interests are subordinated the demands of his career – after all the backing-up woman life mode is a female, empowering life mode and the woman's time belongs to others.

The independent life mode

Outside the formal labour market, but connected to the productive economy, we find the independent life mode. This is based on a combination of the love form of the empowered and the work form of self-employment. This life mode is lived by private entrepreneurs, including farmers and fishermen, with no, or few, employees. In this case one is the producer, while at the same time owning the means of production and the work product.

This social category is sometimes referred to as 'petty bourgeoisie', but it should be emphasized that self-employment does not constitute some 'lesser' form of capitalism. Self-employment and capital ownership are two qualitatively distinct work forms.

The independent life mode does not maintain any specific concept of work, as formed in contrast to any other sphere or activity. This practice gives rise to an ideology where both day and night take on that character of work or activity. Everything you do might appear as work – a useful activity for yourself, and perhaps also your family, in upholding the life mode. Work and leisure time melt together in a way that tends to make the concept of 'leisure' meaningless.

It is important to realize that the central goal in this life mode is not, first of all, to develop the business, as in, for example, increasing profit or making the firm grow. On the contrary, such development might even be problematic. It is independence as such – to be one's own boss, to work for oneself – that represents both the goal and the good life according to this life mode. Employing people might, among other things, mean that one becomes tied up in unwanted relationships of dependence and responsibility. Independence – activity in one's own interests – is the central value and ideal in this life mode.

The family business, then, is in fact a means of upholding the goal of independence. In this way the business is at the same time both its own goal and means, and no effort is too great if it is in its interest. Hence the life mode ideology also contains an ideal of hard work and loyalty to the demands of the business. From another and more established (at least in Sweden) perspective on work, that of the worker life mode, it might even appear that people living the independent life mode work in order to be able to continue to work, something that appears highly irrational to people living the worker life mode.

However, the independent life mode too has access to a supporting and empowering female life mode, namely the assistance life mode. An assisting wife (sometimes also other family members) is part of the 'work force' of the independent man's firm.

The assistance life mode

The assistance life mode is based on a combination of the love form of the empowerer and the work form of assistant work. This denotes the position the woman has often held, and often still holds, in the family business, that is, in relation to *the man*. It is in the social gender context that the woman's work becomes assistance. In relation to a particular business the woman's work might vary in intensity, perhaps equalling or even exceeding the man's effort. Even so, the gender structure – if it allows for such work at all – determines this achievement to be 'mere' assistance.

Here we are dealing with a female life mode with a history different from those described above. The assistance life mode has not emerged out of the historical split between work place and home in connection with the spread of wage work. In the practice of the independent life mode there is a connection between the business and the family. In typical cases, such as that of family farming, these two spheres almost melt together. Since the woman can have responsibilities and work tasks of her own within the firm, she cannot be regarded as a homemaker. Even so, there is still a specific female practice here.

The assistance life mode shares with other female life modes an emphasis on home and family as the basic area of responsibility and work. Through the production of home and family the woman gains her support, her means; at the same time her own goals are also situated in this type of production. And as we have seen, if such production is to constitute means to the woman, it must be shaped in relation to what the man she lives with can use in his practice. To a man living the independent life mode, however, anything can appear as part of, or necessary for, the continuously ongoing business activity. For the woman married to such a man, then, an overarching and non-specific ideology of assistance 'when and where needed' is required.

The need for a wife's contributions may vary considerably from one family business to another and over time. Sometimes the need is small, and nowadays in such cases the wife probably has wage work of her own 'on the side'. If the need for assistance is great, then family business can become the wife's main occupation too. The wife's contributions to the business, however, allow her to influence her own means and goals, that is, she can influence the family company and the economic status, which is the prerequisite for family welfare. Therefore, her female ideology of means and goals located in home and family precisely includes assisting in the family company. The boundaries between family work and company work are vague, just as they are between work and leisure time. A good life in this life mode is to have home and family directly connected with a sound, independent family business, where the woman's contribution is an organic part of her work for home and family.

Today it is common for the wife of an independent entrepreneur to have waged work of her own. Even so, this may be some sort of assistance as it may provide the family with basic economic security. If the family business is not doing well, the wife's waged work could be essential in enabling the man to continue in the independent life mode. However, the woman's time is still 'other's time', and the demand for assistance when needed remains.

Life mode processes in the public-health sector

Modern women, particularly in Sweden, are usually not considered as living these female life modes, since most of them have paid jobs outside the home. Yet they do – life-mode research very often shows that Swedish women live a *mixed life mode*, consisting of a male life mode in the sphere of economic production *and* a traditional female life mode.

The same goes for the assistant nurses in the study reported above. They live a mixed life mode consisting of both the worker and the housewife life modes – and it is the latter that dominates. The interviews presented considerable evidence that this was so. To begin with, almost all of the nurses grew up in working class families and thus were socialized within the social context of the wage worker–housewife relation. They have also continued to live within this social context and today almost all have husbands who are traditional wage earners.

But they are also workers themselves, and that we are partly dealing with a worker life mode here, is evident from the fact that, despite the assistant nurses' love for their jobs, their life project is not found at work (Lindgren, 1999). Work is clearly seen as a means to goals in terms of leisure, and it is not allowed to 'take over'. This is not a 'pure' worker life mode, however, as these goals are mainly located in home and family, where the women also feel they have considerable responsibilities and *work* to be done. Typically, it is difficult to engage the husbands – the 'real' workers – in these activities (the interviewees made many telling comments regarding this). In any case, home and family takes time. It is important to have a nice home and a reasonably well-run household. It is also important that the children should not be in day care more than absolutely necessary, and that the family should spend time together.

The assistant nurses demonstrate a pronounced caring rationality, both in relation to home and family and in relation to their work. In many cases this is also what lay behind the decision to become an assistant nurse. It is safe to say that we are dealing with a female life mode, and that there are no traces of either the backing-up or the assistance practice. It is also safe to say that the involved male work form is neither career work nor self-employment: the nurses studied live a mixed life mode, consisting of the housewife and the worker life mode.

There are historical and logical reasons for this. As many have pointed out, welfare systems and practices have developed in relation to the current gender order, and there is intricate interdependence between the welfare state and the gender order (Acker, 1992; Connell, 1987; Eduards, 1990; Sainsbury, 1996; Siim, 1990). The public sector in Sweden was built up by the working-class movement, which means that it was mainly men living the worker life mode who shaped its systems, organizational forms and so on. To a great extent they employed 'their own' women, who were housewives, to carry out the welfare tasks in practice. This was not least the case regarding assistant nurses, who in general came from working class families, as did the nurses studied.

Until recently this has worked rather well. The nurses have not experienced any conflicts because of their mixed life mode. They have, of course, suffered from increased work pressure, as do many women today, but at the same time they have literally felt 'at home' with the arrangement. Traditional wage work can quite easily be integrated with a female life mode. The women consider that the work makes an additional contribution to the welfare of their families. Moreover, the work can be done part time or in other ways can be adjusted so as not to interfere too much with home activities.

Nursing and household caring activities are particularly easy to integrate. The housewife working as an assistant nurse is doing and thinking things in line with her household concerns, she need not change manners, attitude, or rationality when she enters the work place. She performs her tasks within the general framework of the (male) worker life mode ideology concerning interest-based solidarity, but she does this together with other women. The practices and ideologies of the 'governing' male life mode are not obvious in the immediate daily work; she can integrate her care-, needs-, and relationship-orientated ideology without disturbance.

When the reorganization of the Swedish public sector began, however, this balanced state started to change, calling forth a process of neoculturation among the nurses.

Neoculturation

Neoculturation is what one 'might call the life mode's struggle for its conditions of existence' (Højrup, 1983:216). The prefix 'neo' in the term indicates that it refers to reproducing the life-mode culture, that is, to consolidating, maintaining and defending the life mode's conditions of existence and thus its culture. The neoculturation of a life mode must therefore be analysed on the basis of its own ideology and worldview. The 'struggle' might take place at the social level, for example in the form of political conflicts, but it also takes place at the individual and personal levels. In fact, the neoculturation of life modes can be aspects of all social processes.

Furthermore, at the individual level, neoculturation can be studied through personal trajectories: when someone sees their life mode as threatened, their actions to uphold the life mode culture are a form of neoculturation. This, I suggest, is precisely what happened with the assistant nurses in the study. When the workplace cut-backs began, these women felt that their life mode was threatened. As low-paid and less-educated workers they were urged to seek education, so they could get new jobs; but this was not what they wanted. They did not think that they could afford or manage education – many of them, especially those with young children, thought it would intrude on family life and household duties. Some could not think of any other job to do. But above all, and despite their recent negative experiences, they were almost all very happy with their jobs. So they did what they could to preserve life just as it was. They neoculturated their life mode – that is they re-established the conditions for its existence – and succeeded, though only partially, for at the work-place things are not as they were, and it is unlikely that they ever will be again.

I believe that what is happening here, is that the career life mode is expanding its spheres. It is doing so, I believe, all over the West, and certainly in Sweden. In the public-health sector this life mode has come in along with market models and this has had several consequences (Lindgren, 1999). It has meant that a certain 'system-rationality' – an ideology of system effectiveness characteristic of the career life mode – is spreading at the expense of the solidarity rationality of the worker life mode and the caring rationality of the housewife's life mode.

The assistant nurses studied have had various reactions to different aspects of this development. In the workplace they directly experience the presence of this 'new' male life mode. This has given rise to one of the single most significant themes present in the material: the feeling that the system is totally incomprehensible, 'upside-down', 'so stupid' and so on. They cannot understand the priorities of the employer. The staff has been reduced so much that often they cannot manage to care for the patients; yet the employer will not hire more personnel. At the same time money is being spent on buildings, equipment, and furnishings, and on qualification-raising projects and courses that the women feel simply takes more time from their real job.

As it is now, they are squeezed between the demands of the system rationality of the career life mode and the demands of the caring rationality of their own housewife life mode. They feel inadequate, worn out, and suffering from stress. Notably, for some time, long-term absence due to illness has been increasing considerably in the Swedish public sector.

Apparently the processes involved in public sector reorganization have meant that the current gender order has been heavily reproduced. The assistant nurses contributed actively to this themselves, although it was an unintended consequence, since their only intention was to secure what they felt to be good everyday lives. Simultaneously, the events underline the interdependence of the public sector and the gender order.

But what of the six assistant nurses, two men and four women, who planned for futures outside nursing? These cases do not invalidate our analysis of the situation, but rather confirm it. One of the men has obtained a more secure and considerably better paid job in the manufacturing sector and intends to stay there. The other man obtained education and has started an administrative career in his old department; he feels quite satisfied with how things have turned out. Both these men have become re-installed in traditional male jobs and life modes.

As regards the women, one seems to be on her way back to working as an assistant nurse, because after all, she says, this is what she prefers. Another has become a registered nurse, hoping this will mean more job security. The third is obtaining further education, but is unsure where this will lead and she finds it hard to combine it with her family responsibilities. She says that if worst comes to worst, she could temporarily return to her old job again, as her former employer keeps calling.

The fourth woman has undergone the same education as has one of the men. She will soon begin a similar administrative job, and this may be the only example in the study where neoculturation in some form is not directly evident. Unlike the man, however, who feels very happy with the changes, this woman thinks it is 'scary' to think about the future: How will she find the time to work full-time hours, sometimes perhaps more, without it affecting her family? This case strikingly demonstrates that different opportunity costs are attached to making the same choice in different social positions.

Taken together, the study emphasizes that socio-structural life modes are strong causal mechanisms, having the ability to operate in different ways in different contexts, yet to the same ends.

References

Acker, Joan (1992), 'Två diskurser om reformer och kvinnor i den framtida välfärdsstaten', in J. Acker, A. Baude, U. Björnberg, E. Dahlström, G. Forsberg, L. Gonäs, H. Holter, A. Nilsson (eds), *Kvinnors och mäns liv och arbete*, SNS, Stockholm.

Archer, Margaret S. (1995), *Realist Social Theory: The Morphogenetic Approach*, Cambridge University Press, Cambridge.

Christensen, Lone Rahbek (1987), *Hver vore veje. Livsformer, familietyper og kvindeliv*, Etnologisk Forum, Köpenhamn.

Connell, R. W. (1987), *Gender & Power*, Polity Press, Cambridge.

Danermark, Berth, Mats Ekström, Liselotte Jakobsen and Jan Ch. Karlsson (2002), *Explaining Society: Critical Realism in the Social Sciences*, Routledge, London.

Eduards, Maud (1990), 'Att studera och värdera välfärd', *Kvinnovetenskaplig tidskrift*, no 2, pp. 3–12.

Højrup, Thomas (1983), 'The Concept of Life Mode: A Form Specifying Mode of Analysis Applied to Contemporary Western Europe', *Ethnologia Scandinavia*, 1983.

Højrup, Thomas (1989 [1983]), *Det glemte folk. Livsformer og centraldirigering*, Statens Byggeforskningsinstitut, Köpenhamn.

Højrup, Thomas (2003), *State, Culture and Life-Modes: The Foundations of Life-Mode Analysis*, Ashgate, Aldershot.

Jakobsen, Liselotte (1999), *Livsform, kön och risk. En utveckling och tillämpning av realistisk livsformsanalys*, Arkiv, Lund.

Jakobsen, Liselotte and Jan Ch. Karlsson (1993), *Arbete och kärlek. En utveckling av livsformsanalys*, Arkiv, Lund.

Jónasdóttir, Anna G. (1994), *Why Women are Oppressed*, Temple University Press, Philadelphia.

Karlsson, Jan Ch. (1994), 'The Concept of Work on the Rack: Critique and Suggestions', in Richard L. Simpson and Ida Harper Simpson (eds), *Research in the Sociology of Work: A Research Annual. Vol 5: The Meaning of Work*, JAI Press, Greenwich, Conn.

Karlsson, Jan Ch. (2004), 'The Ontology of Work: Social Relations and Doing in the Sphere of Necessity', in Steve Fleetwood and Stephen Ackroyd (eds), *Critical Realist Applications in Organisation and Mangement Studies*, Routledge, London.

Lindgren, Gerd (1999), *Kön, klass och kirurgi*, Liber, Stockholm.

Sainsbury, Diane (1996), *Gender, Equality and Welfare States*, Cambridge University Press, Cambridge.

Siim, Birthe (1990), 'Feministiska tolkningar av samspelet mellan kvinnor och välfärdsstaten', in *Kvinnovetenskaplig tidskrift*, no. 2, pp. 13–25.

Chapter 8

Employment, Flexible Working and the Family

Rosemary Crompton

Introduction

In this chapter, we bring together academic debates in two large areas – employment and the family. It will be argued that insights into the nature and direction of contemporary social change may be gained by addressing these debates simultaneously, rather than, as is more often the case, as separate topic areas. We begin by examining two contemporary themes. First, we will briefly address arguments relating to the significance of growing individualism in 'late modernity'. This trend is associated with economic liberalism or 'marketization' – and its consequences. The second theme is concerned with the consequences of changes in women's employment and gender relations following the impact of 'second wave' feminism.[1] We will examine arguments (from rather different quarters) to the effect that despite apparent shifts there has been 'no real change' in the gender division of labour. That is, that as women's entry into the labour market has been concentrated in lower-level occupations, and as women still retain the major responsibility for domestic and caring work, there has been a modification rather than a fundamental change.

As we shall see, there is empirical evidence to support the arguments above. However, and in some contrast to both of them, the argument will be developed that parallel developments in respect of both employment and the family might be the source of 'counter-movements' against the effects of economic liberalism.

Economic liberalism and individualism

In the world of work as employment, individualism is associated with an emphasis on the marketization of the self, of the development of what Rose (1993) has termed the 'entrepreneurial self' within the workplace. It is associated with the growth of individualized pay schemes, the conscious development of individual and inter-team competitiveness within organizations, the development of self-directed training and

---

[1]   In Europe, US and Australasia at any rate.

career paths, and 'high commitment' management practices. More broadly, the turn to economic liberalism has been associated with the deregulation of the labour market and the growth of flexible, short-term and self-employment.

Changes in the family have also followed upon the development of an 'extreme' or 'pure' capitalism in which individualized, marketized, identities and perspectives have penetrated ever deeper into the social fabric. There has been a growth of family instability, reflected in increased rates of divorce and single parenthood, as well as a (Europe-wide) decline in fertility (Sporton, 1993). Abstractly, it is the case that capitalism undermines the family form via its indifference to the 'private' lives of the labour power it purchases (Seccombe, 1993, p. 19), and as Beck has remarked, 'The market subject is ultimately the single individual, "unhindered" by a relationship, marriage, or family' (1992, p. 116). Thus although economic liberalism or 'marketization' has powerful political and economic advocates, its resurgence has been accompanied by changes in both employment and the family that are widely regarded in a negative light.

Changes in gender relations/gender division of labour

Changes in employment and family relations have run in parallel with the growth of women's employment and changes in gender norms. The increase in married women's employment has often been held responsible for the growth of family instability briefly discussed above. Indeed, many have argued that there is a 'crisis' in the western family. Commentators of the right advocate a return to the traditional breadwinner model, in which men would be constrained to take on their breadwinning responsibilities and women would rediscover their nurturing role (Fukuyama, 1999; Morgan, 1995; Kristol, 1998). Indeed, taken to its logical conclusion, increasing individualism might mean a virtual end to human reproduction for, as McInnes (2001, following Davis) has pointed out, the cost of rearing children makes little sense as far as an *individual*'s economic maximization is concerned.

Other authors, however, have suggested that the consequences of the increase in women's employment and changes in the gender division of labour have been less dramatic. For example Crouch has argued that the gender divisions of labour characteristic of the 'mid-(20th) century social compromise' have been modified rather than transcended. That is, women's employment tends to be concentrated in servicing work and is often marginal and low paid, and women also continue to take the major responsibility for domestic and household work thus: 'the segregations of the social compromise are reproduced but in a different institutional location' (1999, p. 67). Arguing from a rather different perspective Hakim (2000) has suggested that a majority of women are family-centred or adaptive, and therefore committed to child rearing and domestic labour. Her arguments imply that women will continue to take the major responsibility for caring work, presumably thus underwriting a modest level of human reproduction. Both of these kinds of arguments suggest that, despite the very extensive indications of transformations in gender norms and women's social claims over the last fifty years, in broad outline, the division of labour between the sexes in fact remains more or less as it has always been.

'Pure capitalism' or 'second modernity'?

An influential strand of debate suggests that contemporary social changes – including those discussed above – are truly 'epochal' (Urry, 2000). For example:

> ...epochal change is based on the fact that the guiding ideas and core institutional responses of the first modernity no longer appear self-evident or even convincing... The West's guiding ideas about modernity ... are in the process of falling apart. (Beck, 2000, pp. 23–24).

Thus Beck argues that the 'work society' or 'first modernity' – that is, industrial societies organized around full-time, stable, 'breadwinner' jobs – is in the process of being transcended. It is being replaced with 'second modernity', in which work as employment is fluid and transient, the nation state has to a considerable extent lost its regulatory capacities, and risk is universal. Beck argues that the old certainties can never be recovered, and new ideas and institutions must be developed.

The stable jobs of 'first modernity' were underpinned by the 'male breadwinner' model, in which men were held responsible for providing for the family via market work, whilst women were responsible for caring work within the household and the servicing of the breadwinner's maintenance needs (Pateman, 1989; Barrett and McIntosh, 1980). This model reflects a particular form of what has variously been described as a gender regime or arrangement (Connell, 1987; Pfau-Effinger, 1999; Gottfried, 2000; Lewis, 1992). The ideology of the male breadwinner was and is a powerful one, and indeed, cross-national attitudinal evidence continues to indicate that a very substantial minority (and in some countries, a majority) of people still support it (Scott et al., 1996). The breadwinner model tends to be associated with a set of beliefs expressive of relatively traditional or conventional gender relations and of the 'proper' roles (and jobs) for men and women. In Europe, welfare states were, characteristically, initially constructed with reference to the male breadwinner model.[2]

In some contrast to authors such as Beck, other commentators have suggested that the current scenario is not one of 'epochal change', but rather, reflects the development of 'pure capitalism' and the intensification of exploitation (Crouch, 1999). Proponents of 'second modernity' argue that national welfare states can no longer offer adequate social protections to their (vanishing) worker-citizens, thus the need for radically new thinking. Other authors, however, suggest that historical legacies of national institutional developments and patterns of innovation remain of

---

[2]   It should immediately be acknowledged that considerable generalization is inherent in this statement. Welfare states represent a variety of regime types (Esping-Andersen, 1990) and, as Holmwood (2000) has argued, some states have been positively oriented towards gender equality.

considerable significance. Thus Esping-Andersen's (1999) analysis of the 'Social Foundations of Postindustrial Societies' emphasizes the persisting variation in the capacity of national welfare regimes to accommodate to changing circumstances (for example, he attributes the lower fertility decline in the Scandinavian countries to the provisions made for working mothers).[3]

It may be suggested that these two, rather different, emphases concerning the nature of contemporary social change have different consequences for our approach to empirical research. If change *has* been truly 'epochal', then previous approaches to the analysis of change will be redundant, and new strategies and frameworks are required. However, if change represents the *intensification* of particular phenomena, rather than a fundamental transformation of society, then existing approaches to the analysis of change will still be relevant. In this chapter, we will take the latter view, and in our concluding discussion, we will suggest how a programme of social research addressing the issues dicussed in this chapter, that draws upon established frameworks, may be developed.

However, a feature common to both 'epochal change' and 'capitalist intensification' arguments is that they both acknowledge the importance of changes in women's employment. Indeed, Beck suggests there is a danger that work in general is becoming 'feminized' (2000, p. 64), in that ways of living will 'be more akin to those which women have known in the last few decades...that is, they will not involve careers, but rather combinations of part-time work, casual contracts, unpaid work and voluntary activity for the public good' (ibid. p. 92). Esping-Andersen has suggested that 'women are the vanguard force of change in the new economy' (2000, p. 759) – that is, that women's employment outside the family will contribute to a 'virtuous circle' of job creation. However, it may be argued that both of these authors, despite their differences, focus primarily on the *economic* significance of women's behaviour, and that neither gives adequate attention to the *social* dimension of changes in gender relations.[4]

In contrast, Irwin and Bottero (2000) have argued that rather than perceiving social relations as being driven by changes in the economy, we should recognize that 'the economy' is itself constituted by social claims. Thus (married) women's entry into employment should be seen as reflecting 'not an undoing of social relations by a logic of market capitalism...but rather a reconfiguration of the relative positioning of gender and generational groups' (p. 273). They argue that such groups are constituted within a 'moral economy' within which groups articulate social claims that are themselves a constituent part of change. Thus their approach may

---

[3]   It is not possible to state conclusively whether we are in the process of transformation to a completely new era, or whether we are witnessing the intensification of old problems, but nevertheless it is appropriate to recall Savage's comment that we should not mistake an economic cycle for an 'epoch'.

[4]   Beck (1992, 2000; Beck and Beck-Gernsheim, 1995) has written extensively of the transformation in the situation of women, but as Irwin and Bottero (2000) argue, Beck sees the changing position of women as being largely a *reflection* of economic developments, rather than as contributing to them.

be seen as paralleling an established critique of neoclassical economics in which the 'economic' is seen as irretrievably embedded in the 'social' – and vice versa (Granovetter and Swedberg, 1992). Irwin and Bottero are correct in their emphasis that the *social* claims made by and on behalf of women have been neglected by many commentators.

Like Irwin and Bottero, this chapter argues that the 'economic' and the 'social' are intertwined. Nevertheless the fact that social claims *are* perceived as being in conflict with market imperatives is itself of some significance. Irwin and Bottero suggest that the way ahead lies in the 'detailing of shifts and variations in the composition of the moral economy' (p. 277). However, in order to move our discussions beyond (improved) description alone it is also necessary to emphasize and identify the tensions in the articulation of the economic and the social as part of our efforts to understand, develop, and adapt to changing circumstances.

Polanyi's (1957) classic text focuses directly on these tensions. Indeed, he argued that the truly self regulating market would result in the 'demolition of society', given the fragmentation of social bonds this would imply. Thus, Polanyi argues, capitalist development has historically been characterized by a 'double movement'. On the one hand, the principle of economic liberalism aims to establish a 'self-regulating market', whilst on the other, there is the 'principle of social protection aiming at the conservation of man and nature as well as productive organization' (p. 132). Thus typically, capitalist expansion has been followed by a counter-movement checking this self-destructive capacity (ibid. p. 130).[5] In this chapter it will be suggested that developments in gender norms and relations, and in the division of labour between the sexes, might be a major source of a Polanyian 'counter-movement' in the 21st century. That is, the growing tensions between employment and caring brought about by the erosion of the male breadwinner model, together with the increase in women's aspirations, will be reflected in organizational and institutional adaptations.

We will develop these arguments by first, re-examining some aspects of earlier feminist debates on the family, and the contemporary emergence of 'family-friendly' employment policies. Next we will examine employment flexibility, particularly in relation to its supposed role in achieving 'work-life integration'. An examination of flexibility in practice, and employment careers, will focus on the tensions associated with efforts to achieve such integration. In the final section, we will return to the arguments raised in this Introduction, and suggest directions for future research.

Families and feminist debates

Given that the family is a crucial site for the reproduction of labour power, it is not surprising that the various ways in which it has been meshed with economic activity have been widely discussed. The theoretical debates initiated by 'second-wave'

---

[5]　Many parallel arguments have been formulated. For example, T. H. Marshall's (1948) influential account of the development of 'social citizenship' describes it as being 'at war' with the capitalist class system.

feminism followed a decade – the 1950s – in which the traditional male breadwinner model of the family had reached its apogee. The question of domestic labour and the family, therefore, assumed a high profile in feminist debates of the 60s and 70s.

The influence of Marxist theory during this period resulted in an extended debate as to whether the domestic labour of women might be theoretically analysed in a parallel (Marxist) fashion to that of wage labour, thus rendering women a 'class' within capitalist relations of production. Closely associated with these debates was the question of the source of women's oppression, and of who or what benefited from the 'male breadwinner' model. Some argued that men were the main beneficiaries of women's work within the household. Others, however, argued that domestic labour, being unpaid, was of primary advantage to capitalism (for a summary, see Molyneux, 1979). A further strand of argument relating to the explanation of women's inequality was concerned with the question of the relative significance of material, as opposed to cultural and ideological, factors. Put crudely, the debate centred on whether women's subordination was to be seen as being largely a consequence of the material exigencies of human reproduction in the circumstances created by the development of industrial capitalism (for example Brenner and Ramas, 1984), or whether the systematic ideological denigration of femaleness and femininity should be accorded more explanatory prominence (Barrett, 1984).

In practice, 'materialist' debates within feminism were overtaken by the cultural and Poststructuralist 'turn' in feminist theorizing (Barrett and Phillips, 1992; Maynard, 1995). However, the issues raised by materialist debates remain of considerable contemporary relevance. It will be argued that issues relating to the work of caring remain central – and indeed have assumed considerable significance within contemporary political debates.

As we have noted in the Introduction, there is a widespread assumption as to a state of 'crisis' in the contemporary family. Others, however, have argued that rather than the development of a 'crisis' in family arrangements, these have in fact returned to previous fluidities (McRae, 1999; Gittins, 1993). For example, Seccombe (1993) has argued that:

> The golden age of the male-breadwinner form of the nuclear family, culminating in the 1950s, is an unusual era in family history. Its present decline leaves families today in a transitional state which is, in significant respects, more typical of family life in the past than the period of stability and conformity of recent memory. (p. 208)

In the 1980s, Brenner and Ramas had argued that 'the qualitative changes that would solve the problem collectively by relieving the family of care for dependants could only be gained at the expense of capitalist profitability...and they will therefore meet consistent resistance from employers' (1984, p. 63). In consequence, they suggest, the recognition of and assistance with caring work would only come about as a consequence of class struggle: 'The amount of necessary labour workers have to perform in addition to waged work...will...depend on the class struggle: on whether the working class can force capitalists to underwrite the labour involved in child-rearing (and incidentally, the care of older people, the sick, disabled, and so on)' (1984, p. 61).

With hindsight, Brenner and Ramas may be characterized as working within an excessively 'fordist' set of assumptions relating to both the division of labour between the sexes as well as the likely origins of social change. For in Britain, a government ('New Labour') that would not be considered particularly radical has taken a number of initiatives and the private sphere of the family has become the focus of a range of policy developments. Within the centre left, women's claims to the right to employment have been recognized. There has been a considerable increase of government emphasis on the development and introduction of 'family friendly' policies in respect of employment and the possibilities of 'work-life integration'. However, this shift does not simply reflect the recognition of women's employment aspirations, but is also part of a broader policy objective that emphasizes the beneficial economic effects of maximizing rates of employment in general (DTI, 2000). It is increasingly being suggested that increasing the employment rates of women will create a 'virtuous circle' contributing to economic regeneration, and 'family friendly' policies, therefore, are widely advocated. The discourses of flexible work and flexible families, therefore, are increasingly brought together in positive association.

Employment flexibility and women's work

In the literature on flexible employment, a distinction is drawn between numerical and pay flexibility, which allows the number of workers or amount of labour time to be varied, and functional flexibility. Strategies of numerical and pay flexibility are guided by neo-liberal economic theory, which stresses the efficiency gains that come from making the costs of factors of production as flexibly responsive as possible (Crouch, 1999, p. 79. See also Atkinson, 1984; Smith, 1997). 'Functional' flexibility, in contrast, has been regarded more positively and incorporates the kinds of innovations in production often associated with New Management Techniques and 'high commitment' management – teamworking, upskilling and multiskilling, and so on. Advocates of functional flexibility see flexible specialization as facilitating innovation in both productive activities and institutional regulation, allowing for the exercise of strategic choice and the positive development of productive resources (Hirst and Zeitlin, 1997). Critics of neo-liberal numerical flexibility, however, tend to regard flexibilization as part of a package of measures that facilitate the super-exploitation of the workforce (Pollert, 1988). However, both approaches to flexible working may be used at the same time, as O'Reilly (1992) has demonstrated, and as we shall see in our discussion of 'Shopwell' later in this chapter.

Women's employment has been an integral part of discussions relating to employment flexibility from the point at which academic debates emerged in the 1980s. This is not surprising, given that women have always worked flexibly – in both the numerical and functional senses of the term. For example, Glucksmann's

(2000) account of working class women's work in Lancashire in the 1930s describes how they fitted casual factory work, cleaning, canteen work and so on around household routines which were often extremely rigid.[6]

Nevertheless, as we have seen, despite the fact that flexible forms of employment are not exactly new, many commentators have been pessimistic about their recent growth. This is largely because the 'standard' jobs characteristically associated with the male breadwinner model were, over a period of time, hedged around with various protections such as seniority rules (for both layoffs and promotions) that gave security as well as prospects for the future, employment associated benefits such as pension schemes, sick pay and paid holidays, a predictable income and, in many cases, the possibility of lifelong employment. In contrast, flexible working is often insecure employment, offers less (proportionately and absolutely) by way of employment-related benefits and, in many cases, insufficient income to support a one-person household, let alone a household with any dependants. As a range of empirical investigations have demonstrated, the effect of flexible employment (indeed, one of the aims of neo-liberal flexibility) is to push employment costs onto the individual employee and their families, rather than their being borne by the employer (Dex and McCulloch, 1997; Capelli, 1995). Nevertheless, one of the advantages of flexible employment is that it does enable paid employment to be combined with caring responsibilities (Yeandle, 1984).

However, if women's paid work remains concentrated in flexible service employment, it is possible that the broad division of labour by sex may not be substantially altered – men will continue to be main breadwinners, and women will continue to take the larger responsibility for caring work. Thus as we have seen, Crouch has suggested that the increase in women's employment and the associated rise in flexible working do not in fact reflect 'a transcendence of mid-20th century principles of social organization, but their extension' (Crouch, 1999, p. 67). That is, women continue to carry out the greater part of caring and domestic work, but as market work, rather than within the household. Similarly, Castells has described new social relationships of production as translating into 'a good fit between the "flexible woman" [forced to flexibility to cope with her multiple roles] and the network enterprise' (2000, p. 20).

Arguing from a rather different perspective, Hakim (1996, 2000) has suggested that part-time work has emerged as a suitable compromise employment status for women whose major commitment remains with the home and family, rather than employment. Hakim argues that socio-economic factors are no longer dominant as far as the sexual division of labour is concerned in that, in countries such as the UK,

---

6   As expressed in the traditional rhyme which concludes:

Them as wash on Thursday are folk that wash for shame
Them as wash on Friday most likely wash in need,
And them as wash on Saturday – they are sluts indeed.

It should also be noted that, in the first half of the last century, many men only had access to casual, temporary – that is, flexible, work. See Capelli (1995).

the barriers to women's economic participation have been removed and women's employment rights recognized. Women are therefore free to choose but nevertheless, the preference of the majority of women is to give priority to their domestic lives. These preferences, she argues, are the major explanation for the polarization of women's employment – and indeed, socio economic polarization more generally. [7]

A wide range of empirical evidence may be drawn upon to support these kinds of arguments. Purcell et al. (1999) have argued that the 'uneasy reconciliation of work and family life in Britain has largely been achieved by means of a gender-segmented labour market and the part-time work of women'. Perrons' (1999) cross-national European study of flexible working in the retail industry demonstrated that in all of the countries studied (Britain, Sweden, France, Germany, Spain and Greece) it was women who worked flexibly, and took the major responsibility for caring work as well. As Lewis (1997) has argued, the fact that women continue, in aggregate, to be less advantaged in the labour market is the major reason why the 'modified male breadwinner' model of employment/family articulation persists empirically, despite the fact that in many states, official policy endorses an 'adult worker' model of state welfare.

The fact of women's flexible working, together with the difficulties of career commitment when family responsibilities are considerable and/or pressing, is of course a major explanation of the fact that the most senior positions in organizations are usually held by men. In general flexible employment patterns are not conducive to an individual's career. If, therefore, women continue to predominate amongst those working flexibly, then the chances of achieving gender equality in employment will be severely reduced. A wide range of studies has demonstrated that flexible employment, and part-time employment in particular, is detrimental to promotion prospects and that managerial employment is almost invariably full-time (Crompton and Birkelund, 2000; Rubery et al., 1994; Perrons, 1999).[8] Nevertheless, as more women seek organizational careers – and as more men seek to spend more time with their families – it is reasonable to raise the question as to what a family-compatible organizational structure would look like. Weber's original formulation of the bureaucratic ideal-type characterizes office-holding as a 'vocation', demanding the 'entire capacity for work for a long period of time' (Weber in Gerth and Mills, 1958, pp. 198-199). However, can such career bureaucrats be flexible, or part-time, employees? As we shall see, in present circumstances, the answer has to be 'no'.

Nevertheless, in the present climate, flexible working is increasingly being presented as a possible 'win–win' combination as far as employment and family life is concerned. Thus the more negative aspects of neo-liberal numerical flexibility

---

[7]   Hakim's arguments are controversial and have been widely criticized, see Ginn et al. (1996); Crompton and Harris (1998).

[8]   Highly trained professionals, such as doctors, may work part-time without loss of employment status (Crompton, 1999). It is also the case that in general, individuals possessing sought-after skills – such as IT specialists – are often in a position to name their working hours – as well as their price.

are being glossed as a positive contribution to the reconciliation of employment and family life, and employment and families may be viewed as changing in tandem with each other. However, as we have seen, this emphasis on the 'positive' aspect of employment flexibility is in some contrast to recent research that has revealed its more negative aspects – particularly for women.

We thus return to the conundrum raised in the Introduction to this chapter. That is, despite widespread assertions as to the coming of 'epochal change', there has in fact been 'no real change' in the underlying division of labour between the sexes. In order to proceed beyond this apparent *impasse*, it will be argued that we should develop an approach parallel to that advocated by Irwin and Bottero. That is, we might adopt a perspective that views the 'social' not as being merely shaped or constrained by the economic, but rather focus upon the embeddedness of the economic within the social. This perspective would see 'families' and 'employment' as intertwined with each other, and would give due weight to the transformation of gender relations and the impact of the social claims made by women. These are both factors which, it has been argued in this chapter, have not been consistently taken into account by authors such as Beck and Esping-Andersen.

Flexible work, flexible careers?

In this section we will first, examine the consequences, for families, of lower-level flexible employment. We will then raise the question of employment careers, and the extent to which these are compatible with caring and family responsibilities.

'Shopwell'[9] is a major supermarket that has extensive and high profile family friendly employment policies. Employment at Shopwell is also characterized by the enthusiastic application of the 'high commitment' management techniques briefly discussed in the Introduction. Bureaucratic hierarchies are de-emphasized and everyone within the company is known (and addressed by) their first names. All employees are regularly consulted on working practices, there is a well-publicized suggestion scheme, and bonus-linked competitions (relating to sales figures and so on) both within and between stores abound.[10] Family friendly policies include enhanced maternity and paternity leave, as well as recently introduced grandparental leave. There is also considerable flexibility in working hours. The supermarket operates on a 24 hour basis (although not all stores are open for 24 hours), and a majority of employees work part-time. Employees are entitled to make shift swaps (which they arrange between themselves).

---

[9]   This is a pseudonym. This research is sponsored by the Joseph Rowntree Foundation and is being carried out in collaboration with Prof. S. Yeandle, Sheffield Hallam University.

[10]   More negatively, there is also a high level of employee surveillance, particularly by 'mystery shoppers' who score both the store and individual employees. The mystery shopper reports – positive and negative – are then posted in prominent positions throughout the staff areas of the store.

The level of employee flexibility at Shopwell can be achieved because employees are highly substitutable with each other: 'If you work on groceries, although it's different in terms of products you're selling you could put them on to home and leisure...It would take ten minutes to show them the differences but other than that they can get on with it' (Manager, Shopwell). In short, this is relatively deskilled service sector employment and is paid accordingly. Employees aged 18 and over earn £4.35 an hour, craft workers (butchers and bakers) £6.24 (2000 rates).[11] Managers earn considerably more.[12] Nevertheless, considerable efforts are made to accommodate staff who are often in multi-earner households, as in the following example from the same manager's interview cited above: 'One of my staff, her sister had cerebral palsy and was quite poorly, so she had two weeks off completely...her dad also works for Shopwell...just so they could visit her...we are now in the process of just tweaking her hours around slightly because her dad works at night and sleeps during the day.' This example, therefore (and there were others) might be seen as a contemporary return to previous patterns of work and family life amongst the less well-off, in which household strategies invariably involve more than one family member's income and employment itself might be shifting and variable (Gittins, 1993; Glucksmann, 2000; Pahl, 1984).

Shopwell managers work full-time, and it is a feature of managerial employment that considerable mobility is required in order to build a career. For example, a manager aged 22 (who joined Shopwell after A levels) had already made a move from his first store, and described his career plans as follows: 'I would hopefully come to a duty manager in this store. I would like to open (that is, join) a new store next, hopefully the one in X and go in there as duty into deputy. In a year's time I see myself going into the general store manager's role' (that is, another move). If his career plans come to fruition, they will mean working in four stores over a five year period. Efforts have been made to control the hours worked by store managers through a 'Friends and Family' rota that gives managers one long weekend a month and ensures at least eleven hours between shifts. However, managers interviewed report that they routinely work more than fifty hours a week. In consequence, as another manager replied to a direct enquiry about 'family-friendliness':

> Family-friendly for colleagues (that is, non-promoted employees) yes...family friendly for managers...to a point...then the more senior you are you really – you've got to make a commitment to the company...half of (managers) are family-oriented, they have partners at home that have never worked and the other half are single – someone who's got family commitments, it's very unlikely that their partner would have ever worked.

As has often been noted, both breaks in employment, and part-time working, are problematic for those wishing to build a career (Crompton and Sanderson, 1990;

---

[11] Bonuses and so on will raise earnings above these basic levels, up to several hundred pounds a year extra.

[12] Official pay scales are not available but a twenty two year old manager reported that he was earning £25 000 p.a. (2000).

Halford et al., 1997). Recent research comparing male and female bank managers in Britain and Norway (a country with generous family friendly entitlements at the national level) showed that despite the differences in entitlements available, bank managers in Norway felt under similar pressures to bank managers in Britain, as far as time for their family lives was concerned (Crompton and Birkelund, 2000).[13] Moreover, women managers are far less likely than male managers to have a partner who takes responsibility for domestic arrangements (Wacjman, 1998, p. 140). Women managers have fewer children than male managers, and indeed, are frequently childless (ibid.; Crompton, 1996, 2001). In short, a wide range of evidence demonstrates that women's conventionally-assigned domestic responsibilities continue to operate as a major restriction as far as their employment careers are concerned.

Nevertheless, these elements of continuity should not obscure the fact that women's orientations to career development have not remained static. Cross-national biographical evidence suggests that in some contrast to older women managers, who were often 'accidental' careerists, younger women managers have systematically set out to build organizational careers (Crompton, 2001). Aggregate level data suggests that the number of women training for and entering higher level occupations shows no sign of slackening and in Britain, well-qualified young women with children under five are the fastest growing segment of the labour force (Thair and Risdon, 1999).

As we have seen in the Shopwell family-flexible example cited above, men can care, as well as women. Recent cross-national research (in Britain, Norway and France) has demonstrated that when male managers have had to assume caring responsibilities, then their careers are affected as well (Crompton, 2001). As a British bank manager who had brought up his children on his own (from the ages of 7 and 9) said:

> I wish I'd started earlier…turned down quite a few opportunities 'cos of my own domestic circumstances…turned down jobs, it would have been disruptive for them (that is, his children)…I feel I can get higher but it will be very difficult – certain constraints on me now… (British banker, two children)

In short, it is important to remember that caring is gender *coded* rather than 'gendered' in any essentialist sense, and that men who have to (or choose to) assume a major caring role will also face problems in developing managerial careers. In practice, however, few men in managerial careers choose to share fully in caring responsibilities and as Wacjman concludes: 'Men's careers are underpinned by the domestic labour of their wives' (1998, p. 141). Nevertheless, is it reasonable to assume that this state of affairs will continue, given the shift in women's gendered expectations? Moreover, recent evidence suggests that *fathers* experience more 'extreme' reactions to high pressure at work than mothers (Nolan, 2002).

This brief review of some empirical evidence relating to flexible employment and the family suggests that for many families, flexible working and multiple jobs might

---

[13]   A similar pattern was also found amongst bank managers in France.

be seen as a return to the *status quo ante*, even though it may be a new experience for the contemporary participants. What *is* different about the current situation, however, is that more and more women are seeking to develop employment careers, and there have been substantial changes in gender role attitudes and the social 'claims' made by men and women. However, it would seem that a feature of employment that has not changed is that employment careers are difficult to develop in conjunction with caring responsibilities.

Historically, family life has changed in close association with economic transformations, and changes in structures of state authority and provision (Levine, 1987). However, there have also been strong pressures for change from *within* families, in particular from women, who have sought to control their fertility, gain property rights, and who are the major instigators of divorce (Seccombe, 1993, pp. 209–210). Theorists such as Esping-Andersen have recognized the significant role of the family as far as contemporary economic and political changes are concerned. However, his analysis has a bias towards the economic dimension and fails to take sufficient account of pressures brought about by social and normative changes – in particular changes in gender relations and the increase in women's aspirations. He is 'not interested in women *per se*', (2000, p. 759) and rejects the arguments and insights of 'gender regime' feminist theorists. Normative assumptions are central to these theories (for example, Hirdman, 1989). Esping-Andersen's recognition of the significance of the family to current social and economic developments focuses largely on the anticipated economic consequences of new employment in market jobs in restaurants, daycare nurseries and convenience food manufacture and so on, following the abandonment of domestic labour by women, thus generating more employment and revenue in society as a whole. Indeed, Esping-Andersen agrees with Hakim that the underlying distribution of different attitudes amongst women may be seen as a relative constant, and thus the impact of normative shifts in attitude and aspiration need not be taken into account (ibid., p. 764).[14]

However, in this chapter it is being argued that pressures generated by changing gender roles and attitudes might bring about social transformations at the workplace, as well as within the family. As we have seen, in the current economic climate it is very difficult for managers to combine employment and caring unless there are others available to take on caring work. National trends show no diminution in the proportion of women moving into jobs associated with bureaucratic careers.

---

[14] Hakim argues that 'Affluent and liberal modern societies provide opportunities for diverse lifestyle preferences to be fully realised' (2000, p. 273). That is, as the full range of occupations and so on is now accessible to all women, women's employment patterns now reflect the distribution of their 'preferences'. Clearly, preferences (for a particular combination of employment and family life) *do* shape behaviour, and preferences are heterogeneous. However, it is important to address the question of the origins of these 'preferences', and here contextual and situational factors will clearly be very relevant. It is also important to recognize that 'preferences' in relation to gender roles and the gender division of labour will change over historical time. In this paper, the change in the nature of women's social claims is being emphasized.

Individual women may sacrifice their childbearing potential, or work a 'second shift', but for many this is not considered to be a satisfactory situation. Women may put more pressure on their partners, thus increasing the proportion of employer-carers within organizations as more men take on caring responsibilities. Thus a mounting tide of dissatisfaction may bring about changes within the workplace itself, and in particular, pressures for the introduction of shorter hours working and more 'family-friendly' employment policies.

Work-life balance pressures have increased in parallel with the employment of women because 'workers' have conventionally been assumed not to have other 'imperatives of existence' that impinge upon the job (Acker, 1990). Increasingly, however, the 'worker' – and this 'worker' could be male or female – may be assumed to have caring responsibilities. 'Workers' without career aspirations may be able to cope with caring responsibilities via a number of strategies, including buying in services as well as sharing care with other 'workers'. For those wishing to build a career, however, this combination of care work and market work will be problematic, even if services are bought in, and there are considerable costs for individuals. These may be illustrated by an extract from an interview with a British woman doctor (Surgeon, aged 39):

> I consider it a lot of personal sacrifice to have to keep moving around and not to have a family – a huge amount of sacrifice which I didn't think I was going to have to do...I hope things change here – I don't think it's right that a woman should have to give up a family – men are wary of married women – they don't want to pick up the slack if a woman has a sick child. People have to rethink fundamentally.

Such a fundamental rethinking would contribute to the societal changes necessary for the emergence of a counter movement against the 'self-regulating' market.

Discussion

In this chapter, we have examined a number of debates relating to contemporary changes in both employment and the family. It has been argued that although it is, increasingly, recognized that changes in the structure of both families and employment are inter-related, nevertheless, 'the economy', in the guise of economic liberalism and its effects, is seen by many as the major driver of change in women's (and therefore families') behaviour. It has been argued that the significance of normative shifts in gender relations, and changing attitudes to gender roles, should be more systematically integrated into these debates. At present, even when the significance of women's attitudes is recognized, as in the case of Hakim's work, they are frequently assumed to be relatively fixed.

'The economy' is embedded in institutions and in normative assumptions, and there is nothing inevitable about the 'end of history' (Fukuyama, 1992) or the triumph of neo-liberalism. Our discussion of flexibility in practice, although by no means exhaustive, has noted increasing tensions between employment and family life. Jobs in the service economy (such as retail) may be extremely flexible at the lower level, but these jobs will not generate sufficient income to support a household. Career jobs in the service economy demand long hours and total commitment. 'Careerists' (men or women) might be able to buy in substitute care but this capacity does not completely remove work-family tensions. In the concluding discussion of this chapter, therefore, we will suggest the outline of a programme of social research that would both further investigate these and other employment–family tensions as well as help to develop possible responses to them.

In the Introduction to this chapter, we have noted that commentators differ in their understandings as to whether the present time is one of 'epochal change' or rather, the intensification of capitalism. Authors such as Beck, who have asserted that epochal change is in process, have argued that new institutions, particularly 'transnational interest groups', will have to be developed in response. Whilst one might be broadly sympathetic to such clarion calls for action, it may be suggested that a systematic programme of research is an equally, if not more, important element in achieving change. It may be further suggested that established traditions of research into counter-movements against extreme capitalism, as represented by research on the development of welfare states, may be fruitfully developed here.

In the recent past, this work has been dominated by two major (and apparently opposed) theoretical perspectives, functionalist modernization theories, and power-centred theories (Esping-Andersen, 1990). The former asserts that social policies emerge in response to social needs once a certain level of economic development has been achieved. In contrast, power-centred theories insist that there is no inevitability in the development of market protections, rather, whether or not they are achieved will depend upon the balance of power between opposing (class) forces.

Esping-Andersen's comparative empirical investigation concluded that *both* modernization and power-centred explanations are relevant. For example, pension provisions were developed in response to population ageing and economic growth (as 'modernization' arguments would have predicted), but the *form* taken by pension provision depended on the national balance of political forces (1990, Chapter 5). Feminist comparativists have carried out similar analyses. For example, O'Connor et al.'s comparison of 'liberal' welfare states (the US, UK, Canada and Australia) demonstrated that variations in the political opportunity structure of these countries were crucial 'in facilitating and/or constraining the options open to gender equality advocates' (1999, p. 230). They also point to the similarities between these liberal regimes, noting that their common emphasis upon marketized childcare provision reinforces the good jobs-bad jobs division in all four countries. In contrast, at the present time, the Scandinavian welfare states offer the most favourable national and labour market contexts in which employment may be combined with caring responsibilities, and/or work-life balance achieved. Thus comparative work may not only facilitate our understanding of different policy outcomes, but also indicate examples of 'best practice' in relation to these issues.

It is being argued here that regulation will be required in order to secure the conditions in which the conflict between the need for caring and economic maximization may be resolved – that is, *contra* modernization theory, the institutions concerned with the amelioration of this conflict will not simply emerge of their own accord. State regulation is required in order to moderate the tensions that have been brought about by changes in gender relations and women's expectations in the 20th century, much as the regulation of factory hours and working conditions followed upon the shift to industrialism. For example, in 1993, the Norwegian state introduced a paternity quota of four weeks' paid leave for fathers, to be forfeited if not taken up (that is, not transferable to the mother). By 1998, the percentage of eligible fathers using this leave was 80 percent. However, *optional* sharing of parental leave via a time account system (introduced at the same time as the paternity quota) has not been widely taken up, suggesting that 'mild state coercion' (Brandth and Kvande, 2001) is an important ingredient in securing these kinds of changes.

Indeed, even those who have suggested that with globalization the era of the nation state has passed have nevertheless emphasized the continuing need for state action: 'What is required is the exact opposite of neoliberal deconstruction: namely, strong states capable of transnational market regulation both within and beyond frontiers' (Beck, 2000, p. 175). A re-emphasis on the state brings with it the question of who or what influences and shapes institutions and state policy – in short, we return to the concerns of the 'power relations' theorists. With considerable over-simplification, two broad categories of 'influence' may be identified. First, social trends (in attitudes and expectations, as well as in behaviour) that maintain and/or intensify societal tensions and contradictions. These may give rise to changes in behaviour, and resistances to the market, at the level of the individual or family, and would include the changes in women's aspirations and 'social claims' that have been emphasized in this chapter. Second, social and political groupings, organized around reform or amelioration, will increasingly focus on employment/family issues.

A major social trend that is unlikely to be reversed is the increase in levels of education and qualification amongst women. We may anticipate that in Western-influenced countries at any rate, the increase in women's levels of education and entry into employment positions will not be checked. Parallel with the increase in women's educational and employment levels, attitudes to gender roles, and the domestic division of labour, are also changing. Attitudinal evidence suggests that beliefs in domestic egalitarianism are increasing (Sullivan, 2000). These changes are generating individual 'resistances to the market'. One way in which these issues may be explored is by identifying and researching the circumstances in which men become 'more like women' (Fraser, 1994). For example, in Germany, fathers are more likely to take parental leave if they are highly educated (the educational level of the woman was even more important); if the mother's income was higher than the fathers; and if their attitudes to domestic and caring roles were egalitarian (Rost, 1999).

An emphasis on work-life balance for men is even being identified as a response to anticipated economic downturn. For example, the financial page of the London *Evening Standard* reacted to the resignation of Danny O'Neil from the Britannic Group to spend more time with his family as follows: 'If the rewards go down, so does the incentive to burn the midnight oil in the office. Executives at even top-tier investment banks are therefore quietly calculating how to reduce the hours employees spend at work. They talk of work/life balance, of part-time opportunities and even the need for a more diverse workforce' (18ᵗʰ January 2002).

The example of Danny O'Neil (a top executive) serves to underline the point that some individuals are more able to resist the market than others. Those towards the apex of the income hierarchy have always been able to cushion themselves more effectively against the adverse impact of market forces. However, even amongst the well-off, there are occupational variations in the extent to which individual resistance is an option. As we have seen in the example of Shopwell, and in banking, senior managers – particularly in the private sector – are subject to organizational demands that make flexible and short hours working highly problematic. In contrast, individuals with greater individual occupational power, such as highly skilled and qualified professionals and experts, may choose to work flexibly without loss of occupational status and may even bring about changes directed at work-life integration within their own sphere of employment (Crompton, 2001).

However – and particularly in a period of 'extreme' capitalism – most individuals have only limited options for resistance. Thus we may anticipate that social and political groupings, oriented towards reform, will develop, suggesting another area for future research. Polanyi's account of the generation of resistance to previous periods of extreme marketization emphasized that there have been multiple sources of opposition promoting social and economic controls over the market (Block and Somers, 1984). Historically, given their association with the work of caring and the domestic sphere, women have taken a leading role in pressing for welfare reforms (Skocpol, 1992). Increasingly, however, both men and women will have an interest in policies that moderate the impact of extreme capitalism. Counter-movement coalitions might be drawn from a number of sources, and will include transnational interest groups (Beck, 2000) organized around European institutions (including Trade Unions).[15]

A number of inter-related research topics, therefore, may be identified as contributing to a programme of research that would systematically investigate the impact of one of the major social changes of the twentieth century – the transformation of the status of women. First, systematic comparative research is required in order to explore the impact of different policies that have been developed in response to changes in employment and the family. Second, individual responses reflecting 'resistances to the market' need to be both contextualized and explained. It is important that this kind of research has a focus on both economic *and* normative dimensions of behaviour. The evidence generated by such research will make a contribution to the arguments of organized 'counter movements' against the impact of unregulated market forces. Indeed, the investigation of such movements is yet another potential avenue of research.

---

[15]   At the present time, the question of 'work-life integration' has become a central element in the policies of a number of Trade Unions, including UNIFI and UNISON.

It is unlikely that the conflict between caring and economic maximization can ever be resolved completely. Family friendly policies such as paid leave, shorter hours, help with childcare, and so on, are widely acknowledged to be under increasing pressures on account of 'market making' pressures towards economic deregulation (Glass and Estes, 1997). Non-family care alternatives (and other aspects of welfare) sponsored and organized by the state tend to generate reasonably stable and well-protected forms of employment. However, marketized non-family care alternatives have a tendency to generate 'junk jobs', thereby contributing to social polarization.[16] Women (and men) in economically successful partnerships in such marketized contexts may do well, and occupational segregation has actually declined most rapidly in societies, such as the UK and US, that approximate to this model. Nevertheless, in terms of the increase in social and economic inequality, the damage to the social fabric of such societies may be extreme. We would do well to heed Polanyi's warning as to the dangers of unregulated markets.

References

Acker, J. (1990), 'Hierarchies, Jobs, Bodies: A Theory of Gendered Organisations', *Gender and Society*, vol. 4, pp. 139–158.

Atkinson, J. (1984), 'Manpower Strategies for Flexible Organisations', *Personnel Management*, vol. 16, pp. 28–31.

Barrett, M. (1984), 'A Reply to Brenner and Ramas', *New Left Review*, no. 146, pp. 24–30.

Barrett, M. and M. McIntosh (1980), 'The "Family Wage"', *Capital and Class*, Summer, pp. 51–72.

Barrett, M. and A. Phillips (eds) (1992), 'Introduction', *Destabilising Theory*, Polity Press, Cambridge.

Beck, U. (1992), *Risk Society*, Sage, London.

Beck, U. (2000), *The Brave New World of Work*, Polity Press, Cambridge.

Beck, U. and E. Beck-Gernsheim (1995), *The Normal Chaos of Love*, Polity Press, Cambridge.

Block, F. and M. R. Somers (1984), 'Beyond the Economistic Fallacy: The Holistic Social Science of Karl Polanyi', in T. Skocpol (ed.), *Vision and Method in Historical Sociology*, Cambridge University Press, Cambridge.

Brandth, B. and E. Kvande (2001), 'Flexible Work and Flexible Fathers', *Work, Employment and Society*, vol 15, pp. 251–267.

Brenner, J. and M. Ramas (1984), 'Rethinking Women's Oppression', *New Left Review*, no. 144, pp. 33–71.

Capelli, P. (1995), 'Rethinking Employment', *British Journal of Industrial Relations*, vol. 33, pp. 563–602.

Castells, M. (2000), 'Materials for an Exploratory Theory of the Network Society', *British Journal of Sociology*, vol. 51, pp. 4–24.

Connell, R. W. (1987), *Gender and Power*, Polity, Cambridge.

---

[16]   The most extreme example of such 'junk jobs' in the private care sector would be the employment of immigrant workers, often without even minimal legal protections (as in the case of illegal migrants) as domestic and care workers.

Crompton, R. (1996), 'Women's Employment and the "Middle Class"', in T. Butler and M. Savage (eds), *Social Change and the Middle Classes*, UCL Press, London.

Crompton, R. (ed.) (1999), *Restructuring Gender Relations and Employment*, Oxford University Press, Oxford.

Crompton, R. (2001), 'Gender Restructuring, Employment, and Caring', *Social Politics*, Fall, pp. 266–291.

Crompton, R. and G. Birkelund (2000), 'Employment and Caring in British and Norwegian Banking', *Work, Employment and Society*, vol. 14, pp. 331–352.

Crompton, R. and F. Harris (1998), 'Explaining Women's Employment Patterns', *British Journal of Sociology*, vol. 12, pp. 297–315.

Crompton, R. and K. Sanderson (1990), *Gendered Jobs and Social Change*, Unwin Hyman, London.

Crouch, C. (1999), *Social Change in Western Europe*, Oxford University Press, Oxford.

Dex, S. and A. McCulloch (1997), *Flexible Employment*, Macmillan, London.

Department for Trade and Industry (2000), *Work & Parents: Competitiveness and Choice*, Stationery Office, London

Esping-Andersen, G. (1990), *The Three Worlds of Welfare Capitalism*, Polity Press, Cambridge.

Esping-Andersen, G. (1999), *The Social Foundations of Post-Industrial Societies*, Polity Press, Cambridge.

Esping-Andersen, G. (2000), 'Interview on Post-industrialism and the Future of the Welfare State', *Work, Employment and Society*, vol. 14, pp. 757–769.

Fraser, N. (1994), 'After the Family Wage', *Political Theory*, vol. 22, pp. 591–618.

Fukuyama, F. (1992), *The End of History and the Last Man*, H. Hamilton, London.

Fukuyama, F. (1999), *The Great Disruption*, Profile Books, London.

Ginn, J., S. Arber, J. Brannen, A. Dale, S. Dex, P. Elias, P. Moss, J. Pahl, C. Roberts and J. Rubery (1996), 'Feminist Fallacies: A Reply to Hakim on Women's Employment', *British Journal of Sociology*, vol. 7, pp. 167–174.

Gittins, D. (1993), *The Family in Question*, Macmillan, London.

Glass, J. L. and S. B. Estes (1997), 'The Family Responsive Workplace', *Annual Review of Sociology*, vol. 23, pp. 289–313.

Glucksmann, M. (2000), *Cottons and Casuals: The Gendered Organisation of Labour in Time and Space*, Sociology Press, Durham.

Gottfried, H. (2000), 'Compromising Positions: Emergent Neo-Fordisms and Embedded Gender Contracts', *British Journal of Sociology*, vol. 51, pp. 235–259.

Granovetter, M. and R. Swedberg (eds) (1992), *The Sociology of Economic Life*, Westview Press, Boulder.

Hakim, C. (1996), *Key Issues in Women's Work*, Athlone, London.

Hakim, C. (2000), *Work-Lifestyle Choices in the 21st Century: Preference Theory*, Oxford University Press, Oxford.

Halford, S., M. Savage and A. Witz (1997), *Gender, Careers and Organisations*, Macmillan, London.

Hirdman, Y. (1998), 'State Policy and Gender Contracts', in E. Drew, R. Emerek and E. Mahon (eds), *Women Work and the Family in Europe*, Routledge, London.

Hirst, P. and J. Zeitlin (1997), 'Flexible Specialisation', in J. R. Hollingsworth and R. Boyer (eds), *Contemporary Capitalism*, Cambridge University Press, Cambridge.

Holmwood, J. (2000), 'Three Pillars of Welfare State Theory', *European Journal of Social Theory*, vol. 3, pp. 23–50.

Irwin, S. and W. Bottero (2000), 'Market Returns? Gender and Theories of Change in Employment Relations', *British Journal of Sociology*, vol. 51, pp. 261–280.

Kristol, W. (1998), 'A Conservative Perspective on Public Policy and the Family', in C. Wolfe (ed.), *The Family, Civil Society, and the State*, Rowman and Littlefield, Oxford.

Levine, D. (1987), *Reproducing Families: The Political Economy of English Population History*, Cambridge University Press, Cambridge.

Lewis, J. (1992), 'Gender and the Development of Welfare Regimes', *Journal of European Social Policy*, vol. 2, pp. 159–173.

Lewis, J. (1997), 'Gender and Welfare Regimes, Some Further Thoughts', *Social Politics*, vol.4, pp. 160–207.

MacInnes, J. (2001), *The Nanny State, the Narcissism Taboo and the Lethal Mutation*, BSA, Manchester.

Marshall, T. H. (1948, reprinted 1963), 'Citizenship and Social Class', in *Sociology at the Crossroads*, Heinemann, London.

Maynard, M. (1995), 'Beyond the "Big Three": The Development of Feminist Theory into the 1990s', *Women's History Review*, vol. 4, pp. 259–281.

McRae, S. (1999), 'Introduction', in S. McRae (ed.), *Changing Britain: Families and Households in the 1990s*, Oxford University Press, Oxford.

Molyneux, M. (1979), 'Beyond the Domestic Labour Debate', *New Left Review*, no. 116.

Morgan, P. (1995), *Farewell to the Family?*, IEA Health and Welfare Unit, London.

Nolan, J. (2002), 'The Intensification of Everyday Life', in B. Burchell, D. Ladipo and F. Wilkinson (eds), *Job Insecurity and Work Intensification*, Routledge, London.

O'Connor, J. S., A. S. Orloff and S. Shaver (1999), *States, Markets, Families*, Cambridge University Press, Cambridge.

O'Reilly, J. (1992), 'Where Do You Draw the Line?', *Work, Employment and Society*, vol. 6, pp. 369–396.

Pahl, R. E. (1984), *Divisions of Labour*, Blackwell, Oxford.

Pateman, C. (1989), 'The Patriarchal Welfare State', in C. Pateman (ed.), *The Disorder of Women*, Polity Press, Cambridge.

Perrons, D. (1999), 'Flexible Working Patterns and Equal Opportunities in the European Union', *The European Journal of Women's Studies*, vol. 6, pp. 391–418.

Pfau-Effinger, B. (1999), 'The Modernization of Family and Motherhood in Western Europe', in R. Crompton (ed.), *Restructuring Gender Relations and Employment*, Oxford University Press, Oxford.

Polanyi, K. (1957), *The Great Transformation*, Beacon Press, Boston.

Pollert, A. (1988), 'The Flexible Firm: Fixation or Fact?', *Work, Employment and Society*, vol. 2, pp. 281–316.

Purcell, K., T. Hogarth and C. Simm (1999), *Whose flexibility?*, Joseph Rowntree Foundation, York.

Rose, N. (1993), 'Government, Authority and Expertise in Advanced Liberalism', *Economy and Society*, vol. 22, pp. 283–299.

Rost, H. (1999). 'Fathers and Parental Leave in Germany', in P. Moss and F. Deven (eds), *Parental Leave: Progress or Pitfall?*, NIDI/CBGS Publications, The Hague/Brussels.

Rubery, J., S. Horrell and B. Burchell (1994), 'Part-Time Work and Gender Inequality in the Labour Market', in A. M. Scott (ed.), *Gender Segregation and Social Change*, Oxford University Press, Oxford.

Scott, J. D., F. Alwin and M. Braun (1996), 'Generational Changes in Gender-Role Attitudes: Britain in a Cross-National Perspective', *Sociology*, vol. 30, pp. 471–492.

Seccombe, W. (1993), *Weathering the Storm*, Verso, London.

Skocpol, T. (1992), *Protecting Soldiers and Mothers*, Harvard University Press, Cambridge, MA.

Smith, V. (1997), 'New Forms of Work Organisation', *Annual Review of Sociology*, vol. 23, pp. 315–339.

Sporton, D. (1993), 'Fertility: The Lowest Level in the World', in D. Noin and R. Woods (eds), *The Changing Population of Europe*, Blackwell, Oxford.

Sullivan, O. (2000), 'The Division of Domestic Labour', *Sociology*, vol. 34, pp. 437–456.

Thair, T. and A. Risdon (1999), 'Women in the Labour Market', *Labour Market Trends*, March, pp. 103–114.

Urry, J. (2000), *Sociology Beyond Societies*, Routledge, London.

Wacjman, J. (1998), *Managing Like a Man*, Polity Press, Cambridge.

Weber, M. (1958), 'Bureaucracy', in H. Gerth and C. W. Mills (eds), *From Max Weber*, Routledge, London.

Yeandle, S. (1984), *Women's Working Lives*, Tavistock, London.

Chapter 9

Men's Parental Leave: A Manifestation of Gender Equality or Child-orientation?

Lisbeth Bekkengen

Introduction

Alongside the issue of equal pay for equal or equivalent work and that of equal opportunities in the labour market, the taking of parental leave is probably one of the most frequently-discussed issues in the Swedish debate on gender equality. These issues are often linked together and attention is drawn to the fact that women are paid lower wages and have fewer opportunities for career advancement since they have the main responsibility for children and the home, that is, a responsibility often developed, or indeed increased, as a result of routines established during the period of parental leave.

From this perspective, parental leave which is more evenly divided may be a key to equality in many spheres. When men take more parental leave and women less, one would expect the domestic work and child care to be more evenly shared. Furthermore, men as well as women should be regarded as parents from a labour market point of view and women's periods of absence from work could become shorter. Taken together this might promote an upward trend in women's wages and increase their possibilities of pursuing a career.

With these high aspirations in mind, a look at the parental leave statistics makes for gloomy reading. For more than 30 years now, men and women in Sweden have been able to divide the parents' allowance days evenly. In practice, however, men do not take 50 per cent of their entitlement. Indeed, statistics for the year 2003 show that they take only 17 per cent.

Considering the unique position of parents' insurance in equality politics, one question needs to be asked: 'How is it possible that women still take the major share of the parental leave allowance?' There is a great difference between men and women but there are also great variations among fathers. In my study of men and women's parenthood and parents' leave I found that men can openly express – without fear of being politically incorrect – that a longer period of parental leave is 'a woman's thing'. Other men maintain that the natural thing is for women and men to share the parental leave, but then they come to the conclusion that it was just not practicable in *their* case, as some obstacles appeared along the way. But there were also men who took parental leave despite problems in the workplace and a financial loss (Bekkengen, 2002). How are we to understand these variations?

The discourse of impediments to men's parental leave

The most common arguments for men not taking parental leave are that attitudes and conditions in the workplace do not permit it, it is not economically feasible, or the woman does not want to share the parental leave with him. In my analysis of men and women's parental leave I have chosen to label the arguments as the discourse of impediments to men's parental leave (Bekkengen, 2002). I do so because I found that the notion of impediments is not always in accordance with their own practice or with the actual experience of others around them. Moreover, when problems, which are often taken as a pretext for men not being able to take parental leave, occur in the workplace in connection with women's parental leave, there is no talk of them being possible impediments. Although the problems are the same, the effects are interpreted in a gender-specific manner. Let us examine more closely the three arguments about the workplace, the financial situation and the woman as the impediments to men's parental leave.

Workplace-related problems

The key factor in the problems that may arise, and the negative reactions in the workplace that may occur in connection with parental leave, is the type of work the parent has. I have chosen to make a distinction between collectively, individually and team-based work. When the work is collectively based, there are many in the workplace with the same or equivalent competence. In everyday work they cooperate a great deal and they have the knowledge and skills to perform each other's tasks. When one of the employees is taking parental leave there are usually two alternatives; either the employer allocates the tasks of the parent on leave to the others in the work team, or else he/she employs someone else to do the work. Both alternatives result in higher work load for the colleagues since there are fewer people to do the job or they have an untrained colleague in the team. In these circumstances there *may* be negative reactions from the colleagues. However, the employer gets the goods and/ or services produced without major problems, and therefore there is little reason for a negative reaction.

The situation is different when the work of the parent on leave is individually based. In this case the colleagues rarely suffer through the absence of the parent concerned. An individually-based work implies having a special competence. There is no other person who can perform the absent parent's job. Thus, it becomes the employer's headache to find someone with the special competence to take their place. The colleagues will be less involved since they usually do not enter each other's fields of competence in everyday work. In these circumstances there *may* be negative reactions from the management.

In some workplaces the work is organized through projects, which usually means that the employee has a team-based job within the framework of the project. This means they have a special competence, while at the same time they are very much dependent on the others in the project to be able to do their job. In connection with parental leave both colleagues and management are affected. The management might have to replace the special competence, and the colleagues will be affected negatively since their working process will be changed when one in the project group disappears. Thus, there *may* be negative reactions from both colleagues and management. Whether the tasks are bound to time and space, and whether they can be put on hold or not are also matters of importance, but it would lead us too far to look at this now (for further reading, see Bekkengen, 2002).

I reiterate that there 'may' be consequences in the form of negative reactions and attitudes. In my study I was surprised to find that a parental leave, which had been planned and/or taken, caused so few negative reactions in the workplace. Since I have interviewed both the parents and their managers and colleagues, I can disregard any suspicion that the positive picture is just a sign of wanting to give a politically-correct impression.

Interestingly, the above-mentioned conditions are in no way specific for men but are very much the same for women's parental leave. There is one important aspect, though, where men differ from women: for fathers there are more options. Men can choose if, when, and how long they will be on parental leave to a totally different extent. Although fathers today are expected to avail themselves of at least part of their entitled parental leave, the risk is very small that they would be seen as bad parents – or men for that matter – if they should choose to refrain from taking it. A mother, however, would in all probability be questioned both as a woman and a parent, if she should start to negotiate her parental leave. 'If women do not want to take parental leave, they should not have children' (Ahrne and Roman, 1997). *As soon as there are alternative modes of action, identified problems are seen as impediments.* But if there are no alternatives, the problems simply have to be solved. This is the most common situation when a woman is concerned, but it might also apply to men when they have decided to take parental leave. *One must distinguish between problems and impediments.*

Financial problems

Another weighty argument often given in response to the question as to why men refrain from parental leave is that it is not economically feasible, as the man often has a higher income than the woman of the family.[1] But even on this point my study yields a surprising result: The interviewees have not – with few exceptions – discussed the division from a financial point of view, even though there is a fairly wide variation

---

[1]   The Parental Allowance has varied during the years. At the time of my study the benefits were 80 percent of the income. The upper limit to the amount of parental allowance that can be paid – the so called ceiling – equalled a yearly income of 284 000 SEK.

in income among the different groups of parents, and there are couples where the woman or the man can be the high income earner (see Bekkengen 2002, app. 3).

Of course there are many parent couples who de facto lose more when the man is on parental leave than when the woman is. But this gives rise to many questions. To what extent do the financial reasons actually serve as an explanation, when one considers the number of men who refrain from or just take shorter parental leave? One of the studies conducted by the National Social Insurance Board (Riksförsäkringsverket) shows that 80 percent of those questioned considered that the financial situation determines the taking of parental leave. When they examined how the participating parents actually divided the parental leave, however, it turned out that those parent couples who had the highest income difference – to the woman's *or* the man's advantage – were also those who shared their days most equally (Riksförsäkringsverket, 2000). Statistics from the Central Bureau of Statistics (SCB) further show that the higher income men have, up to the income ceiling,[2] the greater the share of the parental leave they actually take (Nyman and Petterson, 2003).

Furthermore, one may well ask how many of the parent couples that belongs to the category where the man has an income high above the ceiling, that is, fathers whose income decreases by more than 20 percent. A study carried out by the social insurance office in Jönköping showed that this category was fairly small (Linderoth, 2001). The statistics from SCB indeed show that the number of fathers who are above the ceiling has increased from 15 percent for children born in 1993, to 24 percent for children born in 1996. At the same time we can observe that 76 percent have incomes below the ceiling (Nyman and Petterson, 2003).

Other questions involve how much the family loses when they compare the alternatives. And do they calculate this as carefully as they do when for example their housing loans are to be renewed? What weight is attached to the financial arguments in this case compared with other financial priorities? Another question of interest is how large a part of the parental leave do those men take who have the possibility of obtaining further compensation in addition to the parents' allowance. Here there are big information gaps.

My point is that while the financial argument is both logical and rational, one is justified to ask a critical question, namely to what extent the financial situation actually is the motivating factor behind the division of parental leave. It is easier to consciously or unconsciously resort to logical and rational arguments than to make norms and conditions for men and women's parenthood visible; norms and conditions that are not always aligned with the strong gender equality discourse existing in Sweden.

Even if there is not much discussion about economy in my study, the arguments are nevertheless present. However, they appear to be less rational and logical in the light of other aspects. For example, the man's income can be used as an argument both by couples where he earns more than she does and where he has the lower income. In the former, the argument is that the couple would lose too much money

---

[2]   The upper limit to the amount of parental allowance that can be paid.

since his income will be substantially decreased during the parental leave. In one case a couple had actually planned to share the parental leave. The financial argument only arose when the man, as a new father, changed jobs and got a large salary increase. Effectively, they considered they could afford to share when there was less room for manoeuvring, from an economic point of view, but not when the space for manoeuvring was extended. Moreover, it later turned out that the man changed jobs again, as he was not satisfied at his well-paid workplace, and the new job meant a lower salary. Financial considerations appear to be taken into account on a short-term basis and as an argument for not taking parental leave, but not in the long run when it comes to choosing a job.

Interestingly, there are cases where financial reasons are cited as a motive for the man to refrain from parental leave, although it is the woman who has the highest income. They turn the argument round and claim that the man has too low a parent's allowance to stay at home. It is also clear that how much the man as an individual gets into his wallet is more important than the family's joint income. In this light it becomes quite logic and rational to refrain from parental leave; it is always the parent on leave – regardless of whether the parent is a man or a woman, a high-income or a low-income earner – who gets a decreased income during that time. An important factor in the debate should therefore be whether the parents practice a joint domestic economy, or if each has his or her own room for manoeuvring, independent of the other's income.

The woman as a problem

Another, not altogether unknown argument, is the statement that it is the women who *want* to stay at home during all of the parental leave, thereby preventing the men from availing themselves of their opportunities. In this discussion people tend to obscure the rules on which the parents' insurance is based. When the woman stays home during all or most of the parental leave, it is not she who refrains from transferring her days to him; instead, it is the man who transfers his days to her. Since 1995, if the parents have joint custody, the mother and father each have the same number of days. At present, this means 240 days for each parent. There is, however, a possibility for both the mother and the father to transfer a maximum of 180 days to the other parent. If you strain the argument of the woman as an obstacle, it could be suggested that the man, against his will, transfers his days to the woman. As far as I know, there is no research indicating this, but like the other arguments about impediments for men, there are strong notions about the woman actually being the obstacle.

In my studies I have never come across any mothers, fathers, colleagues or managers who have been able to confirm the hypothesis that it is actually women who do not want to share parental leave (see Bekkengen, 1996, 1997, 2002). On the contrary, it has largely been men's wishes and needs that have been decisive for the division. The tendency is that women enter into and understand men's situations and problems while men look at women's situations more from a distance. The fact that there may be problems which are just as difficult for a woman as for a man, and that her conditions for parental leave may be just as difficult, is something which is concealed even from the woman herself. If there is one thing everybody agrees upon – fathers, mothers, colleagues and managers alike – it is that men's parental leave should be voluntary. You cannot force a man to take parental leave; it would neither benefit the man, the woman nor the child. The result is of course – however cynical it sounds – that women's parental leave of necessity must be based on adaptation, since a small child needs practical and emotional care for its survival and progress.

Consequently it is men and how they choose to use their freedom of choice – and not women and their power at home – that determines the division of parental leave. Not all couples have direct negotiations or discussions about any division; it only happens when the man has openly expressed that he wishes to take a share of the parental leave. With other couples the question is never raised; it is taken for granted that the woman is the parent who should stay at home.

It turns out that men on parental leave – or those who were at least planning for it – made this decision long before the child was born, maybe even long before they met their present partner. A man's parental leave seems to have very little to do with pressures from the woman. And there is nothing to suggest that men's wishes appear only when they are becoming fathers. How then is one to understand that some men wish to take parental leave while others do not? And why do some men refrain while others put their plans into effect even when conditions are not favourable?

In my analysis of men and women's parenthood and parental leave I came to the conclusion that to a large extent it is about whether men embody a child-oriented masculinity. However, it is quite possible for men to limit their child-oriented masculinity to a discursive level only without having to put it into practice (Bekkengen, 2002). Let us take a closer look at the arguments behind my reasoning.

The child-oriented masculinity

Society's increased focus on children's well-being has made new demands on parenthood. As I see it, this focus also influences the norms of what a man should be like, more precisely, it gives rise to what I call a child-oriented masculinity.

At least at a discursive and ideological level, an increasing value has been placed upon children. During the 20th century there have been great efforts to strengthen children's rights and position in society (Holmdahl, 2000). A strong focus on the child is characteristic of the Nordic countries, and maybe Sweden in particular (see for example De Bouczan, 2000; Haas, 1993; Hirdman, 1998). For most parents it is natural to try to organize their everyday life from what is assumed to be in the best interest of the child. Few people question the discourse that the child's best interest is of primary importance and that the child is one of life's great subjects for celebration (see for example Bejerot and Härenstam, 1995; Bekkengen, 2002; Bäck-Wiklund and Bergsten, 1997; Holter and Aarseth, 1994). Nowadays it is also declared in political discussions that there should be a child perspective in all decisions, and it is maintained that children must have greater influence in more spheres in the community. The importance of children's rights has been confirmed through the United Nations Children's Convention and the Social Services Act, for example.

This discourse, however, does not imply that actions and decisions automatically result in what is best for the child *in reality*. On the contrary, we are constantly confronted with alarming reports about children who fare badly in today's Sweden within the family, in child care and at school. Likewise, the Swedish equality discourse does not govern all decisions and actions towards a more even division of power, resources and responsibility between men and women. But I dare maintain that the discourse about a child-centred focus is much less questioned than the equality discourse. Very likely this also influences the shaping of the 'new man' and modern fatherhood. Thus child-oriented masculinity becomes legitimate without the obligation of equality between men and women. The development of a child-oriented masculinity alongside the child-centred focus can be regarded as a manifestation of 'men always fit', irrespective of radical social changes and irrespective of what society is like (see for example Kimmel, 1996).

Bergman and Hobson (2002) also point out that there has been a political shift in the view on men as fathers, from a focus on economy and responsibilities to care and rights (Björnberg, 1994). The main objective is to safeguard the child's welfare and interests, specifically understood as placing the contact with the father first. This contact must not be jeopardized by financial demands (see also Björnemalm et al., 2001). If one compares the conditions of Swedish fathers to those of fathers in other European countries, the trend becomes clearer. A consequence of the Swedish Rights scheme is, for example, that joint custody has become the norm, which was one of the so-called Daddies Group's [Pappagruppen] (Socialdepartementet, 1995) most important proposals for change.

Following the development of a common debate and the political message, one can see that the issue of parental leave has begun to lean more and more towards a relationship between dads and their children, taking the focus away from the relationship between women and men. Men should take parental leave and have good relations with the children for their own sake (see Carlsen, 1995; Huttunen, 1996). The idea is that this will result in happier, healthier men who live longer. Another strong argument is that children should have access to both parents, and that children get on better when they grow up together with – or at least in contact with – their father (see for example Socialdepartementet, 1995). It is largely a matter of masculinity and focusing on the child and the interaction between these. Let us now take a closer look at the characteristics of a child-oriented masculinity.

Characteristics of a child-oriented masculinity

A child-oriented masculinity implies having space for close relationships with children in general and parental leave in particular. Children constitute an important part of the good things in life and relationships are a central part of being a man. I am not just referring to being the father of a child; rather it is about attaching great value to relationships and contact with children, as well as having an express interest in children's welfare. Children are associated not only with women's responsibilities and duties but also as part of men's commitments beyond the responsibility of simply providing for them. Men need the relationship with children in order to develop as human beings (Björnberg, 1994; Brandth and Kvande, 1998; Carlsen 1995).

But a child-oriented masculinity may well imply that the child-orientation is stronger at a discursive level than in practice, or that it exists only at the first level without influencing the latter. When practice fails to correspond with the discourse there is a discrepancy. This is due to the fact that men can choose whether they want to put the child-oriented discourse into practice or not. When they choose to refrain, it neither threatens fatherhood nor masculinity. Men remain good fathers, and a child-oriented masculinity does not demand a child-oriented practice, which would, for example, entail a longer paternity leave. When the discrepancy occurs the explanations seem to be shifted to another discourse, namely the one about impediments to men's paternal leave.

Conversely, the men who represent a child-oriented masculinity and who unconditionally put it into practice are also the men who take relatively long parental leave. As I mentioned before, these men made up their minds long before the child was born, and in some cases even before they entered into a partnership (Olsen, 2000). Representing a child-oriented masculinity does not presuppose one's own fatherhood, any more than fatherhood automatically entails a child-oriented masculinity. In my study there are male colleagues who do not have children themselves and who regard parenthood something akin to science fiction but still embrace values in line with this masculinity (see Bekkengen, 2002). Young men without children can take for granted that once a man becomes a parent he should also be a committed father, including the idea of taking parental leave. This attitude can be taken-for-granted although parenthood in itself may seem distant.

Alongside men's entitlement to space for manoeuvring and freedom of choice in relation to commitment to parenthood and parental leave, there is also the strong discourse of focus on the child. Therefore it is not totally legitimate for men not to represent a child-oriented masculinity or to refrain from putting it into practice. The discrepancy between practice and the prevailing discourse can be solved, however, by making regret into a form of amends. Regret legitimizes 'wrong' choices and decisions. The argument is that the men did not realize what was best for them but now they regret it, or they will probably do so later in life. In this way men are released from potential guilt and liability.

In my study there is an example of a man who in his new family looks back to his previous relationship with regret in his eyes. Here there is a strong motivation for not repeating his mistakes. When the man becomes a father in a relationship with a new partner he is given a new chance to live up to the discourse and also the practice of child centring. But this new chance does not apply to his children in the family he left behind; it applies only to himself in the new family. Regret becomes a form of amends for the man's own sake. Thereby the risks, too, are reduced – the risks of not putting the child-oriented masculinity into practice, for example by refraining from taking parental leave. If it turns out that it was a mistake to do so, it can always be repaired afterwards by regret! This confirms men's scope of manoeuvring still more and indicates that men's freedom of choice rules *parallel with* fatherhood.

The difference between men's orientation towards the child and the family

In recent years many researchers have discussed the ongoing change regarding masculinity. It is spoken of in terms of men becoming everyday dads (Åström, 1990), and that men nowadays want to *be part of* the family rather than *having* a family (Holter and Aarseth, 1994). That men take parental leave is seen as a manifestation of this change. A great number of researchers have discussed the 'new man' in terms of a family-oriented man (for example Björnberg, 1994, 1998; Bäck-Wiklund and Bergsten, 1997; Holter and Aarseth, 1994; Johansson, 1998; Kugelberg, 1999; Nilsson, 1992; Olsen, 2000). From my analysis – and seeing the research results of others – one has reason to wonder if it is really men's *family* orientation we are witnessing. Given that the discussion concerns heterosexual parent couples, a family orientation should also include an orientation towards and/or closer relations to women, since men's families do not only consist of children. This is not the case, however, when we talk about the 'new man'. What we witness is a *child orientation*.

Statistics also show that even if women spend more time with their children than men do, men's time together with children has increased between 1984 and 1993, while there is no change for women during the same period. At the same time men's share of the domestic work has increased, but not by men spending more time on this work but because the time women spend on domestic work has decreased (Flood and Gråsjö, 1997; SOU, 1998, p. 6; Pleck, 1993).

The 'new man' and child-oriented masculinity is more about the relationship between parent/dad-child than about the relationship woman-man. This may be an answer to the question of how the gender relationship can remain almost unchanged despite men's seemingly increased orientation towards family and despite far-reaching reforms (see Bäck-Wiklund and Bergsten, 1997).

Child-orientation or equality?

Thus, a child-oriented masculinity does not necessarily imply a masculinity directed towards femininity. Nor can one equate child-oriented men and egalitarian men. A child-oriented masculinity refers to men's relationships with children, while a move towards femininity, or equality, is about the relationship between women and men.

In my study I could identify three dominating discourses: that mothers and fathers are essentially different (that is, the concept of difference), the equality discourse, and child-centring. Both the man and the woman support the child-centred focus at a discursive level, but in practice it is usually the woman who is responsible for bringing about the best interests of the child. At the same time she is sensitive to the man's wishes and needs (see Bekkengen, 2002). There is indeed a strong political discourse that there should be equality between men and women, but it is, above all, the man's interest in and good relations with the child that the woman appreciates. Making demands on equality could be seen as a threat to the best interests of the child. A focus on the child remains an unquestioned, self-evident and normative discourse, in a totally different way than the equality discourse. The notion that men and women are essentially different also legitimizes the notion that they do not necessarily have the same obligations and rights in the family.

A partner relationship consisting of a man who represents a child-oriented masculinity does not necessarily mean that he will share the responsibility and the practical tasks associated with the child on the same terms as the woman. It is obvious, not least by men's motives for parental leave, that it is their relationship with the children – that is, child-orientation – and not the relationship with the women – that is, equality – that is central. Both the parents, the managers and colleagues in my study see the advantages of shared parental leave, mainly from the point of view of the relationship between parent and child. That the result should be gender equality is seldom mentioned. Actions taken with the aim of increasing men's use of parental leave would probably lead in different directions, depending on what the primary goal is: to achieve equality, the child's access to both parents, or a changed masculinity. The child's access to both parents concerns the relationship between the child and its parents. The idea that men, through parental leave, will develop stronger and better relations with their children is also associated with the parent–child relation. It is believed that masculinity will change when men are able to have these good relations. In this way men will come into contact with their feelings and will develop their capability of care-giving, which can also be useful in other relations, such as working-life (see for example JämO, 1992; Socialdepartementet, 1995). However, the goal that men's parental leave will lead to equality does not primarily concern the relationship parents/dads and children, but the relationship between men and women. If you do not keep these different relationships apart, there is a risk of simplifying the situation and jumping to the conclusion that good fathers equate to egalitarian men (Björnberg, 1994).

Ongoing changes

The picture of modern fatherhood is often described as being contradictory and divided (see for example Plantin, 2003). There is a difference in opinion about how great the changes have actually been during the most recent decades. As I see it, this seemingly ambiguous picture can be explained by the fact that on the one hand researchers are at different analytical levels, on the other, they are discussing different kinds of relations. Firstly, it is about what values and ambitions men express, and then how men act in practice; there can be great discrepancies between expression and practice. Secondly, one must – as I have argued above – keep apart the concept of men's relations to children and that of relations between men and women. These social relationships constitute two different social structures.

In my opinion it is uncertain whether parental leave results in men being regarded as parents by the labour market on the same terms as women. It is also uncertain if men on parental leave share the parental responsibility with women, which was the original intention of parents' insurance. That fathers today are *encouraged* to take parental leave seems to affect the relations between fathers and children in a positive way, while the conditions of women in parenthood and gainful employment are being neglected.

In answer to the questions whether, and for that matter, in what way modern fatherhood is a result of a systematic development, I maintain that the changes have mainly taken place at a discursive level and in the relationship between men and children. This implies that we see a child-oriented masculinity which is not necessarily put into practice. Men retain their space for manoeuvring, while at the same time there is a strong discursive stress on focusing on the child; the consequence of this is that relations between men and women are not correspondingly affected.

Among the parent couples and in the workplaces of my study there is a notion that it is common today for men to be on parental leave and that, nowadays, men take longer parental leave (Bekkengen, 2002). 'I believe it [paternity leave] is becoming more and more common. It's almost a modern thing now,' as one of the fathers-to-be expresses it. To take parental leave is now considered the norm for fathers (see Carlsen, 1995). In the same way there are notions that fathers today reduce their working time as a consequence of parenthood. But the notion fails to correspond with current parental leave statistics (see Riksförsäkringsverket, 2003), and part-time work for men as a result of parenthood is principally non-existent (Flood and Gråsjö, 1997; Hörnqvist, 1997; SOU, 1998, p. 6).

The notions of the interviewees do not only deviate from available statistics but also from their own experiences and practice. On one hand they say that it is common today for men to take parental leave, but on the other they know of few, if any, who have actually done so. The reasoning may start with the comment that there is a considerable proportion of men on paternity leave within their own organization and then end with the report of one man who had stayed home with his child after it had had an operation. Or 'the men on parental leave' may be transformed into one individual father in another department, when it comes down to actual fact. That one individual man takes his parental responsibility and makes his parenthood visible, can be transformed into a pattern, which is then applied to many men in the workplace. The discourse of the 'new man' who has a great deal of time and space for parenthood – that is, the child-oriented man – has had a huge impact (see Hearn, 2002). But how is the child-oriented masculinity to be assessed in relation to other types of masculinity?

There is an order of precedence of masculinities, where men take an attitude to a hegemonic masculinity (Connell, 1995). This involves a ranking of men leading to a hierarchy within the category of men. Where child-oriented masculinity is placed within the masculinity hierarchy is, however, unclear. On the one hand there are signs indicating that child-oriented men encounter resistance from other men. It is not uncommon to hear examples of men who have met negative reactions and sanctions in the workplace in connection with plans for parental leave. Whether it is about the discourse of impediments or of obstacles in the practice is not quite clear but, all the same, it could be seen as an indication that child-oriented masculinity is not at the top of the hierarchy.

On the other hand one may observe that it is the 'new man' who actually represents the child-oriented masculinity; a masculinity described in positive words and pictures. The positive pictures are there literally in advertisements as well as on newspapers' sports pages (see for example Hagström, 1999). This should indicate that, in this connection, it is about a masculinity of high ranking in the hierarchy (cf. Brandth and Kvande, 1998). Besides, paternity leave is regarded as a benefit and a competitive means to attract and keep desirable workers. It is considered 'modern' to be *in favour of* paternity leave. An attractive and 'modern' workforce consists of men representing a child-oriented masculinity (Bekkengen, 2002). This could suggest that modern fatherhood and child-oriented masculinity are related to class (Plantin, 2003; Åström, 1990). But as I see it, it is more about a reflective fatherhood rooted in a cultural capital than about financial conditions.

Not only encouragement and positive pictures suggests that child-oriented masculinity is hegemonic or in the progress of becoming so, but also the fact that people have an impression of men's parental leave being much more widespread than statistics and experience suggest. One of the most important characteristics of the hegemonic masculinity is the fact that there are few men living up to it, but that everybody has to relate to it, either directly or indirectly (Connell, 1995).

There are indications that the child-oriented masculinity is on its way to getting a hegemonic status (see Bergman and Hobson, 2002; Morgan, 2002; Plantin et al., 2000). However, this means that not only does child-oriented masculinity become highly ranked among men, but also that it will very likely be placed above femininity. Therefore, when interpreting changes to masculinity it is also important to consider the change in the light of men's structural power positions (see also Brod, 1994; Connell, 1987, 1995; Hondagneu-Sotelo and Messner, 1994; Kimmel, 1994; Segal, 1997). On the one hand masculinity could change without noticeably affecting the social and societal gender relationship. But on the other hand it is hardly likely that the gender structure would change if masculinity does not. A change of masculinity is therefore necessary but not enough; on its own it means that the relational state between men and women can endure and that the order of gender power hardly changes at all, not even with a child-oriented masculinity. Conversely, a change of the gender power order would presuppose a child-oriented masculinity. The most important point is to keep the parents/dads-children and men-women structures apart, when analysing the changes.

References

Ahrne, Göran and Christine Roman (1997), *Hemmet, barnen och makten. Förhandlingar om arbete och pengar i familjen*, SOU, 1997:139, Fritzes, Stockholm.
Åström, Lissie (1990), *Fäder och söner*, Carlsson, Stockholm.

Bäck-Wiklund, Margareta and Birgitta Bergsten (1997), *Det moderna föräldraskapet. En studie av familj och kön i förändring*, Natur och Kultur, Stockholm.

Bejerot, Eva and Annika Härenstam (1995), 'Att förena arbete och familj', in G. Westlander (ed.), *På väg mot det goda arbetet. Om akademikers arbetsvillkor*, Arbetslivsinstitutet, Stockholm.

Bekkengen, Lisbeth (1996), *Föräldraledighet om man så vill*, Jämställdhetscentrum 1996:15, Högskolan i Karlstad, Karlstad.

Bekkengen, Lisbeth (1997), *Föräldraledighet och pappaledighet – skyldigheter och rättigheter*, Högskolan i Karlstad, Karlstad.

Bekkengen, Lisbeth (2002), *Man får välja – om föräldraskap och föräldraledighet i arbetsliv och familjeliv*, Liber, Malmö.

Bergman, Helena and Barbara Hobson (2002), 'Compulsory Fatherhood: The Coding of Fatherhood in the Swedish Welfare State', in Barbara Hobson (ed.), *Making Men into Fathers: Men, Masculinities and the Social Politics of Fatherhood*, Cambridge University Press, Cambridge.

Björnberg, Ulla (1994), 'Mäns familjeorientering i förändring', in Ulla Björnberg, Anna-Karin Kollind and Arne Nilsson (eds.), *Janus & Genus. Om kön och social identitet i familj och samhälle*, Brombergs, Stockholm.

Björnberg, Ulla (1998), 'Family Orientation among Men: A Process of Change in Sweden', in Eileen Drew, Ruth Emerek and Evelyn Mahoon (eds), *Women, Work and the Family in Europe*, Routledge, London.

Björnemalm, Maud, Gustav von Essen and Börje Nilsson (2001), 'Tilltron till välfärden är hotad', *Dagens Nyheter, DN Debatt*, 2001-07-24.

Brandth, Berit and Elin Kvande (1998), 'Masculinity and Child Care: The Reconstruction of Fathering', *The Sociological Review*, vol. 46, no. 2.

Brod, Harry (1994), 'Some Thoughts on Some Histories of Some Masculinities: Jews and Other Others', in Harry Brod & Michael Kaufman (eds), *Theorizing Masculinities*, Sage, London.

Carlsen, Sören (1995), 'Når menn får barn. Om menns bruk av omsorgspermisjon osv', *Kvinneforskning*, no. 1.

Connell, R. W. (1987), *Gender & Power*, Polity Press, Cambridge.

Connell, R. W. (1995), *Masculinities*, Polity Press, Cambridge.

De Bouczan, Nicole (2000), 'Barn i sängen – men det är bara i Sverige som våra små får vara överallt', in *Nya Wermlandstidningen, Helgmagasinet*, 2000-12-16.

Flood, Lennart and Urban Gråsjö (1997), 'Tid för barn, tid för arbete. En undersökning av svenska hushålls tidsanvändning', in Göran Ahrne and Inga Persson (eds), *Familj, makt och jämställdhet*, SOU, 1997:138, Fritzes, Stockholm.

Haas, Linda (1993), 'Nurturing Fathers and Working Mothers: Changing Gender Roles in Sweden', in Jane C. Hood (ed.), *Men, Work and Family*, Sage, London.

Hagström, Charlotte (1999), *Man blir pappa. Föräldraskap och maskulinitet i förändring*, Nordic Academic Press, Lund.

Hearn, Jeff (2002), 'Men, Fathers and the State: National and Global Relations', in Barbara Hobson (ed.), *Making Men into Fathers: Men, Masculinities and the Social Politics of Fatherhood*, Cambridge University Press, Cambridge.

Hirdman, Yvonne (1998), *Med kluven tunga. LO och genusordningen*, Atlas, Stockholm.

Holmdahl, Barbro (2000), *Tusen år i det svenska barnets historia*, Studentlitteratur, Lund.

Holter, Öystein Gullvåg and Helene Aarseth (1994), *Mäns livssammanhang*, Bonnier, Stockholm.

Hondagneu-Sotelo, Pierette and Michael A. Messner (1994), 'Gender Display and Men's Power: The "New Man" and the Mexican Immigrant Man', in Harry Brod and Michael Kaufman (eds), *Theorizing Masculinities*, Sage, London.

Huttunen, Jouko (1996), 'Full-time Fathers and their Parental Leave Experience', in Björnberg, Ulla and Anna-Karin Kollind (eds), *Men's Family Relations*, Almqvist & Wiksell, Stockholm.

Hörnqvist, Martin (1997), 'Familjeliv och arbetsmarknad för män och kvinnor' in Göran Ahrne and Inga Persson (eds), *Familj, makt och jämställdhet*, SOU, 1997:138, Stockholm: Fritzes.

Johansson, Thomas (1998), 'Pappor och deras pappor', in Claes Ekenstam, Jonas Frykman, Thomas Johansson, Jari Kuosmanen, Jens Ljunggren and Arne Nilsson (eds), *Rädd att falla. Studier i manlighet*, Hedemora, Gidlunds.

Jämo (1992), *Det borde vara en merit*, Jämo:s rapportserie Nr 1.

Kimmel, Michael S. (1994), 'Masculinity as Homophobia: Fear, Shame, and Silence in the Construction of Gender Identity', in Harry Brod and Michael Kaufman (eds), *Theorizing Masculinities*, Sage, London.

Kimmel, Michael S. (1996), *Manhood in America: A Cultural History*, The Free Press, New York.

Kugelberg, Clarissa (1999), *Perceiving Motherhood and Fatherhood: Swedish Working Parents with Young Children*, Uppsala Universitet, Uppsala.

Linderoth, Kerstin (2001), *Uppföljning. Enkät om männens uttag av föräldrapenning*, 11/01, Försäkringskassan Jönköpings län, Jönköping.

Morgan, David (2002), 'Epilogue' in Barbara Hobson (ed.), *Making Men into Fathers: Men, Masculinities and the Social Politics of Fatherhood*, Cambridge University Press, Cambridge.

Nilsson, Arne (1992), 'Den nye mannen – finns han redan?,' in J. Acker, A. Baude, U. Björnberg, E. Dahlström, G. Forsberg, L. Gonäs, H. Holter, A. Nilsson (eds), *Kvinnors och mäns liv och arbete*, Stockholm: SNS.

Nyman, Håkan and Joakim Petterson (2003), 'Fler är pappalediga', *Välfärd*, nr 2, Statistiska Centralbyrån, Stockholm.

Olsen, Bente Marianne (2000), *Nye fædre på orlov – en analyse af de könsmässige aspekter ved föräldreorlovsordninger*, Köbenhavns Universitet, Köpenhamn.

Plantin, Lars (2003), 'Det "Nya faderskapet" – ett faderskap för alla? Om kön, klass och faderskap', in Johansson, Thomas and Jari Kuosmanen (eds), *Manlighetens många ansikten – fäder, feminister, frisörer och andra män*, Liber, Malmö.

Plantin, Lars, Sven-Axel Månsson and Jeremy Kearney (2000), 'Mäns föräldraskap. Om faderskap och manlighet i Sverige och England', *Socialvetenskaplig tidskrift*, vol. 7, no. 1–2.

Pleck, Joseph H. (1993), 'Are "Family-Supportive" Employer Policies Relevant to Men?', in Jane C. Hood (ed.) (1993), *Men, Work and Family*, London: Sage.

Riksförsäkringsverket (2000), *Både blir bäst*, RFV 2000:1.

Riksförsäkringsverket (2003), www.rfv.se.

Segal, Lynne (1997), *Slow Motion: Changing Masculinities, Changing Men*, London: Virago.

Socialdepartementet (1995), *Pappagruppens slutrapport*, Ds 1995:2.

SOU (1998:6), *Ty makten är din... Myten om det rationella arbetslivet och det jämställda Sverige. Betänkande från Kvinnomaktutredningen*, Fritzes, Stockholm.

Chapter 10

Dualities and Contradictions

Lena Gonäs and Jan Ch Karlsson

Introduction

We started this book by stipulating the objective to be a discussion of if and to what extent we can see changing gender relations in working life. In the book we present studies that are focusing on different analytical levels and are situated in different socio-economic settings. In the long perspective it has happened a lot, women's employment levels have increased and occupations do change their gender composition. But to what extent can we say that the power relations between the genders have changed in working life? Can we say that the divisions in work tasks are changing, that the ideas and values concerning what are female and male tasks are different? Are the interactions between women and men in workplaces different and have our inner mental perception of what women and men shall do changed? Joan Acker uses the concept 'ports of entry' when analysing the genderization processes in organizations (Acker, 1999). She says that it is not only how we put the demarcation lines and divides the work processes between women and men; it is also our values and ideologies, our actions and interactions with each other and how we relate mentally to these actions that form the gendering organizational processes. And one question is of course under what conditions new sets of values can develop. Let us turn back to the discussion in the introductory chapter on openings for change. Do our authors give us any hopeful examples of developments towards a more egalitarian working life?

Widening class differences

Chris Tilly concludes his chapter by focusing on the importance of the socially driven account of labour market inequality, after having taken his point of departure in the standard, efficiency-driven economic narrative of labour market inequality. Norms and stereotypes channel action in labour markets. Power disparities and the imperatives of organizational maintenance decisively shape labour market outcomes. Labour markets are constructed not simply of striving individuals, but of pervasive networks. Tilly has to a large extent the same approach as Acker, even though he is focusing on labour market inequalities instead of processes on the organizational level. His conclusions point to the fact that gender and ethnicity seems to have a reduced importance in relation to class. Income inequalities broaden among genders and among groups in the population with different ethnical background. Class is re-entering as the most important socially structuring factor in the data from the United States.

As categorical distinctions are persistent they often reappear in new forms and Tilly's message is that the inequalities within groups increases as the class differences grow. He discusses the concepts of 'Laissez-faire racism' and 'Laissez-faire sexism' referring to Afro-Americans and single mothers. When civil rights have been removed the obstacles to advancement for the Afro-American groups, unemployment and low incomes can be explained as individual shortcomings. The same type of reasoning can be used in relation to single mothers, and motivated according to Tilly the 1996 welfare law in the US with work requirements and time limits among other things on single mothers receiving government assistance. Any inequality between people belonging to the same category will thereby be explained by individual shortcomings, not just formal education and training but also skills in terms of 'soft' skills or social interaction skills. This leads Tilly to a discussion about the process of sorting of people and the question of who gets the good jobs. But it is also a question of the ranking of jobs and the value, working conditions and remuneration put to certain work tasks. The socially driven analysis focuses the explanation on norms and values, while the economic narrative stresses productivity differences. Tilly remarks that in many ways a close relationship can exist between efficiency and equity and that redistribution and attempts to change the market results can support economic growth. He implies that we can within limits choose the amount of inequality we want in a society by the institutions, policies and norms we adopt.

Restructuring gender divisions

Also Lena Gonäs discusses in her chapter the relations between policies, institutions and individual outcomes. Her empirical examples are taken from employment policies and economic change discussed on different analytical levels where gender divisions are in focus. The economic crises of the 1990s resulted in differentiation in the labour market along gendered lines. Swedish experiences show that the employment level is still lower than at the beginning of the 1990s and in a European context the decrease in female participation level in Sweden had few parallel examples. The cutbacks in the public sector, still continuing, has decreased the participation level among young women and increased the number of women not in the labour force. This means that the restructuring of the female dominated parts of the labour market has caused long lasting effects that have not caused general problems, but struck certain groups very hard, like the lower skilled occupations and specific socioeconomic categories, like single mothers. In the chapter by Liselotte Jakobsen we get an illustration of what these changes meant on an individual level, in this case for the assistant nurses – a traditionally female occupation. Using the framework of life mode analysis Jakobsen discusses the individual adaptation processes to reorganization and new working conditions. She uses the concept of neoculturation to explain how the assistant nurses tried to reorganize their life mode under new conditions. They were asked to seek education, being both low paid and less educated. Many of them refused as they were not in a position to make this effort, due to their family situation. Instead they tried as much as possible to recreate the conditions as they existed before the restructuring took place. This was possible to a certain extent, but they had to accommodate to new working conditions that collided with their values, ambitions and possibilities, not least the caring rationality of their life mode, the housewife's. The assistant nurses became squeezed between the demands from the system rationality of the career life mode and the care rationality of the housewife life mode. They felt inadequate, worn out and they suffered from stress. One result of the restructuring of the public sector in Sweden, seen from this perspective, is that the traditional gender order was reproduced, albeit in a slightly different form.

Developments of the gender divisions in the new media industry are discussed by Diane Perrons. She concludes that though the information and communication technology permits flexibility in working hours and location of work, the uneven distribution of domestic work and caring responsibilities is a constraint on that flexibility. As long as the uneven gender distribution of the unpaid reproductive work exists, again the new technology is just another tool for making it possible for women to adjust to growing demands from work and gender inequality in the domestic sphere. It is therefore necessary to take a wider approach and go beyond the workplace issues to the societal systems and the social support for caring and to issues of resolving inequalities in time use between women and men. Otherwise new technology introduced in existing social and economic settings will lead to further pressures and constrains on the already heavy total workload of the female labour force.

Epochal change and successive market adaptation

Rosemary Crompton raises the issue whether the contemporary changes in society can be seen as epochal and profound or more as an intensification of the existing exploitation under a capitalistic market system. Post-industrial welfare states, the third industrial revolution and the second modernity are concepts used by many social scientists to illustrate the profound economic and social changes that have occurred during the post-war period. Common for all these concepts is that the changing gender composition of the labour force or the breaking up of the traditional male breadwinner norm are not regarded as foundations for the invention of concepts for new social formations. An intense criticism from feminist scholars has, for example, been directed towards the work of Esping-Andersen (1991) on the three worlds of welfare state capitalism (for example by Borchorst, 1992; Orloff, 1993; Hobson, 1994). The criticism concerns the failure to take adequate account of the importance of the unpaid reproductive work still mostly done by women outside of paid employment. Specifically the concept of de-commodification has been debated.

In many countries, specifically in Northern Europe, half of the labour force is women. The younger generations of women have on average a higher educational level than men; but the norms and evaluation of what is regarded as women's work leads to much slower changes of the composition of the labour force and its educational structure. The norm of the male breadwinner exists parallel with more modern breadwinner models. And the process of transformation from a traditional male dominated labour market to a gender mixed labour market has taken many different forms. In some countries it has been supported by institutional arrangements politically driven by liberal or labour parties and trade unions, but not everywhere. Other countries have relied on the market or the family for organizing care for children and elderly. This has had the effect that women's participation in paid work has increased at a slower pace, but is still increasing, specifically for the younger age groups (Plantenga and Hansen, 1999). This means that a gender mixed labour market has developed by processes of adaptation to a male dominated hierarchical and occupationally segregated structure. Women's labour market participation has been regulated by possible entrances and a lot of closed doors.

From the different chapters it is possible to draw certain conclusions concerning possible changes and openings for a more egalitarian distribution of jobs and positions. Even though we can say that there have been profound changes in the levels of labour market participation for women, there are still strong gender divisions in the distribution of jobs and positions. Ruth Emerek gives us a thorough examination of the different ways of measuring gender segregation in quantitative terms. She shows that gender segregation in Denmark is decreasing, but it is very much dependent on the occupational categorization. The better the categorization are the higher the measure of segregation, which leads to the issue of the formulation of the measures as such. There is a positive correlation between segregation levels and women's employment rates. When controlling for the latter in a European comparison of EU15, Sweden and Demark usually having the highest segregation levels in Europe, are not significantly different from the EU15 average. This calls for caution when making comparisons between countries.

It is difficult to find evidence that says that we have been or are passing through an epochal change in the labour market. It is more the case of a slow transition, which of course shall not be underestimated, with adaptation to constant negotiations concerning gender divisions. The Finnish sociologist Liisa Rantalaiho uses the concept 'wage-earner motherhood' to illustrate the double position of women as both wage earners and mothers (Rantalaiho and Heiskanen, 1997). In accordance with Acker she also discusses the negotiations of a new gender contract between women and the welfare state in the Nordic context, with a contract that would facilitate women's adaptation to a more stable participation in the labour market over the life cycle. But the structures of male domination and female subordination were really never contested which can be illustrated by the following:

But men as a collective group were left in peace, their potential duties were not discussed – they allowed the contract to take place but did not actively participate in the negotiations. The logics of hierarchy and difference were made to bend a little to give women more room, but were basically never questioned. (Rantalaiho and Heiskanen, 1997, p. 28)

The daily practices imply that women as a group have to adapt to structures that do not easily yield; the mechanisms that work for reproduction of the existing gender structures are strong – and so is the potential of the single individual to adapt to existing conditions.

A dual perspective: Processes for change and for stability

The gendered power structure is shaped and reshaped by processes working on the societal, the organizational and the individual levels. When we are scrutinizing these levels we find ongoing processes involving both politics and market forces, organizational principles and individual choices and actions (Acker, 1992, 1999). Organizations can be seen as processes and practices rather than structures and they constitute important parts of the reshaping mechanisms of the existing gender structures. When we analyse the results from our different studies we can see that we are talking about both hidden and open processes.

To the more clear and open processes we can count the gender divisions of work tasks and women's and men's positions in the organizational hierarchy. As Ann Bergman's studies show us, even when women are in equal proportion at the workplace, the quantitative integration seldom is followed by a change in the hierarchical top positions of the organizations. The hierarchical gender divisions are still in place and the traditional power relations continue to survive. More hidden processes are those that seem not to have anything to do with gender divisions, but anyhow contribute to establish the gender order. One is the physical organization of the workplaces and how informal contacts are established. Recruitment policies also play a central role in the reshaping of the gender divisions in the workplace. We have internalized images of how we see the male and female character of certain occupations and skills. Deep rooted prejudices concerning women's suitability for reproductive work with a care oriented work relation and the suitability for men to have leading positions or work that demands physical strength and technical knowledge reshape the gender divisions in work tasks and organizational positions.

The structural conditions in the labour market have not changed enough to make it possible for both women and men to unite the roles of wage earner and parent. Rather, it seems to be more difficult than ever. Through Lisbeth Bekkengen's study we get a picture of a divided fatherhood. Bekkengen points to two important issues. The first is the difference between on one hand values and ambitions and on the other hand actions and practice. It is important again to take different analytical levels into account. On a rhetorical level fathers' participation in the parental leave and the daily care work in the family is of importance, but on the practical level very few fathers are actually doing that. Secondly, Bekkengen stresses the importance of separating the concepts of men's relation to children and the relations between women and men. This is important as Bekkengen questions if parental leave results in men being regarded as fathers from a labour market perspective. Her results illustrate that men can still keep the traditional male provider role in the labour market and engage in a modern father's role, not at all improving the conditions for women as parents and wage earners in the labour market. This is the effect of a child-oriented masculinity.

Lessons for further research

One important research issue concerns the processes of class differentiation and segregation/ integration by gender and/or ethnicity. What does it mean for different types of welfare state systems to have an increasing proportion of the population outside of the labour force in different types of economic and social support systems, or just outside any support system? Is it so that we will have a decreasing proportion of insiders with a more egalitarian development between classes, women and men and groups with different ethnical backgrounds? Chris Tilly puts this question to us in the beginning of the book and it seems appropriate to conclude the book by saying that these issues have to be analysed in a broader perspective including different employment regimes and welfare state settings.

Some lessons for future research can be learned from this book. We base the following suggestions on recurring themes from the contributions. A first lesson has to do with the technical aspects of measuring gender segregation at the labour market and in work organizations: the male as well as politically grounded biases in national and international occupational statistics. They still make studies of the extent and depth of gender segregation difficult when it comes to both validity and reliability. Better statistics are required.

This is becoming even more urgent – and complex – when we, as a second lesson, consider the contradictions between different forms of gender segregation. To begin with, formal quantitative equality in the labour market at one level can conceal inequality at lower levels. The official definition of sex equality used in many countries is the '40–60 principle', that is, that no sex should make up more than 60 percent in any aggregation. But if we happen to find an industrial branch that lives up to this goal, we often find that many work organizations and occupations in the branch are segregated. Further, if we find an equal organization it is often segregated in its hierarchy and between departments; and if we find an equal occupation, men and women often perform different work tasks despite their common occupational title. The *interplay* of gender segregation at different levels of working life ought to be studied in its own right. Ann Bergman's concept of 'segregated integration' is a source of inspiration, but it can be applied also outside organizations.

A third lesson is the role played by gender segregation in families for gender segregation in working life. Here are several aspects to take into account. An aspect that has been shown to be important is the gender division of labour at home – an area in which change is slower than many of us have thought. In relation to welfare state arrangements it is also crucial that we keep gender structures and parental structures analytically apart. A change in men's way of being a father does not necessarily have positive consequences for the gender practices in the family. Finally, we must also consider the influence of labour market phenomena on gender relations in families. It is, again, the *interplay* of mechanisms in working life and family life that needs to be researched more intensively.

The last lesson for future research that we want to mention is the importance of connecting different types of segregation, such as by gender, class and ethnicity. The interplay of segregation types shapes people's lives to a large extent. In this case too, the *interplay* itself must be studied. We know quite a lot about the empirical patterns of each type of segregation, and some things about the mechanisms behind these patterns, but we seldom regard them in relation to each other.

The general lesson from this book for future research is, we suggest, giving more attention to the interplay between different levels and areas of gender segregation, as well as to the interplay between different types of segregation.

References

Acker, J. (1992), 'Reformer och kvinnor i den framtida välfärdsstaten', in J. Acker, A. Baude, U. Björnberg, E. Dahlström, G. Forsberg, L. Gonäs, H. Holter, A. Nilsson (eds), *Kvinnors och mäns liv och arbete*, SNS Förlag, Stockholm.

Acker, J. (1999), 'Gender and Organizations', in J. Saltzman Chafets (ed.), *Handbook of the Sociology of Gender*, Kluwer Academic/Plenum Publishers, New York.

Borchorst, A. (1992), 'EF, Kvindeintresser og velferdsstatsregimer', Institute of Political Science, University of Aarhus.

Esping-Andersen, G. (1991), *The Three Worlds of Welfare Capitalism*, Polity Press, Cambridge.

Hobson, B. (1994), 'Solo Mothers, Social Policy Regimes and the Logics of Gender', in D. Sainsbury (ed.), *Gendering Welfare States*, Sage, London.

Orloff, A. S. (1993), 'Gender and the Social Rights of Citizenship: The Comparative Analysis of Gender Relations and Welfare States', *American Sociological Review*, 58:3, pp. 303–332.

Plantenga, J. and J. Hansen (1999), 'Assessing Equal Opportunities in the European Union', *International Labour Review*, 138(4): pp. 351–379.

Rantalaiho, L. and T. Heiskanen (eds) (1997), *Gendered Practices in Working Life*, Macmillan, Basingstoke.

Index